ROUTLEDGE LIBRARY EDITIONS:
AGING

Volume 4

GERONTOLOGY

GERONTOLOGY

Social and Behavioural Perspectives

Edited by
D. B. BROMLEY

LONDON AND NEW YORK

First published in 1984 by Croom Helm Ltd

This edition first published in 2024
by Routledge
4 Park Square, Milton Park, Abingdon, Oxon OX14 4RN

and by Routledge
605 Third Avenue, New York, NY 10158

Routledge is an imprint of the Taylor & Francis Group, an informa business

British Library Cataloguing in Publication Data
A catalogue record for this book is available from the British Library

ISBN: 978-1-032-67433-9 (Set)
ISBN: 978-1-032-70988-8 (Volume 4) (hbk)
ISBN: 978-1-032-70996-3 (Volume 4) (pbk)
ISBN: 978-1-032-70994-9 (Volume 4) (ebk)

DOI: 10.4324/9781032709949

Publisher's Note
The publisher has gone to great lengths to ensure the quality of this reprint but points out that some imperfections in the original copies may be apparent.

Disclaimer
The publisher has made every effort to trace copyright holders and would welcome correspondence from those they have been unable to trace.

GERONTOLOGY: SOCIAL AND BEHAVIOURAL PERSPECTIVES

EDITED BY D.B. BROMLEY

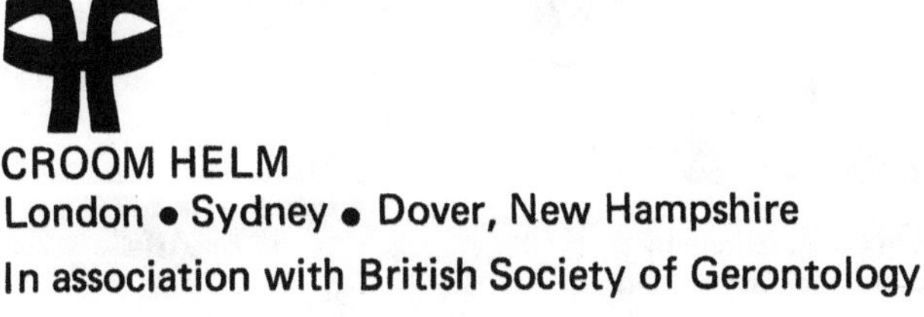

CROOM HELM
London • Sydney • Dover, New Hampshire
In association with British Society of Gerontology

Croom Helm Ltd, Provident House, Burrel Row,
Beckenham, Kent BR3 1AT
Croom Helm Australia Pty Ltd, First Floor, 139 King Street,
Sydney, NSW 2001, Australia
Croom Helm, 51 Washington Street, Dover, New Hampshire 03820, USA

British Library Cataloguing in Publication Data

Gerontology
1. Aged – Great Britain – Care and hygiene
I. Bromley, D. B.

ISBN 0-7099-3283-9

Library of Congress Catalog Card Number and
Cataloging in Publication Data applied for.

Printed and bound in Great Britain by
Biddles Ltd, Guildford and King's Lynn

CONTENTS

THREE : EVALUATION OF SERVICES

PART FOUR : CULTURAL FACTORS

PREFACE

This volume contains a selection of the contributions to the Annual Conference of the British Society of Gerontology held in Liverpool from 23rd to 26th September 1983, in association with the Institute of Human Ageing and the University of Liverpool. It is a matter of some regret that not all the contributions presented at the conference or submitted for publication could be included in the present volume. Those that are included cover a diversity of interests characteristic of those pursued by members of the British Society of Gerontology - a point taken up briefly in the Introduction. The volume is intended to be a worthy successor to Ageing in Modern Society edited by Dorothy Jerrome and published by Croom Helm in 1983.

I have tried to confine my editorial work to clarifying meanings and achieving a reasonable consistency of style and format. I trust my occasional ventures into major textual surgery will not be regarded as butchery by those authors who have fallen victim to it!

The book should appeal to readers interested in contemporary social and behavioural gerontology in the United Kingdom, and in particular to readers interested in issues such as services for the elderly and their effectiveness, policy issues and privatisation, women and ageing, cross-cultural comparisons, approaches to dementia, and the topics of reminiscence, attitudes, education, retirement, visiting and research utilisation.

I should like to take this opportunity of thanking all those - contributors, organisers, secretarial and technical staff - whose efforts made the Liverpool Conference a success and led to the publication of this volume of Proceedings.

D. B. Bromley,
University of Liverpool.

Chapter One

INTRODUCTION. REPRESENTATIVE STUDIES OF AGEING

D. B. Bromley

In what ways are the contributions to this volume representative of different perspectives on ageing? They are representative in the broad sense of illustrating the very wide range of interests and points of view to be found within social and behavioural gerontology.

One of the difficulties faced by the social sciences is that their subject-matter frequently, some would say inevitably, has political and ethical implications. Social gerontology is no exception. In this volume, some of these implications are made explicit - for example with regard to the privatisation of services, financial costing of alternative forms of care, sex discrimination and research utilisation. In other words, the enterprise we call 'social gerontology' is not simply about carrying out systematic surveys, controlled experiments and other forms of 'scientific' inquiry, it is also about advocating and implementing certain forms of social action which, in the last resort, help to determine the fate of individuals. Through the present volume, readers can experience the very wide scope of social gerontology since the contributions range from those concerned with research methodology, through those that report straightforward research findings, to those that strongly advocate particular courses of action or raise ethical issues.

British social gerontology is not insular, although it might seem, from this volume at least, that our links with European social gerontology are not as strong or as numerous as they might be. Arrangements are already in hand, however, to develop and strengthen these European links. Our links with the English-speaking world, by contrast, have always been strong and numerous and show every sign of continuing to be maintained and improved. With reference to our links with the Third-World, I should like to draw attention to Dr. Merriman's contribution on the role of elderly women in India. It raises some interesting issues, and it is by no means clear that the sorts of solutions to the problems of ageing developed in the advanced countries will suit the under-developed countries. Dr. Merriman's sources and references disclose the size and nature of the iceberg of which her chapter is simply the tip.

Although the various contributions to this volume may seem to deal with a variety of specific and somewhat unrelated issues, there are some common themes and persisting issues which give the collection a measure of coherence. Several of the chapters imply or explicitly express the desirability of early detection and intervention in relation to the manifold adverse effects of ageing. Preventive action, however, continues to receive far less attention than it deserves. One of the reasons is that prospective research studies (studies designed to examine outcomes under controlled 'treatment' conditions) are extremely costly, time-consuming and administratively difficult to carry out. Without them, however, we are unlikely to make much headway in understanding processes like dementia, physical fitness and personal adjustment in relation to ageing (where the time period of interest is rarely less than five years).

The topic of prevention and prospective studies leads on to questions about accountability and the evaluation of services. Again, the complexities associated with national and local government policies, financial considerations, administrative organisation and professional interests make it all but impossible to carry out the sorts of research work that stand up to close scrutiny from the point of view of scientific rigour. It is not only the administration of research into accountability and evaluation that is difficult, the basic conceptual and methodological issues in these areas are also difficult to formulate and resolve.

Complexity appears to be a chronic feature of issues in social and behavioural gerontology. As the reader will see, even something as apparently simple as visiting between children and elderly parents turns out, on examination, to be complicated in unexpected ways.

It is interesting and pleasing to observe a tendency in this interdisciplinary area for boundaries between disciplines to dissolve, so that one is not particularly conscious of the fact that what one is reading was written by a sociologist, psychologist, geriatrician, administrator, economist or other specialist. Even the 'jargon', as one contributor fears, seems not to be intrusive. If it is the case that social scientists within gerontology are finding a technical level of discourse that enables them to communicate effectively with each other, this perhaps augurs well for multi-disciplinary endeavours generally. Who knows, before long we may be able to communicate effectively to those outside the social sciences, and make up some of the ground lost in recent years.

The social attitudes that we should be concerned with are not just those that bear directly on ageing and the aged but also those that bear upon our scientific and professional activities. The development of social gerontology, like any other scientific or professional specialism, is conditioned by historical, cultural and broadly ecological circumstances. Among these circumstances we must include the prevailing political and economic climate, public opinion as it finds expression in the media and in a myriad of individual opinions and choices, and the attitudes of our colleagues in other scientific, academic and professional areas. It is obvious that we are currently witnessing a major revaluation of the social sciences (not simply a reduction in resources) and we must be prepared to defend what is of central value and to relinquish what can be shown to be mistaken or of negligible importance.

It is hoped, therefore, that with each succeeding year our beliefs, values, research endeavours and policy recommendations will change as old concepts give way to new, as our interests shift from one set of problems to another, as we develop improved methods of investigation and interpretation, and as we become more influential at every level of decision-making. Those at least are, I think, the aspirations of social gerontologists.

Applied social gerontologists are fortunate, in a way, that the practical problems with which they are concerned are so obvious; but even academic gerontologists, planners and policy-makers, and others, somewhat removed from the practicalities of caring for individual older persons, can, in the last resort, justify their efforts in terms of the short- or long-term benefits they are intended to achieve.

We share, in a general way, an image of a rational, empirical, i.e. 'scientific', enterprise designed to further the interests of common humanity. So, in a sense, understanding and advocacy should go hand-in-hand. In contrast to this albeit vague image we have the reality of a relatively small, far from coherent, collection of individuals and organisations trying to cope with what is, at a world-wide level at least, an immense, difficult and frightening set of problems - the ageing of populations - problems which, in the final analysis, reduce the recognising the differences between people and fostering the health, happiness and achievement of individual persons in later life.

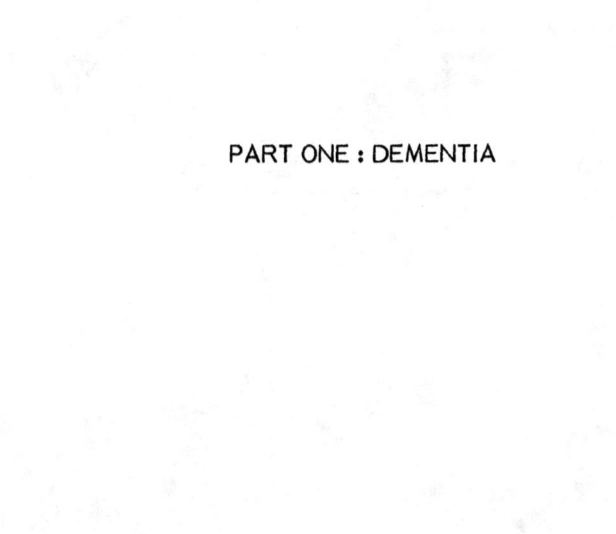

PART ONE : DEMENTIA

Chapter Two

THE EARLY DETECTION OF DEMENTIA. A BASELINE FROM HEALTHY COMMUNITY DWELLING OLD PEOPLE

M. G. Binks and A. D. M. Davies

Introduction

Descriptions of the pattern of cognitive impairment in moderate and severe dementia include fluctuating attention, slow learning, forgetfulness and difficulty in finding words that are appropriate to the conversation. These cognitive losses form the basis of a number of mental status tests and 'dementia scores'. However, much less is known about cognition in the early stages of the disease process - Roth (1980). Yet it is early screening that holds out the best hope of accurate description of the natural history of dementia, and this, in turn, the greatest promise of the effective management of dementia.

This paper is in three sections.

1. It discusses conceptual and empirical problems in devising screeening tests for early dementia.

2. It argues that a baseline of knowledge of cognition in the normal elderly is a necessary preliminary to developing dementia screening instruments.

3. It describes the performance of a healthy group of comunity dwelling elderly on some potentially useful screening tests, in particular the National Adult Reading Test (NART) and the Set Test.

Why Do We Need a Baseline?

Screening for cognitive impairment raises two problems.

1. Normal Versus Pathological Change

Assessment of cognitive impairment requires that an individual's functioning (in say language, memory or orientation) is compared with some standard. For the individual patient and his supporters, the standard used is the person's past level of performance, e.g. relatives notice increasing confusion, forgetfulness or lack of judgement about what is appropriate to the situation. For research and psychological assessment, the standard of comparison is the level of performance of people of similar age and circumstances who show no signs of a dementing process: a matched control group or psychometric norms. Some cognitive changes occur to some extent in most people as they become older. There is a large literature on ways in which the speed and quality of cognition changes with age, e.g. Woodruff (1983). These may be called 'normal' or 'benign' changes in cognition - La Rue (1982). An example is the temporary and occasional inability to retrieve the name of an acquaintance, or not being able to find a word for something wich one feels in on 'the tip of the tongue'. Typically the sought-for name 'surfaces' suddenly, later on, when the active attempts at retrieval have passed. This common cognitive failure can occur at any age but tends to increase in frequency in the elderly. It does not seem to be associated with, or to predict, more severe cognitive impairment. Other memory or orientation errors are 'malignant' in that they occur in moderately demented people but not in the normal elderly, e.g. mistaking your husband for your father. A baseline of normal cognitive function is needed to find which changes are 'normative' and which predict pathology. We already know how to make some gross distinctions, as in the examples above. However, we know insufficient about the finer distinctions which predict further deterioration. For this we need longitudinal studies which provide the harsh but valid discipline of predictive validity.

2. Cognitive Change and Diagnosis

As Roth has pionted out, we are not sure what we should be looking for. The early signs of dementia may differ from those of 'diagnosed dementias'. Screening with established procedures such as Mental Status Questionnaires and the Kendrick battery will of course pick out those people with relatively gross impairment - but tests validated on the criterion of terminal diagnosis have yet to demonstrate sufficient discrimination to pick up early impairment. Recent work suggests that language-based assessments may provide promising test content for early diagnosis.

Psychometric Tests of Language Functioning

Some aspects of language functioning appear to be quite well preserved in mild and moderately dementing people, others appear to be sensitive to disease changes. The 'dementia resistant' functions appear to be syntax, correct use of phonology and oral reading -Bayles (1982). The 'dementia sensitive' functions appear to be semantic - a broadening of word meanings, erroneous object naming and reduced verbal fluency.

The NART test

Nelson (1982) has recently published a word reading test. The aim is to predict the premorbid level of cognition in people suffering cognitive impairment. Typically one has no useful information on how a person performed in the past unless a highly demanding and skilled job has been held. One has to infer past level, observe present level and compared the two to estimate cognitive impairment. Nelson observed that reading ability is well preserved in dementia and based her test on this.

The subject's task is to read a list of 50 irregularly spelled words, e.g. ache, labile. The score is the number of errors of pronunciation. The rationale for the test is that people cannot work out how to pronounce ACHE. It is irregular. If the word is correctly pronounced it must have been learnt in the past, so NART score estimates past vocabulary and hence estimates past cognitive functioning. To justify this, Nelson and McKenna (1975) showed that reading ability and Wechsler I.Q. correlated r = +0.75 in a group of 120 non-demented 20-70 year olds. There was no significant effect of age or social class.

For the NART to be used as a screening test for dementia in the elderly the following assumptions must be made.

1. Reading ability correlates with cognitive function in normal non-dementing old people (The NART standarisation used no over 70s).
2. In dementia, reading ability is near premorbid levels for the short irregular words in the NART, i.e. there are no differences in score between demented and non-demented people. Nelson and O'Connell (1978) showed this was true for younger groups. There is no information on older groups.
3. To be useful as a screening test the NART should not decline with age in the over 70s.
4. For comparison with the NART there should be a 'dementia sensitive' index of current functioning available.

The Set Test

As described above, we do not have good early dementia sensitive indices. The Set Test, however, shows marked differences between moderate dements and non-dements and is a simple highly acceptable test to the elderly. Subjects are asked to name as many fruits, towns, etc. as they can, in this study up to a maximum of 20, compared with 10 for Isaacs' hospital diagnosis version. The ceiling is higher to suit a community survey. Four categories are tested per subject. Gregory et al. (1983) have also constructed a second parallel version. The experimental work on language suggests that the Set Test taps those aspects of language likely to be impaired, e.g. verbal fluency, use of semantic boundaries.

While the Set Test has the advantage of requiring active search and collation of semantic knowledge, it has the disadvantage of age sensitivity. In non-dementing old people performance declines with age as a benign sign of normal ageing. In contrast, tests of present vocabulary, such as the Mill Hill vocabulary (MHV) synonyms scale, are not age sensitive in that non-dementing old people preserve their performance until their 80s - Heron and Chown (1967), while in dementing old people performance declines with age as a malignant sign of pathological ageing - Orme (1957). The MHV makes more passive use of semantic knowledge, particularly in the six alternative forced-choice format used in this study and for which there are age norms for the Liverpool population - Heron and Chown (1967). Each subject in the screeening completed a half-length version of the MHV synonyms test.

Subjects and Methods

In twelve months of screening, about 1100 elderly people living in the community were interviewed. Amongst these a subsample was sought whose illnesses and handicaps, if any, would not hinder their mental functioning. Consequently, those selected were not taking any drugs prescribed by a doctor, and were described in the summary at the end of the interview as definitely not depressed or demented or suffering from any other mental handicap such as a stroke. So far, this gives a sample of 182 people aged from 64 to 84 who were likely to be in better physical and mental health than the parent sample of interviewees. However, they are not necessarily an elite group of old people in optimum health. The selection procedure yielded more men in the sample than in the patient sample, for unknown reasons. Thus men and women may have been selected differently and the sexes should be analysed separately even when there is no significant sex difference on a variable.

Results

To assess the effects of age on the psychological tests, age was recoded into five-year cohorts starting at 65 - see Table 1. The main effect of age cohort was highly significant at the .001 level for MHV and Set Test but not significant for the NART. This confirmed the expectation that it would not be age sensitive and extends to age 84 Nelson's support for this assumption in non-demented people. The effect of age on MHV was negligible from 65-79 as expected for an age insensitive test but reduced scores for the 80-85 year olds were observed. The effect of age on the Set Test confirmed previous reports of age sensitivity -Isaacs and Akhtar (1972).

The main purpose of this study was to assess the prospects for predicting current verbal performance, MHV, from current pronunciation performance, NART. The following results are based on half of the sample and retain the other half for cross validation of the conclusions. The simple linear regression between NART and MHV (MHV = -0.2 NART+18.6) is shown in Figure 1 and the corresponding correlation is -0.65, which is significant beyond the .001 level. The correlations reported for different samples of the screening project used MHV errors whereas this study used MHV correct replies, so this correlation, in a sample that was not mentally ill or taking prescribed drugs, is comparable firstly with the correlation of 0.58 in an

Table 1 The Effects of Age on Mill Hill Vocabulary, National Adult Reading Test and Set Test Scores

	Age Cohorts			
	65-69	70-74	75-79	80-84
MHV	14.7	15.9	14.8	11.5
NART	18.5	15.3	15.7	24.6
Set Test	61.2	60.7	54.4	43.6
N	76	57	38	10

Figure 1 Scatterplot and Linear Regression of Mill Hill Vocabulary on National Adult Reading Test, 95 percent Confidence Limits for Individual Values

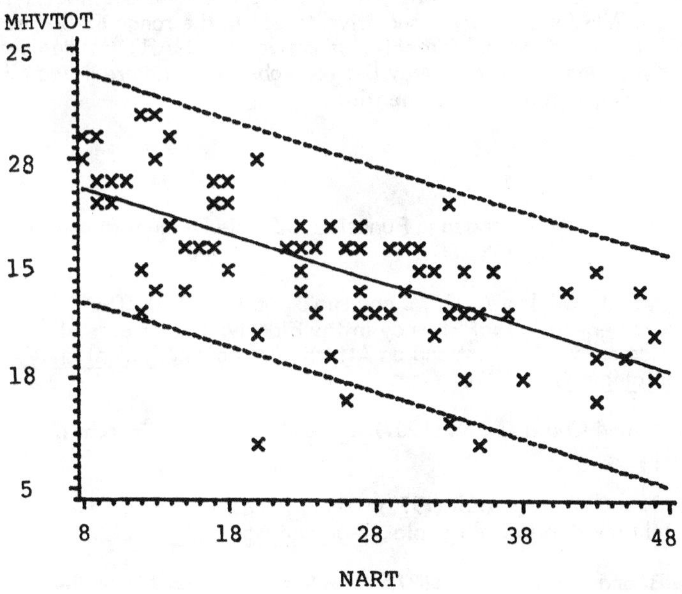

unselected sample reported by Wood and secondly with the correlation of 0.73 in a sample selected to have 50 percent of suspected early or probably late cases reported by Searle in this volume. The usual regression diagnostics confirmed that this simple linear regression was an adequate description of the data. Adding age, sex and interviewer effects did not improve prediction. The corresponding linear regression between NART and Set Test would be a poorer basis for predicting current verbal performance, i.e. Set Test, from current pronunciation, i.e. NART, since the correlation was weaker (-0.30), albeit significant at the .005 level. Thus the NART and MHV tests do not substitute for each other. The best use of an individual's Set Test score would be to compare it with separate psychometric test norms for normal healthy old people, for early dementias and for clearly established dementias. In contrast, the best use of an individual's NART score would be to predict premorbid MHV to reveal a discrepancy with current MHV and indicate the possibility of early dementia.

Conclusions

This study has provided a baseline of functioning on the NART and Set Test in healthy elderly people and centile psychometric norms will become available. It shows that the relationship between reading ability and vocabulary in an old healthy group is strong and linear. The NART and MHV scores are insensitive to age in the range 65-80 years. If MHV is confirmed as dementia sensitive and NART as dementia insensitive, then the discrepancy between observed and predicted MHV is a promising sign of early dementia.

Bibliography

Bayles, K. A. (1982) 'Language Function in Senile Dementia', _Brain and Language_, _16_, 265-280

Gregory, S. J., Davies, A. D. M. and Binks, M. G. (1983) 'The Improvement of Verbal Fluency in the Elderly. The Effects of Practice on the Set Test and an Alternative Form', _Educational Gerontology_, _9_, 139-146

Heron, A. and Chown, S. M. (1967) _Age and Function_. Churchill, London

Isaacs, B. and Akhtar, A. J. (1972) 'The Set Test: A Rapid Test of Mental Function in Old People', _Age and Ageing_, _1_, 222-226

Isaacs, B. and Kennie, A. T. (1973) 'The Set Test as an Aid to the Detection of Dementia in Old People', _British Journal of Psychiatry_, _123_, 467-470

La Rue, A. (1982) 'Memory Loss and Aging: Distinguishing Dementia from Benign Senescent Forgetfulness and Depressive Pseudodementia', in L. F. Tarvik and B. W. Small (eds), The Psychiatric Clinics of North America, W. B. Saunders, Philadelphia

Nelson, H. E. (1982) National Adult Reading Test (NART) for the Assessment of Premorbid Intelligence in Patients with Dementia: Test Manual, NFER Publishing Co., Windsor

Nelson, H. E. and McKenna, P. (1975) 'The Use of Current Reading Ability in the Assessment of Dementia', British Journal of Social and Clinical Psychology, 14, 259-267

Nelson, H. E. and O'Connell, A. (1978) 'Dementia: the Estimation of Premorbid Intelligence Levels Using the New Adult Reading Test', Cortex, 14, 234-244

Orme, J. E. (1957) 'Non-verbal and Verbal Performance in Normal Old Age, Senile Dementia and Elderly Depression', Journal of Gerontology, 12, 408-13

Roth, M. (1980) 'Senile Dementia and its Borderlands', in J.O. Cole and J. E. Barrett (eds), Psychopathology in the Aged, Raven Press, New York

Woodruff, D. S. (1983) 'A Review of Aging and Cognitive Processes', Research on Aging, 5, 139-153

Chapter Three

THE EARLY DETECTION OF DEMENTIA. INITIAL FINDINGS FROM A LONGITUDINAL STUDY

N. Wood, J. R. M. Copeland, D. M. Forshaw, M. S. Muthu, R. Abed, V. K. Sharma and M. E. Dewey

Introduction

The prevalence of senile dementia increases with age and since the elderly population in most Western countries is increasing rapidly the problem is one demanding more current research. In this particular study we have from the outset addressed ourselves to the central question: Can syndrome cases be detected reliably in the initial phases of the disease? The need for early diagnosis is clearly of great importance both for the individuals concerned and for society in terms of providing the required supporting services.

This study was planned from the outset as a longitudinal prospective investigation. We wished to explore which psychometric assessments and clinical features/investigations would be the most reliable and useful indicators of early dementia in subjects aged over 65. In addition it was hoped that the project would help illuminate and clarify details of the manner of the progression of dementia. Variations in the course and outcome could reveal aetiologically distinct subgroups. The successful identification of measures can only be properly validated against outcome. Psychometric measures for example can significantly distinguish between unequivocally 'normal' and demented subjects, but in the area of borderline or early syndrome cases ambiguous results are often obtained. Reversible causes of dementia, drug induced congitive impairment, pseudodementia and low I.Q. subjects can be screened out during a longitudinal investigation involving annual follow-up procedures of the type described here.

Methods

Subjects

Eighty-one General Practitioners in the Liverpool Family Practitioner Committee area were selected randomly. The patient lists of 55 of these were randomly sampled and 3600 names, addresses and dates of birth obtained. Letters from the research team and the General

Practitioners were sent to 2294 subjects and appointments arranged for a visit by one of six non-medically qualified interviewers in the subjects' own homes. Altogether, 1241 subjects were interviewed. Refusal rates varied widely between G. P. populations and averaged overall 21 percent of those contacted. A further group were effectively not in the sample because of recent death, chronic hospitalisation or removal from the area.

Initial Interview

The 1241 subjects interviewed were given a shortened version of the Geriatric Mental State Examination Schedule (GMS) - Copeland et al. (1976) - developed for this study from an analysis of the large US/UK London community study - Gurland et al. (1983), by selecting the items best discriminating depression from dementia and cases from non-cases. Psychological tests given at the same time included modified versions of the Mill Hill Vocabulary - Raven (1938), Set tests - Isaacs and Kenny (1972) and the National Adult Reading Test (NART) -Nelson (1982) to assess premorbid verbal I.Q. A specially devised demographic schedule was also given. Blood pressure was estimated three times during the interview using a standard method (systolic, diastolic phases 4 and 5 estimated using a random zero sphygmomanometer).

Followup Procedures

To facilitate the rapid identification of subjects for further investigation, dementia and depression scores were calculated from appropriate GMS items. The cutoff for nominating the sample to include early syndrome cases was arbitrarily taken at four on the dementia scale. The range four to seven (inclusive) was provisionally taken to nominate early syndrome cases, eight and above on the dementia scale provisionally taken to identify clear syndrome cases of dementia. A random number of subjects scoring below four (provisonally designated as normal controls) were also selected. A Computed Axial Tomography (CAT) scan was performed on a number of subjects (76 at a time of writing this report) identified in this way. A clinical examination on these subjects was undertaken giving particular attention to the CNS. The GMS was repeated by a psychiatrist on these subjects together with a further randomly selected group of subjects seen again in their own homes.

Blood acetyl and total cholinesterases, folic acid, serum B12, Wasserman reaction tests, full blood count, thyroid function tests and standard SMAC procedures were performed on blood samples taken from these 76 subjects.

One hundred and twenty subjects (one half scoring four and above on the dementia scale and one half scoring below as normal controls) were re-interviewed in their own homes by a research psychologist within six months of initial interview and again six weeks and one year later. Instruments included Raven's Progressive Matrices- Raven (1962), Kendrick's battery - Gibson and Kendrick

(1979), the Numbers Test (Unpublished), Misplaced Objects test - Crook et al. (1979) and specially devised schedules to measure activity levels and everyday memory. It is intended to repeat these follow-up investigations at annual intervals for the duration of this study.

Analysis

Data were submited to the SPSSX statistical package using an IBM 4341 computer.

Results

A preliminary analysis of a subset of the data collected so far is presented here. A randomly selected group of cases has been used as a basis of this analysis. Table I presents a breakdown of the sample by age and sex. The mean age of the sample was 74 years.

Table I Age and Sex of a Sample of Subjects Interviewed

Age Group	Males (N)	%	Females (N)	%
65 - 74	95	26.8	119	33.5
75 - 84	39	11.0	76	21.4
85 - 94	13	3.7	12	3.4
95 -	0	0.0	1	0.3
Total	147	41.5	208	58.6

Further analysis of the demography of the sample indicates that some 70 percent were manual or blue collar workers during their working lifetime. Some 34 percent of the sample were living alone and 6.2 percent were receiving some form of practical assistance, e.g. Home Help, Meals on Wheels, from the local Social Services Department. About 20 percent of the sample had little or no contact with friends and relatives on a regular basis.

There were no significant differences between males and females on the calculated dementia score (Males mean = 2.44, Females mean = 2.67, N.S.). A breakdown of the dementia scores is illustrated in Table 2.

Table 2 Dementia Scores in a Sample of Subjects Interviewed

Dementia Score	N	%
0 - 3	259	75.5
4 - 7	55	16.0
8 - 11	19	5.5
12 - 15	7	2.0
16 - 19	2	0.6
20 -	1	0.3

On the basis of dementia score classifications, three quarters of the sample interviewed would be classed as non-dementing, 16 percent as possible early syndrome cases and eight percent as possible late syndrome cases.

The calculated depression scores for this sample indicate that females score significantly higher (more depression) on this measure than the males (Males mean = 8.57, Females mean = 12.57, $p<0.01$). The overall mean on the Set Test was 49.7 (maximum score = 80) whilst errors on the NART (maximum = 50) and MHVS (maximum = 22) averaged 21.2 and 8.5 respectively. Correlations between the cognitive test scores, the calculated dementia score and age are depicted in Table 3 (Pearson r).

Table 3 Correlations Between Cognitive Test Performance, Age and Dementia Score in a Sample of Subjects Interviewed. All correlations significant ($p<0.001$)

	Set Test	NART Errors	MHVS Errors	Age	Dementia Score
Set Test	-	-0.43	-0.54	-0.29	-0.57
NART Errors		-	0.58	N.S.	0.22
MHVS Errors			-	0.23	0.35
Age				-	0.32

The Set test, an established measure of clear dementia, correlates negatively with all the other measures in this table, so the worse the Set test performance the greater the number of errors on the other cognitive tests, the older the subjects and the higher the dementia score.

An analysis of 121 subjects reinterviewed by psychiatrists

provides further evidence of the utility of this measure of dementia. The calculated dementia score correlates 0.58 ($p<0.01$) with a diagnosis of dementia made using the shortened version of the GMS. Table 4 provides a more detailed breakdown of the diagnoses attached to subjects in each of the three dementia score categories.

Table 4 Dementia Scores and Psychiatric Diagnoses Made on 121 Subjects Followed Up.

Dementia Score	N	Diagnosis of Clear Dementia	Diagnosis of Early Dementia	Diagnosis of Other Caseness	Diagnosis of Normality
0 - 3	64	0	1	5	58
4 - 7	38	5	10	8	15
8 -	19	6	6	6	1

Discussion

The shortened version of the GMS developed for use with this study is under continual evaluation as a screening instrument for the detection of early cases. The indications from this study to date are that non-medically qualified but trained raters achieve consistency of performance with this instrument. The calculated dementia score averages do not differ significantly between these raters in this study and provide an objective means of selecting subjects for further investigation. How well is this selection process working? We are aware that selecting subjects who score four and above on the dementia scale for further detailed investigation is missing very few syndrome cases of dementia (Table 4). A high dementia score by itself is not necessarily indicative of a diagnosis of dementia however, and our results to date indicate that about one third of high dementia scoring subjects are psychiatrically classed as other cases (principally depression). If a moderately high dementia score (4 - 7 range) is obtained, we would predict a large number of these subjects may develop psychiatrically diagnosed dementia within a few years.

As we are aware that the successful identification of measures to select early cases can only be properly validated against eventual outcome, it would be precipitous to draw firm conclusions at this time. Our preliminary results indicate that language-based assessment provides promising test content for a screening battery of this nature. Incorrect use of semantics, erroneous object naming and reduced verbal fluency appear important areas to investigate further. Results from the psychological follow-up part of this study are presented elsewhere in this volume, although here it may be metioned that the Set Test is correlating with the dementia score as highly as a psychiatric diagnosis of dementia. That the NART, a test of premorbid ability, should correlate highly with a test of current verbal

I.Q. (MHVS) and also, although fairly weakly, with dementia score is more unexpected. The present analysis does not take account of the existence of possible common factors such as poor sensory acuity on performance on these tests. It may be noted however that the NART has to date been standardised only on subjects up to 70 years of age - Nelson (1982) and the present data will provide norms substantially up to the age of 84 years.

Bibliography

Copeland, J. R. M, Kelleher, M. J., Kellett, J. M., Gourlay, A. J., Fleiss, J. L. and Sharpe, L. (1976) 'A Semi-structured Clinical Interview for the Assessment of Diagnosis and Mental State in the Elderly. The Geriatric Mental State Schedule I. Development and Reliability', Psychological Medicine, 6, 439-449

Crook, T., Ferris, E. C. and McCarthy, M. (1979) 'The Misplaced Objects Test: A Brief Test for Memory Dysfunction in the Aged', Journal of the American Geriatrics Society, 27, 284-287

Gibson, A. J. and Kendrick, D. C. (1979) The Kendrick Battery for the Detection of Dementia in the Elderly, NFER Publishing Co., Windsor, 1979

Gurland, B. J., Copeland, J. R. M., Kuriansky, J., Kelleher, M. J., Sharpe, L. and Dean, L. (1983) The Mind and Mood of Ageing: The Mental Health Problems of the Community Elderly in New York and London, Hayworth Press, N. Y.

Isaacs, B. and Kennie, A. T. (1972) 'The Set Test as an Aid to the Detection of Dementia in Old People', Age and Ageing, 1, 222-296

Nelson, H. E. (1982) National Adult Reading Test (NART) for the Assessment of Premorbid Intelligence in Patients with Dementia, Test Manual, NFER Nelson Publishing Co., Windsor

Raven, J. C. (1938) Manual for the Mill Hill Vocabulary Test, H. K. Lewis, London

Raven, J. C. (1962) Manual for Coloured Progressive Matrices, H. K. Lewis, London

Chapter Four

A COMMUNITY BASED FOLLOW UP OF SOME SUSPECTED CASES OF EARLY DEMENTIA. AN INTERIM REPORT

R. T. Searle

Introduction

The need for early diagnosis of senile dementia is clearly of great importance both to distinguish treatable from non-treatable causes so that treatment regimes may be implemented where appropriate and to allow early implementation of promising treatments before gross behavioural changes have occurred. The problems inherent in any study of early dementia are so extensive, however, that as an area of research it has been largely neglected, with much of the research concerning more advanced "unequivocal" cases.

The main problems are as follows. Depressive symptoms often mask early dementia, or may be confounded with it such that dementia is over-diagnosed - see Marsden and Harrison, (1972) and Wells (1979). Though psychometric measure can significantly distinguish between unequivocally normal and demented subjects, early or borderline cases (or patients with functional disorders) provide ambiguous results on these tests. Selection to various types of hospital can influence the clinical picture; also, early cases of dementia are unlikely to be seen in a hospital setting, thus community studies are needed. The majority of elderly people do not suffer from dementia, so that very large numbers need to be screened. For example, two surveys totalling nearly 800 random sample subjects yielded less than 50 subjects with a definite diagnosis of dementia - Bergmann et al. (1971). Extensive studies are therefore needed. Lastly, prospective studies are needed to confirm initial diagnosis, to differentiate groups prognostically and to chart the evolution and progression of the illness employing standardised assessment techniques. Longitudinal studies of large, randomly selected groups, involving repeated psychometric testing over a time period of at least two years (to allow for change) are necessary to detect earlier signs of change predictive of the development of a dementing illness. This is a time consuming expensive process characterised by a decrease in the number of subjects at each stage due to illness, death, refusal and so on.

This study, which sets out to determine which psychometric measures are the most useful and reliable indicators of early dementia is part of a larger prospective study using standardised clinical methods and computerised tomography.

Materials and Methods

Subjects

A randon sample of 1200 subjects aged 65 and over was sampled from the lists of G.Ps serving the city of Liverpool. All subjects were seen originally in their own homes by a trained non-medical interviewer. The initial interview consisted of three blood pressure measurements, demographic and medical questionnaires, three cognitive tests comprising the Set Test [Issaacs and Kenny, (1974)], the New Adult Reading Test (N.A.R.T) [Nelson and O'Connell (1978)] and the Mill Hill Vocabulary Scale [M.H.V.S. Synonyms, Raven (1962)] and the Geriatric Mental State (G.M.S.), specially shortened for use in the community - Copeland et al. (1976).

To isolate those subjects who had possible cognitive changes indicative of early dementia a Dementia Scale was developed using data obtained from a previous study in which the G.M.S. formed part of the C.A.R.E. schedule used - Gurland et al. (1983). Those questions of the G.M.S. were elicited for the scale which correlated most highly with a diagnosis of dementia made by a group of research psychiatrists. A Dementia Score (D.S.) was them obtained by summing the subjects' scores for all those questions. At a score of seven (see Table 1) 60% of the dements were successfully diagnosed but 40% were missed. Because this score probably selected subjects with a relatively advanced stage of illness a cut-off point of four was decided upon, in order to include those with more mild cognitive loss. An equal number of control subjects who scored less than four on the Dementia Scale were also included. To avoid interviewer bias those subjects who had been seen at initial interview by the follow-up interviewer were eliminated from the sample pool.

Table 1 Relationship Between Dementia Score and Percentage of People Correctly Diagnosed Demented in Previous Studies - Copeland et al. (1976)

Cut-Off Points (% People Categorised Demented)				
Diagnosis	(4)	5	6	7
Well	-	-	-	-
Demented	85	80	65	60
Depressed	7	-	3	-
Neurotic	0	0	0	0
Other	-	-	-	-
Unspecified	-	-	-	-
TOTAL SAMPLE	N = 396			
DEMENTED	N = 20			

Suspected Cases of Early Dementia: An Interim Report

A total of 178 subjects were selected for follow-up, of which 123 have been seen; 46.3% were male and 53.7% female, sixty came from the "normal controls" and 63 from the "possible dementia" group. Their ages ranged from 65 to 92 years.

Subject Response

Of the 178 selected for follow up, 22.4% have refused further interviews at some stage in the follow-up procedure. A further 4.49% had moved house and were untraceable; 4.49% had died since initial interview and 2.03% were too ill to be seen.

Tests and Procedures

Subjects were interviewed in the same order as for the screening interview, so that the time gap between initial screeening interview and first psychological follow-up interview were roughly equivalent for all subjects. Contact was made by letter with a suggested appointment time, followed by a home visit. If necessary a second letter was sent with a further appointment time and a second visit made. This procedure was repeated until either an interview was obtained, or a definite refusal or notification of illness or death.

Psychological Tests and Questionnaires

The choice of tests for inclusion in the test battery was guided by the need to keep the procedure short and acceptable to subjects, it included the following.

1. Object Learning Test - Gibson and Kendrick (1979). This is a test of recall of everyday objects after viewing them for a short time. It has been validated on psychogeriatric patients with whom it has been reported to have a low refusal rate and high level of acceptability - Kendrick and Moyes (1979).

2. Digit Copying Test - Gibson and Kendrick (1979). This test of speed performance is the second test in the Kendrick Battery for the Detection of Dementia in the Elderly (with the O.L.T.). This study offers a unique oportunity to test the predictive and diagnostic validity of the Kendrick Battery on community residents, including borderline or suspected cases of dementia, against outcome.

3. The Numbers Test - Kendrick (1981, unpublished). This new test is aimed at assessing the subject's ability to make decisions based on past information and a finite number of possible decisions. The subject is shown a card from a series numbered between one and ten and asked to predict whether the next number shown will be higher or lower than the one currently displayed. This is repeated until all cards have been shown. The test of memory is whether or not they can recall the number of the last remaining card. The expectation is that patients with dementia will fail, while early cases will show an

abnormal decision process sequence when compared with elderly normal or depressed subjects' responses. No other available test assesses decision making processes in this way.

4. Misplaced Objects Test - Crook, Ferris and McCarthy (1979). This is a test of working memory. It comprises a diagram of the cross-section of a seven-roomed house, and representations of ten objects frequently misplaced around the house, e.g. keys, spectacles, gloves. The task of the subject is to place the objects in the rooms, and after an interval of 20 minutes to recall the location of each object. The task is appropriate for a broad range of cognitive ability since performance requirements are minimal and readily apparent, the test also has obvious face validity. Discriminant validity for memory impairment has been demonstrated - Crook, Ferris and McCarthy (1979), and test/retest reliability for consecutive days is high (0.84).

5. The Progressive Matrices - Raven (1965) Sets A, Ab, B, Coloured version. This particular set is shorter and more acceptable to the impaired elderly, and correlates well with the longer form. Norms are available for ages 60 to 89, and for groups of demented and depressed subjects. Scores for senile dementia patients have been found to be significantly below other groups, in contrast to tests of vocabulary, socres on which have been found to be relatively stable.

6. Activity Levels Questionnaire (A.L.Q.) This test is inteded to provide a measure of the subject's general level of mental and physical activity. The level of activity maintained by a person, particularly when elderly, may greatly influence performance on cognitive tests - see Diesfeldt and Diesfeldt-Groenijk (1977). We found no scale that was suitable for use with relatively active, community-dwelling residents. A detailed questionnaire was therefore devised to provide an estimate of activity, with a higher score reflecting more activity. This score has been split into two components: the general activity level, comprising the total score, and the score for those low energy activities such as reading, games, T.V., which do not involve actual physical movement, known as low energy activities (passive).

7 Everyday Memory Questionnaire (E.M.Q.) This questionnaire has been devised for the project to provide an estimate of the patients own perception of memory loss and its effects on his day-to-day functioning. It is intended to provide a means of relating the rather artificial test situation to the actual degree of impairment in the patient's life. Tests were administered in a standard order, by the same interviewer alone with the subject.

The first assessment was the longest and usually most stressful of the two including all the tests listed above, and lasting on average between 60 and 90 minutes. The second assessment consisted of the alternative form of the O.L.T. and the D.C.T. and took on average about 15 minutes.

Results

This is an ongoing, prospective study, so these results will be seen at a later date in relation to further results. We examine here the inter-relationships between the measures used. Table 2 shows mean age, occupational level - Goldthorpe and Hope Scale (1974) - and test results for the three groups: (a) normal controls (D.S. less than 4) (b) possible cases (D.S. 4 - 6) and (c) probable cases (D.S. 7 or more). Results are presented in the form of O.L.T. (total recalled), D.C.T. (transformed score), P.M. and M.O.T. (total correct), M.H.V.S. and N.A.R.T. (errors). Activity Levels are presented as General (total and passive).

Table 2 Comparison of Mean Test Results Broken Down by D.S. into Normals (DS<4) Possible Early Cases (D.S. 4 - 7) and Provisionally Identified Late Cases (D.S.≥ 7)

	Controls		Early Cases		Clear Cases		Signif.
Set Test	56.18	15.77	45.57	14.65	33.27	11.29	.0000
M.H.V.S.	6.16	3.74	8.60	3.85	9.55	4.34	.0020
N.A.R.T.	18.59	11.66	24.09	12.75	24.22	13.39	N.S.
O.L.T.1	36.55	9.62	33.45	12.80	21.27	8.82	.0000
O.L.T.2	37.45	9.15	36.13	18.90	23.31	11.90	.0020
D.C.T.1	96.75	28.10	77.72	34.41	70.38	29.35	.0021
D.C.T.2	101.45	31.41	80.73	26.65	62.65	21.05	.0000
P.M.	24.42	4.92	21.18	7.12	18.94	5.04	.0017
M.O.T.	6.56	2.44	5.70	2.46	4.26	2.52	.0083
A.L. (gen)	80.83	21.26	69.57	22.57	56.55	19.90	.0003
A.L. (pas)	25.73	5.33	21.57	5.11	22.33	6.66	.0026
Age	73.89		74.60		76.38		N.S.
OCC	25.50		22.57		28.05		N.S.
S.C.	4.20		3.96		4.50		N.S.

There is no significant difference in age, social class or occupational level between the three groups. A one-way ANOVA shows that there are significant differences between the groups for the results of all the measures used except for the N.A.R.T. When the impaired group are considered as a whole, i.e. all those who score 4 and over, there is a significant difference between group means for the N.A.R.T. for controls versus impaired (control $\bar{X}$ = 18.59, possible cases $\bar{X}$ = 24.14, P<.02). For all other tests and total Activity Levels the difference is in the expected direction, with greater cognitive impairment related to a decline in scores.

Table 3 Relationship between Occupation, Dementia Score (D.S.), Activity Levels [A.L.(G) and A.L. (P)] and Test Results (Pearson r)

	Occupation	D.S.	A.L.(G)	A.L.(P)
Dementia Score	.11			
Activity (Gen)	-.01	-.42***		
Activity (Pas)	-.03	-.30**	.39***	
Age	-.09	.15	-.31***	-.13
M.H.V.S.	.43***	.35***	-.10	-.18*
N.A.R.T.	.39***	.26***	-.09	-.20**
Set Test	-.29**	-.55***	.24**	.27**
P. Matrices	-.23*	-.37***	.27**	.21*
O.L.T.I	-.04	-.50***	.23*	.28*
D.C.T.I	-.22*	-.50***	.52***	.27**
M.O.T.	.12	-.29**	.20*	.17

* P<0.05 ** P<0.01 *** P<0.001

Table 3 shows the relationship between D.S., test results and age. Age does not correlate significantly with D.S. but all the test measures and Activity Levels (total) do correlate significantly, such that as D.S. increases performance declines. The strongest correlation is the Set Test at 0.55 (P<.001) followed by the O.L.T. at 0.50 (P<.001). Age and Activity Levels (total) correlate with all test results except the two vocabulary measures, the M.H.V.S. and the N.A.R.T. Both Activity Levels (total) and cognitive test performance decline as age increases. Performance on the two vocabulary measures, however,seems to be unrelated to total Activity Levels, while Activity

Level (passive) does not correlate with age but does correlate with alltest measures including the two vocabulary measures, the M.H.V.S. and the N.A.R.T. The M.H.V.S., N.A.R.T., P.M. and Set Test all correlate with occupational level while the D.S., Activity Levels and other test results do not.

Discussion

In this study most test measures show an expected decline across the three groups: normal, possible and probable cases of dementia. However, the findings for the N.A.R.T. are different. While the number of errors for the N.A.R.T. increases significantly when a cut-off point of four is used the difference disappears when the groups are further broken down into three groups, as above. Since the N.A.R.T. is designed to measure premorbid I.Q. rather than post-morbid I.Q. this suggests that those subjects who score four or more on the G.M.S. Dementia Scale (and therefore show some signs of "cognitive impairment") may not all be early cases of dementia but include subjects with long-standing low intelligence. In cross-sectional community studies of the prevalence of dementia the group of subjects with non-progressive low intelligence have always been the most difficult cases to diffentiate from true dementia.

An alternative explanation is that the N.A.R.T. is not measuring pre-morbid I.Q. but is simply another measure of post-morbid I.Q., which might be borne out by the correlation with the Progressive Matrices (0.39, $p<0.001$). Unlike the P.M., however, which declines across all three groups, the N.A.R.T. declines between normals and possible cases but not between possible and probable cases. This suggests that the deterioration measured by the cognitive items of the G.M.S. is not simply one of premorbid intelligence but that in the possible cases premorbid intelligence may be a factor in scoring poorly, whereas in the range of probable cases scores do not reflect premorbid I.Q. That low premorbid I.Q. may be a factor in poor test performance is borne out by the finding that occupational level correlates with M.H.V.S. and N.A.R.T. ($p<.0001$) and with P.M. ($P<.05$). The problem is whether low intelligence is a factor in subjects performing poorly on cognitive items and thus being mis-classified as demented, or that low pre-morbid I.Q. is a factor in the subsequent development of dementia.

A further point of interest concerns the Set Test. Whilst this test obtains the highest correlation with the D.S. even for those with a high D.S. (probable cases) the mean Set Test score is as high as 33.27 which would fall in the normal range, above a score of 15 proposed by Isaacs and Kenny (1972). In fact scores only go below 15 for one subject in this sample. While a higher ceiling was used in this study (subjects were allowed to generate up to 20 items per category compared with 10 for previous studies) this is unlikely to improve scores in the lower range. This suggests that the utility of this type of test is limited to more advanced cases of dementia.

The last point concerns the relationship of Activity Levels to test scores. Activity Levels both total and passive show a significant decline across the three groups (Table 2) suggesting that those who are most active tend to show less sign of cognitive impairment. We have here a problem of cause and effect. Does loss of cognitive function impair activity or is there further evidence for the suggestion, e.g. Diesfeldt, Diesfeldt-Groenendijk (1977), that increasing activity improves performance on cognitive tests? However, while total Activity Levels also decline with age, passive activities do not decline with age but are related to degree of cognitive impairment. The obvious explanation is that as the degree of physical impairment increases with age (due to the illnesses of old age) so the person's ability to be active decreases, whereas passive activities which are unaffected by physical impairment are maintained. It can also be seen from Table 3 that while a relationship exists between both the vocabulary measures, the M.H.V.S. and the N.A.R.T., and passive activities, this is not so for total activities. This could be due to the fact that a large part of the score for passive activities is, in many cases, made up of reading, as well as listening to the radio and watching television, all of which contribute to superior scores on vocabulary measures. Alternatively it could be that those people who have high pre-morbid I.Q. (reflected in N.A.R.T. score) tend to maintain high levels of passive activity even when physical impairment precludes other types, and that these people are less disposed toward cognitive decline in later life.

Later follow-up, which will include a psychiatric interview, will examine these questions in the light of the presence or absence of further decline in test scores and mental state.

Bibliography

Copeland, J. R. M., Kelleher, M. J., Kellet, J. M., Gourlay, A. J., Gurland, B. J., Fleiss, J. L. and Sharpe, L. (1976) 'A Semi-structured Clinical Interview for the Assessment of Diagnosis and Mental State in the Elderly. The Geriatric Mental State Schedule I. Development and Reliability', Psychological Medicine, 6, 439-449.

Crook, T., Ferris, S. H. and McCarthy M. (1979) 'The Misplaced Objects Test: A Brief Test for Memory Dysfunction in the Aged', Journal of the American Geriatrics Society, 27, 284-287.

Diesfeldt, H.F.A. and Diesfeldt-Groendijk, M. (1977) 'Improving Performance in Psychogeriatric Patients: The Influence of Physical Exercise', Age and Ageing, 6, 58.

Gibson, A. J. and Kendrick, D. C. (1979) The Kendrick Battery for the Detection of Dementia in the Elderly, NFER Publishing Co., Windsor

Gurland, B., Copeland, J. R. M., Kuriansky, J., Kelleher, M., Sharpe, L., Dean, L. L. (1983) The Mind and Mood of Ageing: Mental Health Problems of the Community Elderly in New York and

London. Haworth Press Inc., New York

Isaacs, B. and Kennie, A. T. (1972) 'The Set Test as an Aid to the Detection of Dementia in Old People', British Journal of Psychiatry,123, 467-470

Kendrick, A. J. and Moyes, I. C.A. (1979) 'Activity, Depression and Medication and Performance on the Revised Kendrick Battery'British Journal of Social and Clinical Psychology,18, 341-350

Marsden, C. D. and Harrison, M. J. G. (1979) 'Outcome of Investigation of Patients with Presenile Dementia', British Journal of Medicine,I, 249-252

Nelson, M. I. and O'Connell, A. (1978) 'Dementia: The Estimation of Premorbid Intelligence Using the New Adult Reading Test', Cortex, 14, 234-244

Raven, J. C. (1962) Manual for the Mill Hill Vocabulary Test, H. K. Lewis, London

Raven, J. C. (1965) Guide to Using the Coloured Progressive Matrices, Sets A, Ab and C, William Grieve & Sons, Dumfries

Wells, C. E. (1977) 'Chronic Brain Disease: An Overview', American Journal of Psychiatry, 135, 1-12

Chapter Five

A REVIEW OF A STANDARDISED MENTAL STATE EXAMINATION AND COMPUTER ASSISTED PSYCHIATRIC DIAGNOSES FOR USE IN RESEARCH WITH THE COMMUNITY ELDERLY.

J.R.M. Copeland, D.M. Forshaw, and M.E. Dewey.

Introduction

The purpose of this paper is to briefly outline the development of the Geriatic Mental State Examination (GMS) and its associated computer assisted diagnostic system, the Automated Geriatic Examination for Computer Assisted Taxonomy (AGECAT).

To obtain reliable psychiatric diagnoses the clinical interview on which the diagnoses are based must first be standardised. This ensures that important symptoms are not forgotten by the interviewer and his or her style does not colour the symptoms recorded. The most successful attempts at standarding are those which retain, as far as possible, the flexibility and judgement of a normal clinical interview. Although the routine clinical interview has two main components - the history and the mental state examination - efforts to standardise have been aimed at the latter. Diagnosis in psychiatry is essentially classification by symptom profile. Symptom profiles can be derived by a computer from semi-structured mental state examinations. The computer can then derive a diagnosis by applying to these profiles a hierarchy constructed from clinical judgement. Although a computer cannot simulate the subtle factors normally influencing a human choice of diagnosis, it will diagnose the same set of symptoms in the same way on different occasions. A computer derived diagnosis would therefore serve as a reliable standard against which to assess the consistency of the psychiatrist's diagnosis.

The Development of the Geriatric Mental State Examination

The development of the Geriatric Mental State interview was initially reported in 1976 - see Copeland et al.(1976) and Gurland et al.(1976). It is a semi-structured mental state examination for use with subjects over the age of 65. Since its introduction, it has been used in a great number of studies by groups in the United Kingdom, the United States, Australia, Canada and Europe. It has been translated into French,

German, Icelandic, Dutch and Danish. The GMS is a direct descendant from the Present State Examination (PSE) schedule and the Present Status Schedule (PSS). These, like the GMS, are both semi-structured mental state examinations. They were, however, designed for use with younger subjects.

The PSE was developed at the Institute of Psychiatry, London, by Wing et al. (1967). The interviewer using the PSE rates a number of obligatory questions which cover a wide range of psychiatric symptoms. The interviewer uses his judgement and rates that which in the light of his experience he considers to be abnormal. If the rater is unclear about how to rate a particular item after asking the set question, he is permitted to ask additional questions of his own choice. The interview is designed to elicit and record symptoms experienced by a subject in the preceding month.

The PSS was developed by Spitzer et al. (1964) at the Biometrics Research Unit in New York. In some ways it is similar to the PSE but is designed to record symptoms occuring in the preceding week. The exact wording of the set questions must be adhered to, and if the rater is unclear how to rate the item after asking these questions he is permitted to use only non-specific probes. The possible ratings for each of the items are very clearly specified.

For the purposes of undertaking a cross-national (New York - London) comparison of diagnosis in psychiatric patients aged 19-59 years the PSE and PSS were grouped to form the Combined Mental State (CMS) schedule. A factor analysis on the data of the first 500 subjects was performed by Fleiss et al. (1971). These authors demonstrated that 25 factors were valid discriminators of Project diagnoses. These factors were then used as a basis for classifying the subjects by symptom profiles. The groups so arranged were found to correlate well with both Project and hospital diagnoses, with the type of treatment received and with the duration of hospital stay.

The original GMS was constructed from 268 items from the PSE, 64 items from the PSS, together with 209 new items dealing with organic type symptoms such as memory impairment and disorientation. The items taken from the PSE and PSS were selected on the basis of the 25 discriminating factors demonstrated by Fleiss et al. In case elderly subjects found difficulty in understanding a question or in giving a clear answer, many of the items were simplified and shortened and more precise rating instructions were provided. The majority of ratings are made using five-point scales where each point is clearly defined. Key items covering main symptom areas are rated first, so that an overview of the subject's mental state can be obtained should illness or fatigue curtail the interview. These initial items consist of 36 questions covering 15 symptom areas. Like the PSE, the GMS records symptoms experienced in the preceeding one month. Unlike the PSE or PSS, the GMS rates all behaviour variations and not just those considered abnormal by the rater. This approach was adopted because of the unknown effects of normal ageing on behaviour. The rater is required to distinguish between illness, particularly dementia, and normal ageing, at the diagnostic stage of the examination. After completing the GMS the rater is required to state a diagnosis based on the interview he has just completed, and is required to make a judgement about whether or not the subject is a case. A case has been defined as "one having psychiatric symptoms of such quality and quantity as considered to require treatment or management by professional staff". As with the PSE, raters should be trained in the use of the GMS.

An initial assessment of the performance of the GMS as used in the US-UK Diagnostic Project was published by Copeland et al. (1976) (Part I) and Gurland et al. (1976) (Part II). It was based on the data obtained by interviewing 100 hospitalised subjects within 72 hours of admission, who were then re-examinated after one and three months. After the GMS had been given to the subject at the initial interview, a diagnosis was made. The history of the illness was then obtained and the diagnosis reassessed. Of a series of 30 consecutive patients so examined, it was found that a change of diagnosis of some kind was made in only 20% of patients after the history had been taken. There were no changes from a functional diagnosis to an organic one or vice versa. Thus it was concluded that the contribution of the history of the illness to the final diagnosis was rather less than had been anticipated. When information from physical examinations, social histories, biochemical tests and X-ray studies was taken into consideration, this also had little effect on the final diagnosis. It was noted that symptom profiles for organic and functional disorders differed markedly. Comparisons of symptom profiles before and after the three-month follow-up period showed, as expected, that those associated with a diagnosis of affective disorder suffered a significant fall in level of symptoms while those with dementia demonstrated little change. The above findings indicated a measure of diagnostic validation.

Two inter-rater studies were reported in the same paper, which had been performed after a one-year interval. They demonstrated reasonable reliability both for important symptom items and for diagnosis between raters rating together, and between those rating consecutive interviews. A correlative procedure involving clinical and statistical operations was carried out on this same group and produced twenty-one factors.

The original US-UK Diagnostic Project hospital samples were subsequently expanded to include community based subjects. The random samples in New York and London each provided mental state data on approximately 400 community residents while the earlier hospital comparisons provided data on 150 in-patients in London and 75 in New York. The London samples were used as the main source of data for testing AGECAT.

The Development of a Community or Short Version of the GMS

It has been the intention to develop a shortened version of the GMS which would be suitable for: screening for mental illness in elderly populations; recording basic psychiatric symptoms; formulating a diagnosis by major categories.

At present two community versions are being piloted - Version A in Liverpool and Version C in Canberra, Australia. The results of these pilot studies will be pooled and compared in order to derive a standard community version. The full GMS takes on average 40 minutes to give to a sick person whereas the shortened version A can be given in 25-30 minutes. The shortened version A is currently being piloted in the community in Liverpool by both psychiatrists and non-medical personnel trained in its use. Two inter-rater studies have been performed by two groups of workers, one using video recordings, the other using consecutive interviews in the community (medical rater followed non-medical rater in all instances). A provisional analysis of these studies shows that symptoms are rated similarly by both groups in the video tape study, although the non-medical group consistently overestimates 'caseness' compared to the medical group of raters when using intuitive judgement. This bias presumably reflects the different backgrounds of the raters. In the community study however, it appears on first analysis that the non-medical group consistently overestimate both symptom severity and caseness when compared to the medically qualified group. This new bias could reflect the different uses for which the two groups of raters were using the interviews. The non-medical group were screening, i.e. trying to identify cases, whereas the psychiatrists were merely using the schedule as a check on 'caseness'. The presence of these biases, particularly the use-bias, has stimulated a more detailed analysis of the data which will be published later.

The Development of AGECAT

Computer generated diagnostic systems have been developed with the PSS and PSE. These are the DIAGNO - Spitzer et al. (1968, 1969) and CATEGO - Wing et al. (1974, 1978) systems respectively. The AGECAT system has been developed along different lines from the CATEGO system. It is being reported by Copeland, Dewey and Griffiths-Jones (in press). Symptom items from the full GMS are condensed into 160 symptom components. The symptom components are then grouped under eight clinical diagnostic clusters, viz. organic, schizophrenic/paranoid, manic depressive psychosis, obsessional, hypochondriacal, phobic and anxiety neurosis. A clinical hierachy is applied according to the group scores within each cluster resulting in a level of diagnostic confidence on a six point scale for that cluster. Diagnostic clusters are then compared level for level using clinical judgement starting with organic and schizophrenic/paranoid and ending with anxiety, to provide the final diagnosis.

To demonstrate the preliminary success of AGECAT against the psychiatrist's diagnostic decision, Table 1 shows the tentative first comparison of the prevalence of major diagnostic groups in the community study in London for psychiatric judgement and AGECAT. Agreement on diagnostic proportions is fairly good and the overall agreement is close. AGECAT has no means, as yet, of diagnosing most conditions subsumed under the heading 'other' such as alcoholism, addiction and personality disorder.

Table I Prevalence of Major Diagnostic Groups. London Community Sample (Tentative first comparison).

(Age 65+, 408 seen, 396 schedules completed)

	Psychiatric interviews Judgement	AGECAT Diagnosis
%	%	%
Depression	17.2	19.4
Psychotic 1.5 Neurotic 15.7		
Dementia/organic	4.3	3.8
Neuroses	3.3	1.8
Other	2.0	-
Cases - Proportion of whole	26.8	25.8

Table 2 shows the actual agreement on cases, between psychiatrists and AGECAT. The heading 'others' here includes the neuroses. This is an area which needs improvement. The tendency of AGECAT to diagnose some non-cases as depression also warrants further improvement although some disagreement on mild cases is inevitable in a community study. Despite these problems, agreement occurs on 62 cases of depression out of 68, on 14 cases of dementia out of 17, and on 278 non-cases out of 298. Sixty percent of the subjects were followed up one year later. Out of 396 initial cases of illness 51% of AGECAT cases and 65% of psychiatrists' cases were no longer cases at follow up, leaving 49% and 35% respectively still classed as cases. After the year, 6.4% new cases emerged not previously diagnosed by the psychiatrists. Overall the outcome of the two groups of patients diagnosed by AGECAT and the psychiatrists was reasonably similar. In most comparisons involving diagnostic judgements, there are a large body of cases and non-cases on which all raters tended to agree, while decisions on a few borderline cases are often so difficult as to be almost no better than random. The results shown in the Tables are tentative at this stage as work is continuing to refine AGECAT and test it against hospital populations.

Table 2. Agreement on Cases Between Psychiatrists and AGECAT. London Community Sample (Aged 65+)

		AGECAT			
		Depression	Organic	Other	Non-Cases
Psychiatric Interviews	Depression	62	0	0	6
	Dementia	1	14	0	2
	Other	0	0	3	10
	Non-cases	15	1	4	278

There is some way to go yet in developing and improving AGECAT but the initial results are encouraging. Its use is to be extended to the GMS community versions. A standardised psychogeriatric history schedule has been developed (J.R.M. Copeland and D.M. Forshaw) which it is hoped will increase the usefulness of AGECAT and extend the diagnostic discrimination. Eventually AGECAT will make the following information available for each subject:

(1) category of diagnosis; (2) sub-category; (3) alternative diagnosis, if any; (4) level of diagnostic confidence; (5) level of caseness; (6) a diagnostic profile of levels across all eight diagnostic clusters; (7) a symptom profile on 21 symptoms; (8) the presence of emotionally distressing physical illness.

Bibliography

Copeland, J.R.M., Dewey, M.E. and Griffiths-Jones H.M. (in press) 'Further Developments of the Geriatric Mental State Interview (GMS) and the Automated Geriatric Examination for Computer Assisted Taxonomy (AGECAT)', Psychological Medicine

Copeland, J.R.M., Kelleher, M.J., Gourlay, with A.J., Gurland, B.J., Fleiss,J.L., and Sharpe, L. (1969) 'A Semi-structured Clinical Interview for the Assessment of Diagnosis and Mental State in the Elderly. The Geriatric Mental State Schedule. I. Development and Reliability'.Psychological Medicine, 6, 439-449

Fleiss, J.L., Gurland, B.J. and Cooper, J.E. (1971) 'Some Contributions to the Measurement of Psychopathology', British Journal of Psychiatry, 119, 647-656

Gurland, B.J., Fleiss, J.L., Goldberg, K., Sharpe, L. with Copeland, J.R.M., Kelleher, M.J. and Kellett, J.M. (1976) 'A Semi-structured

Clinical Interview for the Assessment of Diagnosis and Mental State in the Elderly. The Geriatric Mental State Schedule. II. A Factor Analysis', Psychological Medicine, 6, 451-459

Spitzer, R.L. and Endicott, J. (1968) 'Diagno: A Computor Program for Psychiatric Diagnosis Utilizing the Differential Diagnostic Procedure'. Archives of General Psychiatry, 18, 746-756

Spitzer, R.L., and Endicott, J. (1969) 'Diagno II. Further Developments in a Computor Program for Psychiatric Diagnosis', American Journal of Psychiatry, 125, 12

Spitzer, R.L., Fleiss, J.L., Burdock, E.I. and Hardesty, A.S. (1964) 'The Mental Status Schedule: Rationale, Reliability and Validity', Comprehensive Psychiatry, 5, 384-395

Wing, J.K., Birley, J.L.T., Cooper, J.E., Graham, P., and Isaacs, A.D. (1967) 'Reliability of a Procedure for Measuring Present Psychiatric State', British Journal of Psychiatry, 113, 499-515

Wing, J.K., Cooper, J.E., Sartorius, N. (1974) 'Measurement and Classification of Psychiatric Symptoms. An Instruction Manual for the PSE and CATEGO Program', Cambridge University Press, Cambridge

Wing, J.E. and Sturt, E. (1978) 'The PSE-ID-CATEGO System: A Supplementary Manual' (Mimeo), Institute of Psychiatry, London

PART TWO : POLICY AND SERVICES

Chapter Six

WELFARE POLICY FOR THE ELDERLY. THE POLITICS OF THE PERIPHERY?

H. Taylor

Introduction

I want to examine some of the consequences of the present government's social and economic policies, specifically in relation to the elderly population. The choice of subject was, for me, a kind of coming to terms with the possibility (to put it as non-politically as I can) of an intensification over the next five years of the kind of policies experienced during the previous four. Even as recently as February, 1983, when an illicit copy of the cabinet Family Policy Group papers found its way into my hands, I recall being somewhat complaisant upon reading what was a relatively small and apparently innocuous section on the elderly. The document itself seemed to pose a much greater threat to the aims of friends and colleagues working in the poverty and family 'lobbies' than to myself in the ageing field. This is not to say that I was unaware of the effects which cuts in health and social services must inevitably have on the care of elderly people. All the same, it seemed reasonable to believe that the inescapable reality presented by an ageing population, particularly the increase over the next 20 years in the 75+ group, which includes some of the frailest members of society, would ensure that even a government committed to Victorian values would seek to protect this 'deserving' section from the worst effects of financial cutbacks and recession.

Was I alone in this total misconception of things? On the one hand, the political Right no doubt believed that temporary policies of tight fiscal and monetary control would create the conditions for economic revival. The Left were equally confident that the failure of these policies would lead to their rejection at a general election. Both have been proved wrong. The increasingly manifest commitment of the Government to a far-reaching re-institution of market forces has inevitably led to a challenging of the centrist consensus, which to a notable degree has existed since the Second World War, regarding the role of the institutions of the Welfare State. What is more, the collectivist middle way, with its high levels of taxation and inefficient bureaucratic administration, has been an easy target for attack. The question is, who are likely to be the most seriously affected victims of any attempts to cut social spending and roll back the statutory welfare services? The answer must be the elderly, since it is they, more than any other group, who are the major consumers of health and social services and whose pension entitlement appears to constitute such a huge threat to the future financial viability of this country. Far from their position as elders rendering them sacrosanct, they have become instead the 'nettle that has to be grasped'.

Monetarism and the Breakdown of Consensus

It is now a familiar tenet of recent social history that during the period of industrial expansion of western countries which followed the Second World War measures to secure full employment and a greater degree of social justice were favoured by all shades of the political spectrum. For a number of years, there seemed to be a convergence of ideas around the political centre. Whether this amounted to a genuine consensus or merely a temporary 'stalemate' is a matter for debate. What is clear, however, is that the situation has been confounded by a Conservative administration which, confronted with long-term inter-related problems of inflation, low investment and overseas competition, has resorted to radical policies of an ideological stance, involving the revival of earlier monetarist assumptions about economic behaviour - thereby overthrowing the delicate social and political balance of the last 40 years. The problems of a post-Keynsian world economy, where growth can no longer be guaranteed, is being tackled by pre-Keynsian techniques - even though they come in an extremely sophisticated package bearing the name of a most eminent economist.

The problem, of course, is that financial, industrial and trading institutions are now international - the national economies do not respond predictably to the regulators applied in a particular country. But more importantly, as far as those of us with a vested interest in social policy are concerned, the institution of full employment and the Welfare State has led to a public sector which does not behave according to the classic principles of supply and demand. This in itself severely restricts the extent to which such policies can be applied in practice. Nevertheless, the current cuts in social spending should be seen, not as a temporary measure necessitated by economic crises, but part of a long-term political strategy. Whether it will prove an irreversible trend or merely one of the swings and roundabouts of history dating back to the medieval Poor Laws need not trouble us here. The fact is that it is significant in the here and now.

The exposure of government thinking over the last years, particularly in the unpublished Think Tank report and the Family Policy Group papers, has been confirmed in circulars and statements issued since the general election in June. It is now clear that a prime objective is to cut back statutory social services and to encourage whenever possible the handover of welfare support to the private and voluntary sectors; this means a yet greater social division of welfare, the encouragement of a pool of lowly paid, and an even heavier burden placed on an already over-burdened informal caring sector. It amounts to a determined rejection of the collectivist middle way. The strategy adopted appears to be to reduce the level of public expenditure by cutting benefits, limiting entitlement and holding down funding to health and social services below the level of actual demand of even our present ill-defined and inadequate standards. The resulting deterioration in statutory services will provide the stimulus to alternative commercial provision. It is, as the general election indicated, a policy which for the present strikes a favourable chord with a large section of the electorate. At the same time, it should be added, surveys have shown - Lansley and Meek (1983) - that when confronted with the implications of cuts in actual services, the majority of people opt for their retention and indicate a readiness to pay the price.

Part of the embarrassment of the Government, we are informed, is that in spite of its declared intentions, public expenditure as part of gross domestic product has actually increased from 41% to 44% since 1979 - Lipsey (1983). Moreover, it is estimated that, short of a rapid recovery of the British economy and unemployment coming down, the percentage is likely to rise sharply over the next decade. In part, this is the result of demographic pressures creating a need for additional social spending. Mainly, however, it is attributable to the cost to the state of paying out unemployment benefit, providing support to ailing industries and increasing the defence budget. In these circumstances, the only way the government can keep its promise to roll back public expenditure and redeem its pledge to reduce taxation is to cut spending on health and social services.

There is, it should be added, increasing doubt as to whether the policy of reducing public expenditure will have the desired effect, that is, of lowering interest rates, stimulating investment and facilitating reduction in taxation. All that seems to have happened so far is that cuts in public expenditure have necessitated further borrowing and a continued high level of taxation in order to finance unemployment. Even with 3.5 million persons unemployed and cuts in existing services, we are still faced with high interest rates, wage awards which run ahead of inflation and one of the slowest economic recoveries in the world. It is a fragile structure, largely balanced, one suspects on the basis of revenues from North Sea oil. Once this particular support is removed in a few years time, the future looks very bleak indeed. What needs emphasising is that the problems and pressures which this situation creates are likely to be the same for whatever government is in power.

Implications for the Elderly Population

Over the next 20 years the pressure of public expenditure is likely to be upwards, while the resources to meet this, on present showing, will decline. During this time, the number of elderly persons over 75 years will rise by 13%. Bessell (1983) in a recent letter to The Times pointed out that, 'Far from being a burden on health and social services, the fact is that over 90% of elderly people live and die in their own homes, making no more than marginal demands on their general practitioner. It is only a small minority who need specialist care in hopsital, old people's homes or sheltered housing, and no more than 7% who receive home help or meals'. This is, on the one hand, very helpful and salutory - if not entirely accurate. For instance, 90% of the elderly do not die in their own homes. On the other hand, it does ignore the costs consequent on the needs of the 10% and also the extent of unmet need. Over half the country's social security payments go to elderly people, whilst in terms of costs per head, they are the main consumers of health and social services - CSO (1982) and DHSS (1978). Looking ahead, by the mid-80's the cost of the State earnings-related pension scheme will begin to expand rapidly. As the ratio of economically active persons to pensioners contracts, unless there is a compensating increase in productivity and economic growth, the National Insurance contributions as a proportion of earnings will also have to increase by as much as 30%. The implications of all this is that a stationary or even falling level of industrial output will be unable to sustain the cost of the level of support to the elderly, to which we are already committed.

In the face of this, the government is attempting to initiate a debate for radical changes in National Insurance provision. Thus, we have internal Whitehall committees, the Policy Studies Institute and the National Institute for Economic and Social Research all being drawn into the process of policy revision, the aim of which is to create a climate of opinion in which, it is hoped, the need for drastic changes can be recognised. The kinds of ideas which are being examined include the scrapping of the 1975 earnings-related scheme and even the withdrawal of the State from the earnings-related sector altogether. Hence, the frantic effort to solve the problem of transferability which 'dogs' occupational schemes. According to Hencke, Social Services Correspondent of The Guardian - Hencke (1983), staff in the social security section of the Ministry are working to a brief ordered by Mrs. Thatcher to look for substantial savings in the scheme without undermining a government commitment to keep its principles intact. Under consideration therefore are: (a) abolition of widows' rights to take over her husband's entitlement; (b) abolition of the right by workers to choose the best 20 years of their life on which to base their earnings-related pensions. Both measures apparently would lead to enormous savings.

The National Health Service, in contrast to the position of personal social services over the last few years, has been largely protected from the cuts in public expenditure. However, at the beginning of July, the situation went beyond the stage of arguing whether growth in expenditure represented real growth or not and the brakes were definitely and officially applied. The Secretary of State for Social Services announced that planned annual increases in health spending would be restricted to half of one percent over the next ten years. This contrasts with the Department's own estimates that 0.7% growth is necessary simply to meet health care needs of the elderly population. However, this has been followed up by a circular to health authorities imposing cash limits which involve substantial reductions in manpower levels within the present financial year. The Department is poised to announce still further cuts.

The attempt to restrain local authority personal social services (in effect, a cut-back in services) started even before 1979. Since then, local authority expenditure has been singled out as the main target for attack under the Conservative Government. The spending targets for English local authorities, announced by the Secretary of State for the Environment at the beginning of August, 1983, require so-called high spending authorities to make a 6% cut in cash terms alone. The scene is now set for an attack on both hospital and community services which will make the cuts of the previous four years seem as mere skirmishes by comparison.

Government Targets for Local Authority Expenditure

Until now, local authorities have borne the brunt of the attack aimed at reducing public expenditure. This is in spite of the fact that it is central government that has 'burst' its own spending limits. Local authorities have become the scapegoats for the failure of successive governments to manage the economy. The Environment and Social Services ministers claim that there are savings to be made from the most cost-effective use of existing resources. No doubt there is room for greater efficiency within local govenment (just as there is within central government), but the costs incurred by the high spending authorities are not the result of waste or profligacy. Rather, they are the consequence, in urban areas, of inner city decay and more generally the attempt by local authorities to develop community services according to central government's own stated guidelines. Having found that Whitehall targets for expenditure and finance under the rate support grant are not sufficient to maintain levels of service, local authorities in many cases have been prepared to raise the additonal revenue through the rates. This they have done in full knowledge that they would be held accountable for their actions at the local elections. According to my understanding of economics, this action does not add to the money supply and therefore cannot be said to fuel inflation, so there would seem to be little justification for central government to block this exercise in local democracy. Nevertheless, a White Paper has just been published which outlines legislation which proposes to do just this - D.O.E. and Welsh Office (1983).

If local authorities had actually stuck to the spending targets set by the DOE, then it would not have been simply a case of services failing to meet increasing demand. This has been the main complaint of Directors of Social Services. The cuts would bave bitten far more deeply, as much as 10% below that for which the authorities themselves have budgeted. The fact is that it is the elected members who have largely protected the personal social services until now - by a combination of juggling the rate support grant and raising the rates. Although the Government has been compelled to make adjustments to its own original targets, a number of authorities have still been hit by penalties for overspending under the rate support grant.

During the present year, local authorities have budgeted (during 1983-84) to exceed their spending targets by £771m - that is by 4% - Jacobs (1983). Within this figure, the percentage for social services, if previous years' experience are anything to go by, can be expected to be much higher. The targets for next year (referred to above), which aim to hit the high spending authorities, will also certainly not leave a low spending authorities unscathed. Thus, while it is the case that levels of expenditure on personal social services have increased since 1979, this has not been sufficient to maintain them in line with inflation and demographic changes - and the present level has been achieved in spite of central government targets.

This situation compares with the spending on the National Health Service which, as already noted, until recently escaped relatively unscathed. This requires some explanation in a situation where it is the Government's declared intention - and one which is widely supported - to move from institutional care to care within the community. In terms of rational social policy, it would have been more appropriate for the NHS to be squeezed and for local authorities to be spared. As Webb and Wistow (1982) have pointed out, it is the personal social services which have to pick up the bill for the policy pursued by the NHS of emptying its wards of long-term patients. To quote them, 'overspending on the PSS simply reflects the continued attempt by local authorities to will the resources needed for community care at a time when central government service and resource policy streams have diverged sharply'. That is, central government no longer itself wills the means to achieve its own policy ends. I think one must look to political considerations - the huge popularity of the NHS and the powerful professional interests within it - to explain why it is only now, after the Government has achieved a second term of office, that is coming under major attack.

Response of Researchers

Having been accustomed for so long to a degree of political consensus in regard to the institutions of the welfare state, the upsetting of this, together with the growth of the private market in welfare, forces one back to thinking about first principles - something which perhaps we have grown unaccustomed to doing. The political Right have taken the initiative and, in monetarism, appear to have a ready-made theoretical position as well as an implementable set of economic and social policies - whatever one may think about the results. Marxists, too, have an immediately serviceable body of doctrine upon which to fall back. It is less easy for those who hold a position in the centre - composed of an amorphous group, ranging over reforming Conservatives, radical Liberals, Fabian Socialists and the Tribunite Left of the Labour Party. Hardly any of these groups can be said to hold a common theoretical position beyond a recognition of the need for collective action, through the institutions of the State mainly, in order to ensure a degree of social justice for the population as a whole.

Although the problem this situation presents to social

researchers is my main concern, the issue is probably much the same for others concerned with the field of social policy, namely, how does one define one's personal position when the common ground has been cut from under one's feet? It is a question which has been focused for me recently in connection with a study which the Centre for Policy in Ageing is presently carrying out of staffing needs in voluntary and private residential homes, and also an earlier study I undertook of the voluntary hospice movement. Since outright opposition to these developments outside the statutory sector was scarcely a feasible option, either I could swim with the political tide or I could try to clarify my assumptions and subject them to objective scrutiny in the light of research findings. In adopting the latter approach, I hope my conclusions were not arrived at in isolation from the wider implications or simply in response to the climate of the time, or the requirements of the funding bodies, but rather in terms of valued ends, clearly stated, which they are intended to serve. No doubt this is a process which most researchers go through when confronted by evidence which questions some of their basic assumptions and beliefs. I suggest that we apply what are the lessons, in fact, of our first-year undergraduate study, and make sure that we carry out this process openly, since we can no longer assume the extent of shared understanding between ourselves and those who commission or utilise our research.

Although in a democratic society there exists the opportunity to argue for alternative policies, the problem for professionals, whose careers and livelihoods depend heavily on government support, is that intelligent self-interest may push them into a position of quietism or simply waiting for the present political storms to blow over. Undertaking research into the role of the private and voluntary sector, for instance, may assure the survival chances of a number of researchers. Indeed, I think it is important that the growing contribution of the private sector should be recognised and understood. Nevertheless, one should also be aware of the limits to that contribution in terms of the immense problems confronting the elderly population and that it may not always be for the good.

Ethrington, (1983), for instance, has made the point that the services which are likely to expand are those which are the most profitable rather than those for which there is arguably the greatest need, i.e. residential care rather than community care.

The difficulty is that trends in research, as in policy, tend to follow a rationale of their own, which is not always justifiable in terms of actual priorities. Loney (1983) gave this very pertinent warning in connection with the development of the voluntary sector, which I think is also relevant to the private sector: 'If the Government can succeed in resituating the debate about welfare into a debate about what should be provided by the family and what should be provided by the voluntary sector, then it will have achieved its objective'. Researchers themselves should be careful not to fall into this trap.

Conclusion

From the point of view of the Government, the social services are entirely secondary to the needs of the economy; the development of the former is dependent on the performance of the latter. This is nothing new. The title of this paper relates to a remark made by the Director of one of the largest agencies concerned with the welfare of the elderly: that as far as all governments are concerned, policy towards the elderly is merely peripheral to their main concerns, which are the economy, defence and foreign policy. Moreover, it seems likely that any future government will be confronted with the same pressures and be compelled to deal with them in much the same way. Sinfield (1983) has been quoted as saying, 'If social work wants to survive in the climate of prolonged recession, it must learn to protest and survive'. How researchers manage this, where dependency on government funding and patronage is usually that much more direct, is also that much more critical.

Bibliography

Bessell, B. (1983) The Times, correspondence, 6th August

Central Statistical Office (1982) Social Trends, 12, HMSO, London

Department of Health and Social Security (1978) A Happier Old Age, HMSO, London

Department of the Environment and Welsh Office (1983) Proposals for rate limitation and reform of the rating system, White Paper, August, London, HMSO.

Ethrington, S. (1983) 'Community wares on the private market', Social Work Today, 14, no. 37, 7th June

Hencke, D. (1983) 'Plan to cut back on state pension scheme', The Guardian, 17th August

Jacobs, A. (1983) 'Councils Set to Burst Spending Targets by £771m', Local Government Chronicle, 29th April

Lipsey, D. (1983) 'Cold comfort for granny', The Sunday Times, 28th August

Loney, M. (1983) 'Private agenda', Social Work Today, 14, no. 26, March

Sinfield, A. (1983) Reported in Community Care, 21st April, 1983, p. 6

Lansley, A. and Meek J. (1983) Booklet on the survey on poverty conducted by MORI for London Weekend Television documentary series 'Breadline Britain', London Weekend Television, London.

Webb,A. and Wistow, G. (1982) 'Over and under', Social Work Today, 13, no. 34, 11th May.

Chapter Seven

PRIVATISING RESIDENTIAL CARE. A REVIEW OF CHANGING PRACTICE AND POLICY

M. L. Johnson

Introduction

In the past decade those who observe health and social services have seen a succession of changes, fashions and developments which have taken root and grown at an alarming pace. Yet few could match the kind of expansion which has taken place in residential care over the past four years.

Before the first Thatcher government came to power one could confidently speak of Part III Homes as a synonym for the whole residential sector. Those who needed residential care received it under the auspices of local authorities, whether they were children, mentally handicapped people, mentally ill or old. Even this this form of expression was an exaggeration, for about a quarter of residents were in voluntary and private establishments. Only about one in ten of the whole residential population were in Homes that were commercially run.

Textbooks on residential care remain focused on what occurs in local authority provision. A vast literature of research studies is almost exclusively about statutory arrangements, with a thin slice of attention going to voluntary Homes. But this is now getting rapidly out of date. Whilst the privatisation of health care has grabbed public and professional attention, a silent and unheralded revolution has transformed long-term social care, particularly for elderly people. For a further account of previous British and American experience in this field see Johnson (1983).

The Changing Pattern of Provision

It is not difficult to detect the causes of growth. The most obvious is the great late life demographic expansion which is now most active in the over-eighty age groups. At the same time this 'rising tide' (as DHSS now term it) is faced with a reduction of places in Part III homes as local authorities respond to cuts and transfer their attention to care in the community. Pressure on hospital beds and the increasing practice of geriatricians to discharge patients who no longer need their specialist services has further inflated the numbers seeking long-term care. As the gap between public provision and manifest demand has widened, the private sector has moved in. Political will (if not active policy) has provided encouragement; the law has been inadequate to stem growth even where it has been considered undesirable and social security 'top up' funding has made private care available to many more people. The residential workers' industrial action in late 1983 only served to amplify a trend which was already established.

Reliable national statistics of the current numbers of private social care Homes and their residents are simply not available. DHSS Research and Statistics Division acknowledge the local authority returns are incomplete for all recent years - particularly in respect of establishments for mentally handicapped and mentally ill people. This deficiency coupled with the inevitable time lag between local collection, dispatch to DHSS and publication, in a fast moving field means that any figures must be taken as under-estimates. Nonetheless the very different trends in the local authority, voluntary and private sectors are unmistakably clear. Written answers in response to a Parliamentary Question about the number of beds in old people's Homes were submitted to Michael Meacher in November 1983, see Commons Hansard (1983). The following material (extract) was supplied:

Table 1 Number of Residents Aged 65+ (England)

As at Dec 31st	Local Authority Homes	Voluntary Homes	Private Homes	All Homes	Number of Residents expressed as a rate/100 aged 65+
1975	95,113	22,454	18,759	136,326	2.11
1980	102,890	25,449	28,854	157,193	2.28
1982	103,668	26,116	35,839	165,623	2.33

Whilst the three patterns are immediately obvious, these 'England only' figures are best taken only as a rough guide. They show at least a doubling of private Homes places in seven years, taking up almost all the growth.

The 1981 green paper A Good Home - DHSS and Welsh Office (1981) - supplied a more detailed breakdown of the 1980 position. Then there were about 37,000 people accommodated in some 1,300 registered voluntary Homes and 33,000 people in 2,400 registered private Homes. This compared with 115,000 people in residential care provided by local authorities. (These figures are for all client groups, England and Wales, and comparable data supplied by DHSS for 1982 show an increase in the number of voluntary homes to 1361, but a virtually static (indeed slightly reduced) population of 36,622 residents.) In the local authority sector the number of residents had dropped to 106,859 - a reduction of approaching 10%. Concurrently the total of registered private Homes had risen to 3,093 and 41,724 residents. My own estimate for the end of 1983 is 3,500 homes with 48,500 residents. Hence, whilst the traditional providers of residential care are declining or in equilibrium, the commercial suppliers are meeting all the increased demand indicated by the greater proportion as well as the greater numbers of retired people. In addition there is an expansion of a more modest sort in all the other client groups as Part III provision contracts. Even on these figures, which underplay the situation, 693 additional private Homes appeared in two years. Taking into account the known failure rate, I estimate that in mid-1983 seven or eight new Homes per week were being opened in England and Wales.

A further indication of the sometimes exponential growth which has taken place, it is instructive to look first at the shire county retirement areas. Kent, Devon and East Sussex are the league leaders, each with more than 350 registered Homes in their areas and enquiries from prospective proprieters running at around ten a week. Already three-quarters of the 6,000 retired people resident in East sussex Homes are in the commercial market. In the sea-side towns of Lincolnshire, Essex and North Wales, where the dying holiday industry has turned to the more reliable business of care, registering authorities have tried to limit the concentration of new premises by applying planning law as their flimsy tool. In 1983 alone the East Sussex Social Services Department increased its list of registered Homes from just over 300 to 380.

Predictably the foci of growth have been in the south of the country and in the county areas rather than in large conurbations. Nonetheless, Norfolk has over 150 registered premises and a very high growth rate, Lancashire rivals many areas in the south, whilst the outer suburbs of big cities are now experiencing the first concerted wave of commercial intrusion. There can be no doubt that a further period of Conservative government will see this growth sustained.

Statutory Provisions Before April 1984

Under the Residential Homes Act 1980, local authorities are required to register and inspect premises offering residential social care. It is a very brief and loosely constructed piece of legislation which has left registering authorities with very little opportunity either to decline undesirable or unprepared proprietors, or to withdraw registration. Fire regulations and physical requirements are easier to enforce, but matters concerned with staff conduct, quality of care and over-charging practices have proved elusive. Even convicted felons are able to have effective control of Homes, by placing the registration in the name of a relative or colleague.

In the growth areas local authorities have been forced to take the tasks of registration and inspection seriously, but in most places there has been great ambivalence. Labour controlled authorities are likely to give minimum resources in the hope of dissuading the private sector. Conservative authorities have often taken the same position for different reasons. They feel that private care should be allowed to grow unfettered by bureaucratic requirements. In all cases finance is a factor. With the current registration fee at a once-for-all payment of £1 social services committees see private care as a drain on their funds with no domonstrable return. Even in Norfolk where the Registration Officer, Bryan Rowe, has led the field in developing a close and reciprocal relationship with the field through information documents, seminars with prospective proprietors, a course at the local Further Education college and taking the lead in setting up a Regional Rest Homes Association, he has had to struggle on alone. Soon to have a support colleague, he has had to deal until now with 150 registered Homes and several new enquiries a week. So, whilst Kent has a dozen officers and East Sussex have recently five new senior staff, many authorities continue to delegate inspection and registration as an extra task to field social workers or even to add it to the job description of not very senior administrator.

In these circumstances of official neglect and legal inexactitude, it is no wonder that anxiety is building up about the worthiness of some of the Homes which have approved status. At this point it is important to say that high standards of accommodation and care are commonly found in private Homes. Probably the best residential provision for elderly people in Britain is to be found within the private sector - but also the worst. yet de-registration of even the most appalling establishments has proved almost impossible. Some proprietors will take off with fright at official warnings. Others, seeing their livelihood threatened, have hired expensive lawyers to engangle ill-prepared local authority solicitors with little law and no judicial precedent to help them. Cases which social services staff have felt totally sure about have been consistently lost when they have reached the courts.

One element in the local authority ambivalence is their sense of unspoken relief that the commercial Homes are able to take the pressure off them. No longer are waiting lists for places in Part III extensive. In Dorset, which includes the great concentration of private care in the Bournemouth area, there is no waiting list and occupancy levels are beginning to fall. In other places where the presence is less prominent, registration authorities are aware that closing a Home will put them in the unmanageable position of having to offer alternative places in their own premises which are simply not available.

Changes in residents' funding have also given quiet pleasure to local authorities. In the past any person placed by social services in a private or voluntary Home with insufficient personal resources to meet the costs had to be sponsored. But over the past year or two it has become the practice for local social security offices to allow the payment of attendance and other allowances previously available only to those in their own homes, to receive these in residential care settings. Moreover, a discretionary topping-up payment is now widely made in accordance with the level of local costs. Thus, across the country there are supplementary benefit supported residents in Homes where the weekly costs until recently ranged from £70 to £125. In October 1983, the Minister for Social Security, making the first public announcement about this major new form of public support to the private residential sector, announced an uprating of DHSS payments by 25%.

In the light of this ministerial action and statements associated with it, there is no indication that DHSS are moving towards a curbing or withdrawal of this considerable source of revenue for proprietors who are increasingly aware of its benefits. One new owner, wishing to fill his beds, recently advertised a free weekend trial stay for elderly people. When the rested carers came to collect their equally satisfied elderly parents, lamenting that it would be nice to continue the arrangement except for the money, the proprietor had a solution. Ready to hand he had a supply of SB forms - and rapidly filled his beds. This facility is undoubtedly costing tens of millions of pounds a year, and some Social Services Directors share my view that it may already have reached £100m in the payment of allowances and top-up awards.

Residents and the Market

Private Homes are clearly becoming more accessible to the least well-off elderly, but the majority of residents are, for the time being, self-supporting. The facilities on offer clearly reflect the financial standing and former lifestyle of residents. Unlike Part III Homes which serve a poor and relatively homogeneous population of frail old people, private Homes exist in great variety. They range at the cheapest end of the market from modest homeliness at as little as £55 a week up to superior residences with 5 star hotel facilities at £200 a week and more. One I know of in Suffolk, housed in a substantial period mansion and requiring all residents to dress formally for dinner, not long ago had an enquiry from a lady who wondered if she could bring her horse. Not an enquiry often encountered in Part III!

Like all of the subjects already discussed, there are few hard data available about the routes by which old people become residents. A handful of research projects are in progress, but firm knowledge is as scarce as official statistics. During the next year the results of these studies and my own should provide a clearer picture. In the meantime, existing intelligence suggests that most prospective residents are guided by professionals. General practitioners provide advice to those who are living at home, whilst geriatricians and psychiatrists are increasingly conscious of the private sector as a way of releasing 'blocked' beds. Social workers are also involved, though now increasingly more cautiously, acting as advisers rather than arranging placements which might involve a claim on the ratepayer.

Predictably it is relatives who are the main initiators of entry to old peoples' Homes. Estimates suggest that about four out of five arrangements are effected this way. Their reliance on professional guidance combined, very often, with a desire to keep costs low, makes a mockery of the claim that private care offers freedom of choice. In the circumstances of weariness, guilt, lack of knowledge (no national handbook of private Homes, their merits, facilities and charges exists; whilst local authorities publish only lists of addresses with brief details) and urgency, it is little wonder that consumer preferences are given restricted prominence.

The dangers of professionals acting as agents for particular Homes are already appreciated within the field. Yet there are no existing mechanisms for searching out the corruption which will inevitably be attracted to long-term care here, as it has in the USA, Australia and parts of Europe. More specifically there is not yet a code of conduct for professional involvement in private residential care, as investors, agents or advisors.

Characteristics of Private Homes

At present Homes tend to be small - 12 to 15 residents is the commonest size, although the presence of some very large establishments takes the average well above these figures. Typically the proprieter and Head of Home or Matron is a woman who has some experience of caring, with her husband a co-worker, dealing with the business side and employing his practical skills in maintenance and decoration. Again, firm information does not exist about levels of training amongst proprietors or staff. It is evident, however, that a substantial group of proprietors are women with nursing qualifications plus a small number with backgrounds in social work, residential care, medicine and psychology.

As registered rest Homes are expressly excluded by the Nursing Homes Acts from providing (or purporting to offer) nursing care, the presence of so many nurses as proprietors is paradoxical but it makes good marketing sense. Relatives are always anxious to ensure that illnesses and medication will be adequately provided for and tend to favour nursing led Homes.

Staff, as in local authority Homes, (though now to a declining extent) are largely untrained. Both day and night staff are likely to be women drawn from the locality of the Home, working on a part-time basis for lower than local authority rates of pay. Registration Officers are constantly concerned about staffing levels and the lack of training, yet have been able to act only in the most extreme circumstances.

The Market

One line of argument suggests that where conditions are poor there will be a lack of clients - the dissatisfied will leave and tarnished reputation will deter newcomers. As with all commercial ventures, market forces will operate. Good service and efficiency will thrive and where there is surplus capacity the less good establishments will go to the wall - for further discussion see Walker (1984) and Judge, Smith and Gooby-Taylor (1983).

In the field of social care there are three important reasons why these general mechanisms should not be allowed to be the principal regulatory force. The first is that the traditional economists' assumption of 'perfect knowledge' of the market is manifestly not the case. The prospective resident (or relative) will find it exceedingly difficult to make an informed choice. 'Which' guides to old people's

Homes do not yet exist. So far, the best that can be offered - see Medical Market Information (1980 et seq.) - is a listing within the Directory of Private Hospitals and Health Services (published annually) for residential Homes, although one local guide has been compiled -see Oxfordshire Community Health Council (1983) - and some others may exist.

Secondly, elderly residents are now quite likely to be so old and so frail (the mean age of entry is 80) that to remove themselves from an unsatisfactory Home is likely to require skills and capacities they no longer have. Residential Homes cannot be changed with the ease of changing one's butcher. Linked with this point is the third. Competition might be a desirable market condition, but if the consequence of it is closure for those which cannot survive the pressure, then a heavy price will be paid by older people in need of care and support, whose security and stability will be put at risk. Given the known mortality rates within the first month of admission to old people's Homes, bankruptcy and business failure will become more than the proprietors' tragedy.

Public Accountability

The maintenance of good standards is a task which has fallen to local authorities since passage of the 1948 National Assistance Act. But statute, as we have seen, has provided them with very little power to intervene and governments have made no financial provision for doing the job. Accompanying regulations have been equally restrained. Revisions of the law in 1962 and in the very recent Residential Homes Act 1980 have retained the original brevity and focus on the registration process. Once registered under these Acts a Home need not necessarily expect any further attention from the registering authority, for no specification of inspection requirements was made. Naturally, prudent Social Service departments have set their own patterns, but many have found it difficult to visit even once a year.

As if to reinforce the insubstantial framework of accountability which the law prescribed, the cost of registration remains to this day a single once-for-all payment of £1. Despite this nominal return local authorities have been aware a long time that neglect of the private sector could cause them trouble and embarrassment. Cases of fire, over-crowding, cruelty or malpractice with residents' money appear with sufficient regularity in the popular Sunday press to ensure a certain minimum of vigilance. Yet even when these circumstances have come to the notice of visiting inspectors, it has proved enormously difficult to achieve de-registration. Recourse to the Magistrates Court or an appeal to the Crown Court by aggrieved proprietors has consistently demonstrated the weakness of the law as it now stands. In effect we have a licensing system which excludes only the most patently unsuitable proprietors and premises.

With the great expansion, the industry itself has become aware of the need for publicly recognised high standards. Established proprietors anxious to retain their share of the market in the face of escalating competition, have banded together in Regional Rest Homes

Associations. Most operate on a single county basis and have, as an important part of their objectives, a concern with high standards of provision. Whilst such requirements are in part self interested (they keep the competition down to ensure a cachet for members) they also reflect a genuine desire to operate self-regulation in the absence of strong public measures.

New as the Regional Associations are, they are already linked by a national body, the National Association of Regional Rest Homes Associations. It has come out strongly in favour of more stringent entry regulations and broadly welcomes the new legislation. Even the increased costs are accepted as a necessary part of the tightening up. For rather different reasons the Association of Directors of Social Services, the British Association of Social Workers and the Residential Care Association have been anxious to increase controls over the private sector. So, the new Act has a wide spectrum of support, but will it, along with ministerial regulations and the Code of Practice, provide the necessary safeguards?

The New Act

Under the anonymous title, Health and Social Security Adjudications Act 1983 (but consolidating legislation now before Parliament would change it to the Registered Homes Act 1984), the new legislation most certainly goes further than all previous law. Schedule 4 (which becomes operative on April 1 1984) uses the term 'residential care Homes' and requires all establishments with four or more residents to become registered. A new annual charge will be made. In addition to having 'fit' premises, the proprietor and the Head of Home will have to be registered as 'fit persons'. They will be required to keep more detailed records about their workings and about their residents and to be open to inspectors on their annual or more frequent visits.

Separate registration of proprietors and persons in charge is a new development, as is the obligation to inform the registering authority of changes in resident structure, numbers and any absences of the Head of Home. A new tribunal will be set up to deal with disputes about registration, closing off previous access to civil courts. Particularly significant is the new opportunity for dual registration as a residential care Home and as a Nursing Home, which is already causing nightmares amongst registration staff.

Almost as important as the Act are the accompanying Regulations. An early draft has already been the subject of consultations and received favourable reactions. It contains requirements for much more detailed records, specification of services provided by the Home and an obligation on non-resident owners (whether individual or corporate) to visit the Home at least one a month.

What the draft regulations do not yet contain is a figure for the annual fee. Early discussion had centred on a £100 fee for all establishments since the local authority Associations pressed for a more 'economic' fee which might cover most or all of the costs of private sector liaison. The figure of £1,000 a year was mentioned, at an early stage, but it now seems likely that a flat fee of £100 per establishment, plus £10 for each registered bed will be the final arrangement. With such an income Social Services departments would be in a position to service the private sector as well as to police it. In the counties with 300 or more Homes, this fee system will produce a 1984 income of approaching £100,000.

Code of Practice

Whilst a number of local authorities have their own codes of practice, there has never been a national and official code. To accompany the new legislation and regulations a Code of Practice has been prepared. Lady Kina Avebury chaired the DHSS sponsored twelve-person Working Party, which was given professional and secretarial support by the Centre for Policy on Ageing.

Some observers have been rightly sceptical about the effectiveness of a voluntary code and would have preferred something which had unequivocal legal standing. American legislation is much more detailed than ours. The Dutch Old People's Homes Act of 1972 incorporates sections on the conduct of Homes, in a way which strengthens regulatory powers. Nonetheless, there is good reason to believe that the British Code will establish principles and standards of care and practice which will gain strength through litigation and their adoption by local authorities. At the time of writing there are indications that the code might be accorded a more official status.

The Working Party, which received over two hundred items of written evidence, saw its task as enunciating clearly the rights of residents and basic ground-rules of good care. Upon this foundation it hoped to build a framework of good practice and guidance about physical standards, staff-resident relations, privacy, staffing, training, resident-proprietor contracts, links with statutory services and with the local community. Plans exist to launch the Code of Practice and the Regulations together with shortly before the April 1st implementation date - see CPA (1984).

A necessary footnote to this brief note on the Code of Practice is to point out that it will, in effect, be a Code for the whole of residential care. Local authorities will be unable to exercise standards prescribed in the Code for the private and voluntary sector if their own Homes fall below these requirements. The significance of this linkage of standards has still to permeate social work circles. Once it does, both private care and the Code will be taken far more seriously than at present.

The Future

With sharper and weightier tools in their hands and revenue to meet much of the cost of inspecting and supporting private Homes, local authorities will find their role in residential care shifting fairly rapidly. They will increasingly act as agents of public accountability and less as service providers. Moreover, as the private sector moves more into the hands of big business and away from the present cottage industry, inspecting authorities will need to be equal in skill to their commercial clients. How long the new tool-kit will prove sufficient remains to be seen.

As dual registration of residential care Homes and nursing Homes tests the ingenuity of statutory bodies, there will - in my view - emerge a need to form a registration system for the whole residential sector. The distinctions between nursing and social care establishments have become so unclear in practice that we face yet another revision of structure before very long.

Acknowledgements

This paper is a substantially revised version of two articles which first appeared in the Health and Social Service Journal. It appears here with the publisher's permission, which is gratefully acknowledged: Malcolm L. Johnson, 'Private Lives' Health and Social Service Journal, July 28, 1983; Malcolm L. Johnson, 'A Sharper Eye on Private Homes', Health and Social Service Journal, August 4, 1983.

Bibliography

Centre for Policy on Ageing (1984) Home Life: A Code of Practice for Residential Care, Centre for Policy on Ageing, London

Commons Hansard (1983) November 11, HMSO, London

Department of Health and Social Security and the Welsh Office (1981) A Good Home. A Consultative Document on the registration system for accommodation registered under the Residential Homes Act 1980. DHSS and the Welsh Office, London

Johnson, M. L. (1983) 'Controlling the Cottage Industry', Community Care, 25 August

Judge, K., Smith, J. and Gooby-Taylor, P. (1983) 'Public Opinion and the Privatisation of Welfare', Journal of Social Policy, 12, 469-490

Medical Market Information (1980 et seq.) Directory of Private Hospitals and Health Services, MMI Medical Market Information Limited, Bishop Stortford

Oxfordshire Community Health Council (1983) A Guide to Old People's Homes and Nursing Homes In Oxfordshire, Oxfordshire CHC, March

Walker, A. (1984) 'The Political Economy of Privatisation' in J. le Grand and R. Robinson (eds) Privatisation and the Welfare State, Allen & Unwin, London

Chapter Eight

A ROUND-THE-CLOCK CARING SERVICE

L. Sawyer

Introduction

'Privatisation' is a dirty word. In the field of care for the elderly it has been used mainly in relation to private residential or nursing homes. In this paper I describe a new concept in community care - a private agency set up in South London to provide care for old people in their own homes. I argue that the nature of a private organisation is such that it can provide a flexible versatile service which really meets the needs of clients. In doing this I draw on statistics from the first one-and-a-half years operation of the agency. I also consider research findings which indicate the needs of clients from community based services, and one research study which suggests the possible characteristics of private sector clients.

It has been said that the 'care system' provided now is no more than notional and that the fragmentation of services and patchy nature of provision is highly unsatisfactory for the elderly in their own homes and for the care of those who can no longer manage at home (Plank, 1977; Wade, Sawyer and Bell, 1982). Looking specifically at care in the community, many writers have drawn attention to the lack of provision for and the failure to meet the needs of old people at home. Hunt (1976) and Chapman (1979), for example, comment on the very small percentages receiving visits from nurses or health visitors. In the latter study, needs were identified but, for a variety of reasons, less than half these needs had been met six months later. Lack of agreement between clients and professionals about the nature of needs was shown by both Chapman (1979) and Farnish (1978).

In 1981/82 I was involved in a study primarily concerned with investigating the possible need for State provision of nursing homes for the elderly. Inter alia, intensive interviews with a subsample of old people and their relatives revealed the dearth of state community services. Some of these old people were in their own homes, but the majority were in geriatric wards, old people's homes, or private nursing homes, care at home having broken down. We found that just over one third of those still at home received none or very little support. This went up to 43 percent of those admitted to hospital, 48 percent of those in Part III, and 61 percent of the private sector. Overhalf had had no meals on wheels and no care from community nurses. Seventy-two percent over all had had none or only what were described as 'unhelpful' visits from social workers. Over three quarters of all groups had not attended a day centre and 90 percent of those subsequently admitted had had no short term admissions to care in the year prior to admission. It was clear from interviews with carers of those who had received this service that this was a crucial support in enabling relatives to continue caring. There was some evidence of a desire for more nursing help, especially night nurses, and for 'granny sitters'. Night time was a particular problem for those who were mentally confused or tending to fall. Some informants commented that nothing but 24-hour cover would have been of any help. The others who thought that nothing would have helped were relatives who had had the old person living with them or totally dependent on them and had had inadequate support over a long period, probably years, culminating in the total breakdown of care at home. In all care sectors, except those in hospital, old people living with relatives had received very much less state support than those on their own.

We also looked at the levels of support from informal carers and concluded that the evidence did not support assertions that admission to institutions is the result of lack of family support except possibly in the private sector where there appeared to be a tendency to employ housekeepers and other categories of staff rather than giving direct personal or domestic care.

It was against this background of potential need that I decided in, March 1982, my future lay not in research but in providing care. From the outset it was implicit in my thinking that the majority of old people do not need 'nurses'. They may well need basic nursing care as part of a 'package of care', but often no more than a caring daughter could provide. What they do need is reliable, kind people who are prepared to be flexible about the services they provide. Coupled with this was the belief that long term institutional care is an unhappy way to end one's life.

Care Alternatives

I set out to provide reliable, caring people who would do anything which needed doing to help old people to stay in their own homes as long as possible. The name 'Care Alternatives' is meant to imply both that we supply alternative carers, and that we supply information about alternative and 'best options' for caring for elderly dependents. We do not do heavy housework, although we are thinking about developing a cleaning team. Apart from that we are as flexible as possible in what we do, the hours we work, about the way people pay. We are informal, friendly and sympathetic in our approach. We realise that it is difficult to get some old people to accept help and that it is important that helper and helped actually get on well together. We are prepared to work very short hours, if that is what the client wants, so we try to place staff with clients as near their own homes as possible. Thus we try to foster the idea of care from within the community.

There are numerous headaches for anyone setting up an enterprise like this: getting a licence, getting planning permission to use you home as an office, or finding an office, deciding whether or not you should be a limited company, finding out how to keep the books, developing a systematic way of working, to mention only a few. We are licensed to run an employment agency, not a nursing agency, which means that our staff can do virtually anything which a daughter could do but even the SRNs on our books cannot give an injection or do sterile dressings.

For me there was another headache - my reaction to the idea of providing a private service, available only to clients who could pay - and all the other arguments against private provision. To balance that, we were going to do something which was not being done by the State. We might release some State services for clients who were currently not being helped at all. We hoped to provide a cheaper service than the existing private provision (private nursing agencies). We might be able to demonstrate a better way of meeting the needs of old people. In my wildest dreams, local authorities would pay for clients who could not afford to buy help themselves.

We started in Wimbledon and in Sutton but by January 1983 we had taken on staff in London. We meant this to be in Kensington and Chelsea - in response to requests from social workers - but although that area remains the main focus of our London work, we now have clients all over the Greater London area.

Staff

Some people have expressed surprise that we can get people to do this work, since we do not pay high rates. Another headache for me is to balance the need for staff to be paid at a reasonable level with the need to provide a service clients can afford. Having had personal experience of being a client in this situation while caring for my own senile parents, I can see both sides only too clearly.

An advertisement in the local paper offering flexible part-time work to mature responsible people - nursing experience an advantage but not essential, produces non-stop phone calls for three days. Of course, not all the applicants are suitable, and not all are seriously interested, but usually a good proportion are taken on each time. Analysing the staff on our books between April 1982 and August 1983 we had: 22 SRNs (+ 2 without finals exams), 15 SENs (+ 1 without finals), 32 auxiliary nurses, 16 who have worked in old people's homes, 10 who have been home helps, 15 who had experience caring for their own elderly parents or nursing someone in the family, and, finally, 22 who had been variously in voluntary work, social work, school welfare, ward receptionists, dental nurses, FSU, meals on wheels or catering. When revising this paper, I found the latest figure for staff was 122. Although we are obviously only a stop-gap for some people looking for work, nevertheless we have a core of reliable people who get to know us and their clients very well.

Using mainly reports from clients, I have rated 29 percent of the staff as excellent. Interestingly, trained nurses do not have a monopoly of excellence. Auxiliaries and those classified as 'other' were the largest part of this group. A third of those rated as bad were SRNs, some of them with an alcohol problem.

Clients

Our referrals come mainly from other caring professionals. We do not advertise our service in the press. By August 1983, we had helped 156 clients. Since then the number has increased dramatically. We have just enlarged our office to cope with the work. Up to that time, the pattern of referrals was that 29 percent were referred by social workers, 16.6 percent by community nurses, 9.6 percent by GPs, and 24 percent by voluntary organisations such as Counsel and Care for the Elderly, Age Concern, Red Cross, Churches and more specialised groups such as the Parkinson's Disease Society.

Because of our flexibility it is difficult to categorise the sort of work we do, but it does appear that in the first year-and-a-half of operation 17 percent of our clients were getting purely personal care, in other words, basic nursing care. A further 20 percent received a combination of personal and domestic care. A typical case would be where one of our carers went into an old couple's home every morning for six months, got them up - dressed, washed, dealt with incontinence, gave them breakfast and ensured that the old lady was ready by the time the ambulance came to take her to the day centre. Requests for companions or 'granny sitters' amounted to 7.7 percent. Sometimes this also involved taking someone out by car or escorting them somewhere. Requests by 7.2 percent were solely for cooking meals and sometimes feeding the old person. Seventeen percent were domestic - shopping, cooking, making beds, etc., although supervision was an important element in many cases. Seven percent required our staff to live in for short periods of up to four weeks, usually when just discharged from hospital, or when the family were away. For similar reasons 11 percent wanted staff to sleep in their homes. Six percent wanted night duty and four percent asked us to find permanent living-in help.

In the research study discussed earlier we found that the old people who were eventually admitted to private nursing homes, the private sector clients, had received a much lower level of help from all sources. Nearly half had received no help from family, friends or neighbours with domestic tasks. This compared with only a quarter of those in State provision or in their own homes. Equally, a much larger proportion of the private sector had received no help with personal care tasks. This dearth in informal support was partly because a larger proportion of this group had no relatives, but we also found that the norm was to pay for help rather than to provide it oneself. When setting up Care Alternatives I had wondered whether we would simply be providing paid help for people who then opted out of taking an active part in the caring. This fear proved to be largely unfounded.

More than half our clients are living with someone else in the family, over 30 percent live with a child. Looking at those who live alone, there was very considerable input by family and/or friends. Nineteen percent of those living alone were visited daily or more often by a daughter who undertook a major part of the caring tasks. A further nine percent had daughters who visited less frequently, but three of these were abroad and one was ill in hospital herself. Eight percent had sons who visited frequently and took on part of the practical caring, and a further 10 percent had sons who took little or no part other than visits at weekends. However, one of these lived a fairly long drive away and had a wife with multiple sclerosis. Three others lived long distances away, and the remainder were all in full time work. Eight percent had friends who took on much of the practical caring. For nine percent, the significant relative was a niece or nephew - in three cases these kin did virtually all the practical caring - the other four clients were visited more or less weekly. I would say that in the vast majority of cases, we are giving back-up help to caring families rather than providing a service for families who are opting out.

Although some clients seem to have no money worries, the majority find it difficult to afford extra help. We try always to tell people about attendance allowances and have helped some clients to obtain them. At the time of revising this report, we are helping an increasing number of clients who are supported financially by home care grants from Counsel and Care for the Elderly. We have also had three clients whose care was paid for by their local authorities, or by DHSS. One case on our books illustrates the way our flexible approach helps us to meet clients' needs: Atypically, Mrs. Desai was ony 49 when she was terminally ill with cancer. We were first asked to go into the home to cope with the domestic tasks as her husband needed to go back to work for both financial and psychological reasons. As we knew her diagnosis, we provided nurses from the beginning. At the outset, they were happy to organise the household and do the cooking, but within a short time they were caring for Mrs. Desai herself. Because they came in initially to care for the home, she was able to accept them. The two nurses were mainly concerned with Mrs. Desai. They made an excellent relationship with her which continued until her death; so she had continuity of care. The relationship was even more important in this case because a culture clash within the family meant that Mr. and Mrs. Desai were estranged from their daughters and Mrs. Desai was extremely lonely and isolated. Towards the end, the nurses put on uniforms and adopted a clear nursing role. This was another important phase in Mrs. Desai's care because it was only by doing this that the nurses had sufficient authority to keep the hordes of relatives, including little children, who arrived as her death grew nearer, out of her bedroom at all hours of the day and night.

Discussion

There is no doubt that there is a tremendous demand for a service of the type we supply and a need which is not being met by the State.

One of the advantages of being a privately run organisation is that we can expand wherever the demand arises and develop and innovate to meet the needs of clients as they express those needs to us. With the current restrictions on spending, or even with a more humane government, it is extremely doubtful whether these needs could be met by State services.

Professor Betty Landsberger has kindly drawn my attention to the work of Svien Olav Daatland of the Norwegian Institute of Gerontology. The hallmarks of the 'care system' which he proposes as appropriate to meet the needs of elderly people are (1) the central role of relationships between helper, family carer and the old person, (2) the designation of care prescription and management to the primary carer or old person themselves, (3) the recognition of the complex and varied nature of care. His first and third criteria are certainly aimed at, if not always met, by our very flexible staff. By being so flexible they ensure that the varied tasks are carried out with the minimum of personnel, thus ensuring continuity and the development of a relationship between themselves and the old person, and with the primary carer(s). The very fact that we are a privately paid agency means that clients or their family retain control over the work. The client can re-arrange the hours of work or the content of work. If they are unhappy with the staff we provide, we try to find someone who suits them better. We recognise that personality is important. The lack of accountability is a criticism frequently levelled at private provision, but our service is far more directly accountable to the people who actually use it than are the services provided by State agencies to their clients.

Bibliography

Chapman, P. (1979), 'Unmet Needs and the Delivery of Health Care', Occasional Papers on Social Administration, Willmer Bros., Birkenhead.

Daatland, S.O. (1983) 'Care systems', Ageing and Society, 3, 1-21

Farnish, E.G.S. (1978), 'A Comparison of Professionally Defined Needs and Self Perceived Needs Among the Elderly', unpublished MSc Thesis, Surrey University

Hunt, A. (1976) The Elderly at Home, OPCS, HMSO, London

Wade, B., Sawyer, L., and Bell, J. (1983) 'Dependency with Dignity: Different Care Provisions for the Elderly', Occasional Papers on Social Administration, No. 68. London: Bedford Square.

Chapter Nine

PRIVATE LIVES

P. McCoy

Introduction

The continuing debate on "privatisation", thrust into prominence specifically by the proposal that Health Authorities could assess the scope for contracting with Nursing Homes for the care of elderly N.H.S. patients, poses some interesting questions to people caring for elderly residents in statutory Personal Social Services agencies. First, perhaps the most significant question is why is not the future of Social Services facilities, rather than just those of the N.H.S., made an issue by any of the parties, despite the clear existence of similar sets of Government suggestions for them? Second, the debate is carried on as if relevant data were completely lacking. I shall base this on two main sources.

1. D.H.S.S. Returns - perhaps an unlikely source of light as opposed to heat but an important national source of important data - see especially D.H.S.S. (1983).

2. A Census in Suffolk of residential care for the elderly, which gathered data from: 32 Local Authority Homes, 15 (out of 17) Voluntary Homes, 27 (out of 36) Private Homes - McCoy (1980).

The Suffolk Census was a replication with considerable additions of the D.H.S.S. 1970 Census of Residential Accommodation, carried out as a pilot for a national sample survey mounted by Robin Darton, Personal Social Services Research Unit of the University of Kent, and thus forms part of one of the few research studies to look at private homes and the only one I know of with national coverage. There are dangers in lumping together homes which happen to be in the same category to produce an average, especially in a broad category like private homes, and in using broad labels such as short-term care which, in a local authority context, can mean one strand of a broad package of domiciliary care services, and in another, such as the private sector, can mean merely a stay of finite duration. Further, residential care is only one aspect of privatisation. It is estimated that nearly 80% of "contracting out" expenditure by local authorities goes on residential care (for all client categories not just the elderly - Social Work Today (1983)). This view is based on a state vs private dichotomy, which is not so useful when applied to non-institutional care such as fostering, good neighbour schemes and even care by the family, where the full costs of care are often not apparent. "Privatisation" as defined here includes voluntary as well as private homes. Many of the labels pinned onto policy initiatives are misleading because the proposing bodies wish to avoid using negatives. For example, 'private', as used in 'privatisation', really means 'non public' in the current debate. This paper limits itself to examining role, siting and recruitment, and does not look at the processes of care within the different types of home.

Trends in Residential Accommodation

Why has privatisation of Social Services residential accommodation not been made an issue? One major reason could be that privatisation is already so well established that it is no longer a contentious proposal but an operating reality, as the first three graphs show. Figure 1 shows the growth in the number of places available in all three sectors, using 1972 as an index value of 100. This relates to places for all ages, and uses the best line curve. It shows: Local Authority places rising till 1978 then almost levelling off at around 122; places in voluntary homes declining till 1972 then climbing to 109; places in private homes declining till 1975 then rising rapidly to 141. Unfortunately the date available to me only reaches 1981. Looking now at the data in Figure 2 for residents aged 65 or more, the overall trend is similar but more marked. Residents aged 65 or more in local authority homes have grown at a slower rate than all places, as have residents in voluntary homes; but residents aged 65 or more in private homes have grown at a rate far faster than all places. Thus the private sector is taking a major influx of elderly people in particular. The data for residents aged 65 or more and supported by local authorities - Figure 3 - show a gradual rise in local authority homes, an accelerating decline in voluntary homes; and fairly wild swings in the private sector - a very rapid rise at the end of the 70s and a subsequent decline in supported residents since then.

It could be argued that it does not matter in which type of home the increases occur, as long as there is some increase somewhere. This argument assumes, amongst other things, that the different types of home provide basically the same sort of service. Data from the Suffolk census gives clear information that this is not so, and highlights some significant differences, which I have grouped under two broad headings.

Role Differences

Local Authority homes aim to provide a continuum of local services for local people; private homes aim to provide residential services only, advertised nationally. The local authority homes are using a growing

Figure 1 Growth in the Number of Places for Residential Care 1972-1981

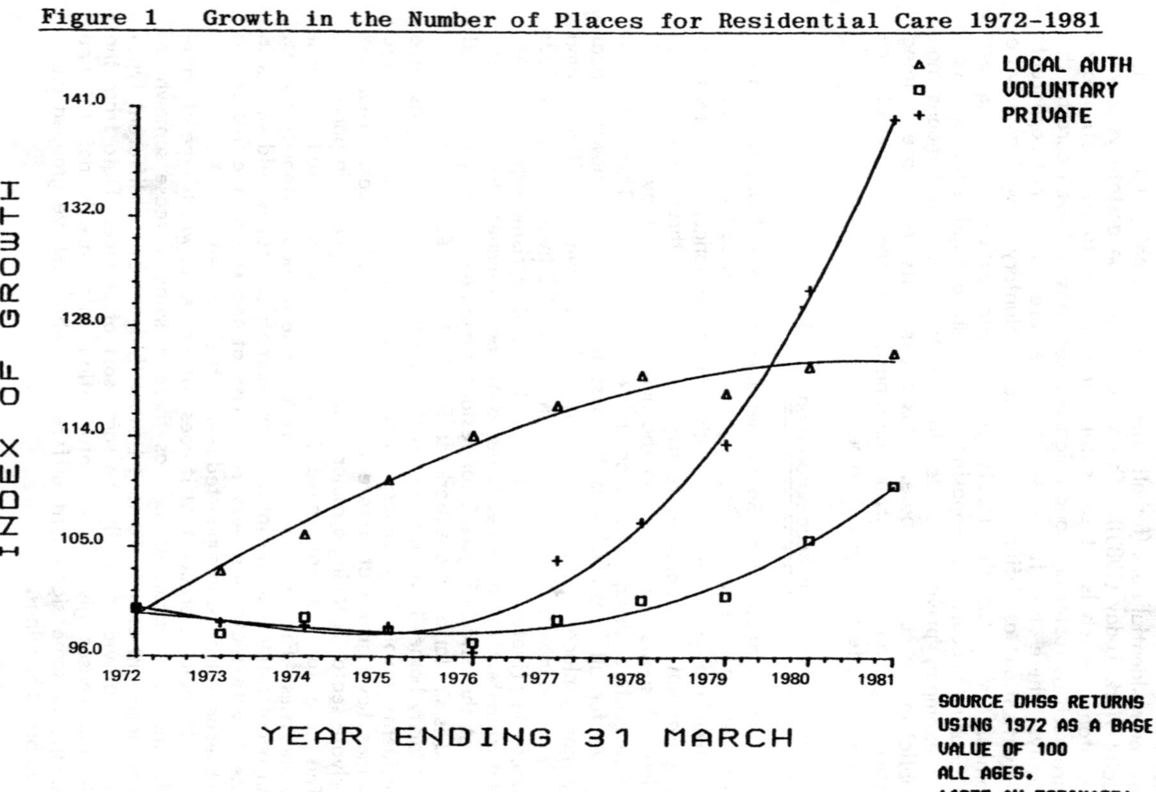

Figure 2 Increases in Residents Aged 65+

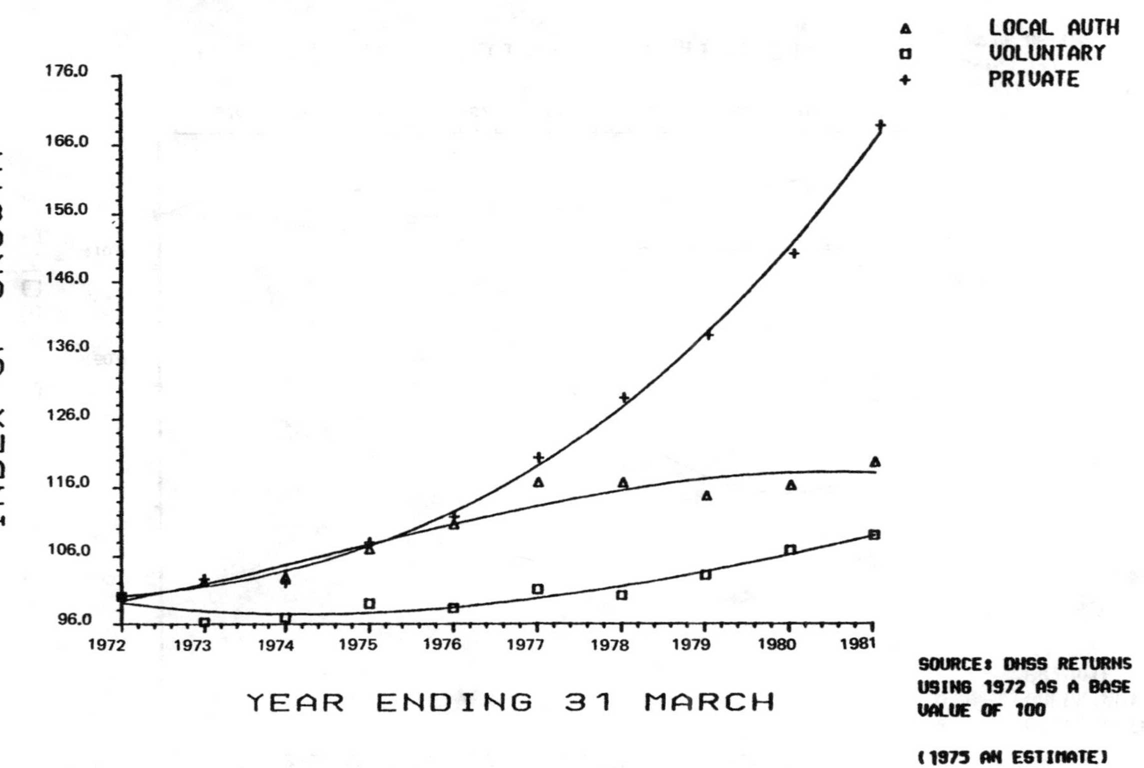

Figure 3 Increases in Supported Residents Aged 65+

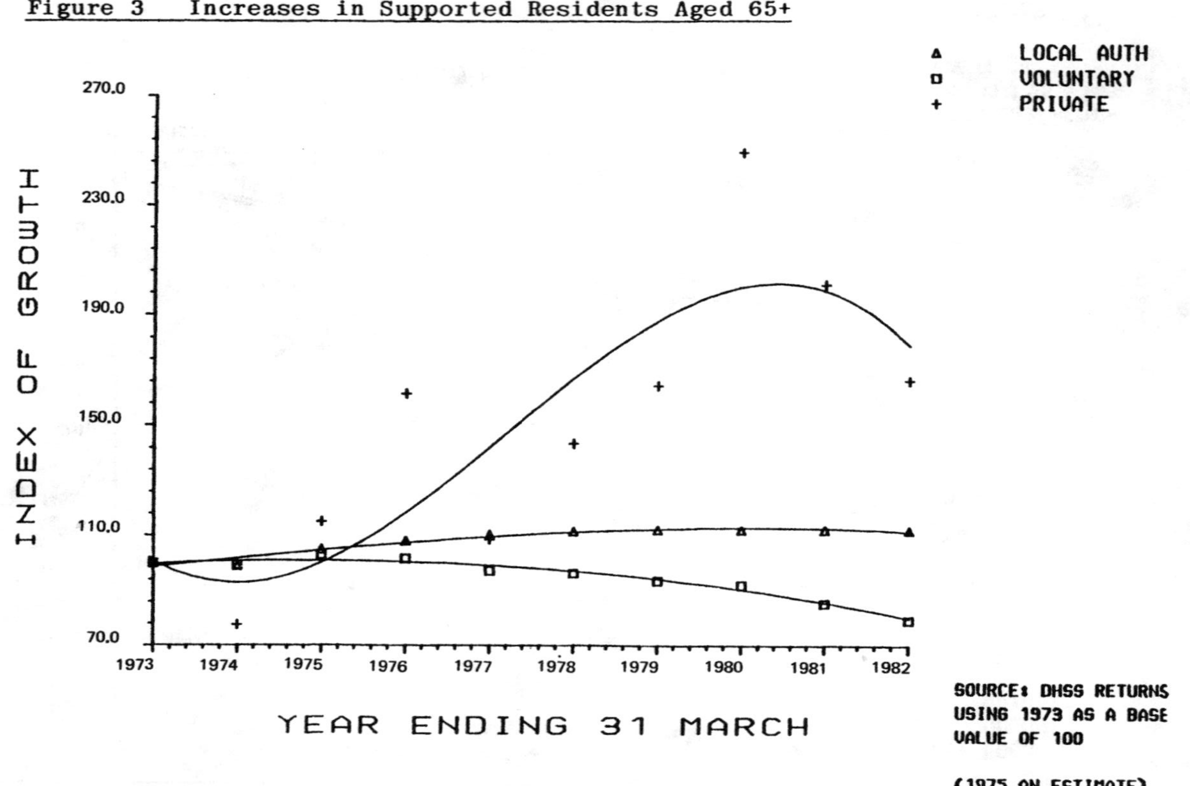

Figure 4 Percentage of Homes by Size and Type

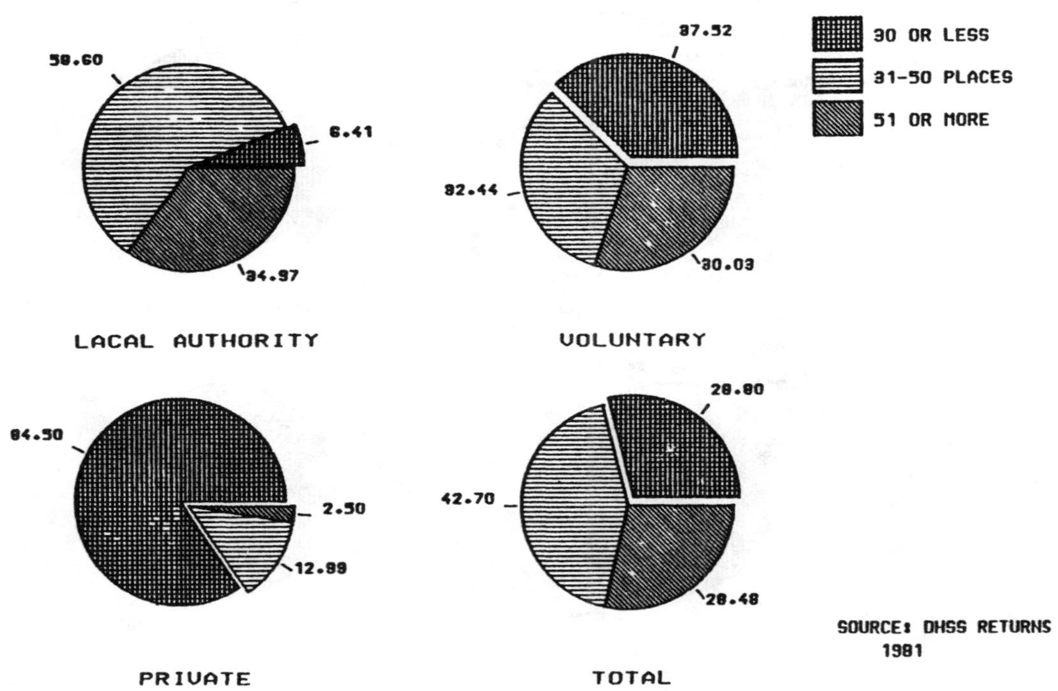

LEGEND

30 OR LESS
31-50 PLACES
51 OR MORE

58.60
6.41
34.97

LACAL AUTHORITY

37.52
32.44
30.03

VOLUNTARY

84.50
2.50
12.99

PRIVATE

28.80
42.70
28.48

TOTAL

SOURCE: DHSS RETURNS
1981

Figure 5 Proximity to Facilities of Local Authority and Private Homes

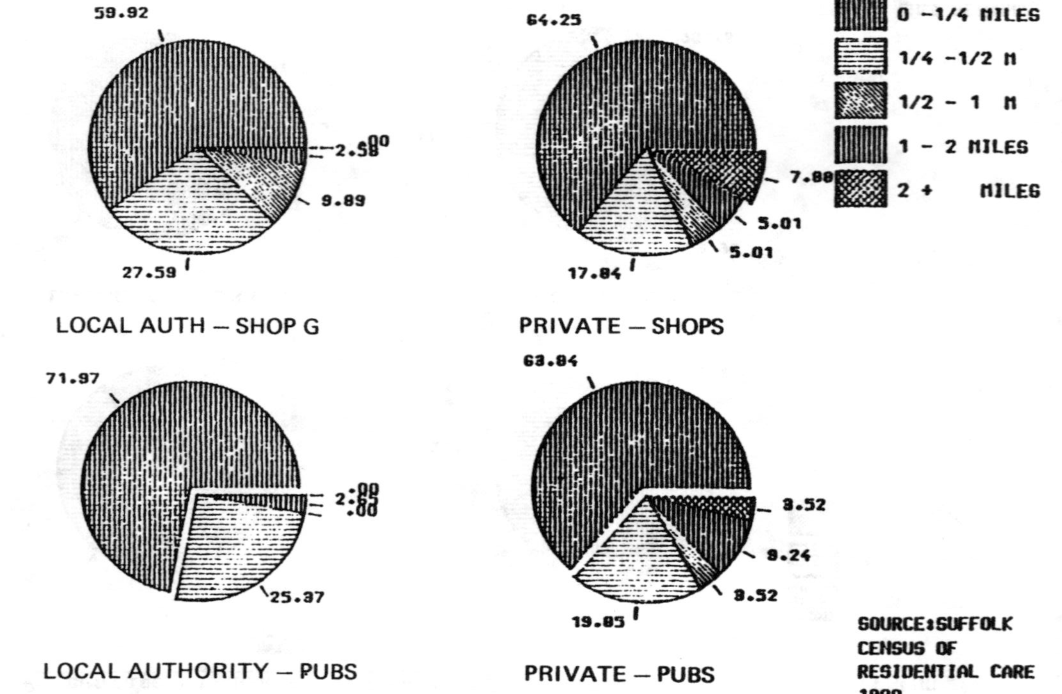

Figure 6 Levels of Dependency in Different Types of Home

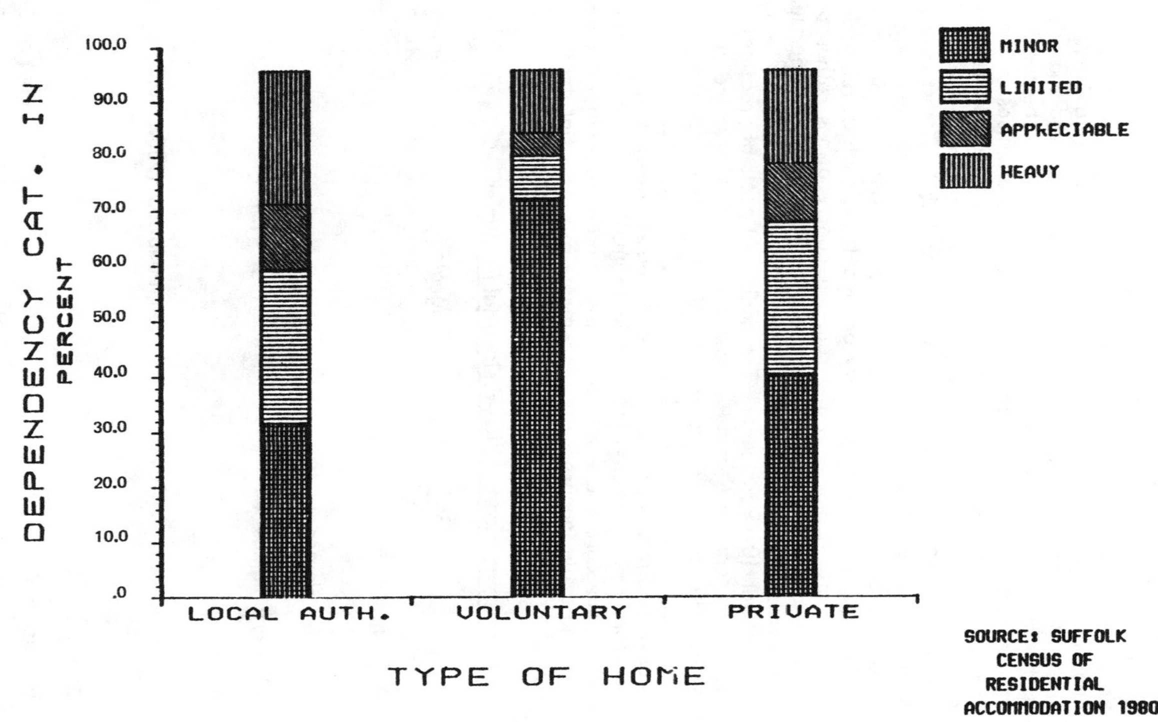

proportion of their facilities to help elderly people who are still living in their own homes supported by domiciliary care services, within a very local catchment area; private and voluntary homes are concentrating on offering long-stay care to clientele from a much wider geographical area. The Suffolk Census showed that the local authority homes had 49 short-term care residents on the survey night, had provided 96 meals for consumption off the premises on the survey day, and had 245 persons attending day care in the week preceding the survey; whereas the figures for private and voluntary homes in the survey were 10,14 and 5 respectively - see Table 1. Most referrals to local authority homes come through local channels, e.g. G.P., hospitals, social service offices, whereas private homes advertise nationally. For many voluntary organisations, such as religious ones, residents are members of the relevant congregations rather than of geographical communities. Private and voluntary homes, particularly the former, are smaller establishments - see Figure 4 - usually catering for 10-15 residents. The additional costs of practices such as short-term care are real disincentives to this practice developing there. This is not to say that local authorities cost such practices adequately. Furthermore, local authorities have responsibilities for local domiciliary services that private and voluntary homes do not, and therefore have a vested interest in promoting 'preventive' services, such as day care and short-term care, in order to promote community care and avoid inappropriate placements in residential care. Private and voluntary homes do not have such an interest or objective.

Table 1 Comparison of Non-residential Facilities

	Short Stay Residents	Meals for Consumption Off Premises	Persons Attending Day Care
Local Authority Homes	49	96	245
Voluntary Homes	6	0	2
Private Homes	4	14	3

Source: Census of Residential Accommodation 1980. Suffolk County Council

Geographical

The vast majority of local authority homes (in Suffolk 26 out of 32) are purpose built and sited establishments, provided more or less evenly throughout the county. Disparities between the three authorities fused together in 1974 have been deliberated reduced. Only one of the 42 private and voluntary homes surveyed in Suffolk is purpose built; many are sited in beautiful, rural but isolated locations, ideally suited to the original function of country retreat. This, of course, can have some advantages - larger rooms, more space for personal possessions -but it does make it more difficult and costly to provide day care and other community servies. As Figure 5 shows, private homes are further on average from facilities like pubs and shops, though this is of more interest to carers than residents. Unlike the local authority homes, in Suffolk the majority of private and voluntary homes are concentrated on the coastal belt, with very few in the inland areas. This geographical disparity in one county is matched by very different rates of growth in private and voluntary homes in different regions since 1972 - see Table 2. There are also small area variations. Boldy (1983) reports a 77% increase in places between 1976 and 1981 in South Devon. Judge et al. (1983) find this increase directly related to a high domestic rateable value per hereditament, and the proportion of pensioners owning cars! This is important because the Suffolk Census shows that local authority homes take the vast majority of their residents from their immediate neighbourhoods, and next to none from outside their District Council area. Less than 30% of the private and voluntary homes said that they took most of their residents from the District council area and many said they took most people from outside the county.

Two further points are worth making. First, on the question of costs, the charges made by private and voluntary homes averaged just over £81 per week, the same as the full charge in Suffok's homes at that time. However, this is a very simple measure of a fairly complex issue. It is relevant to quote Judge et al. (1983) who conclude that "Private Homes were no more expensive than local authority homes" (my emphasis). Second, the survey in Suffolk showed marked differences in the levels of dependency found the different types of homes, as shown in Figure 6. Using a detailed analysis to divide residents into four categories of dependence, the local authority homes in Suffolk were found to be caring for a higher proportion of residents of appreciable or heavy dependency than private homes and in particular the voluntary homes. It is worth noting that the proportion of heavily dependent persons is increasing more rapidly in the private sector. However, mental health and physical frailty should be catalogued separately. The lower cost of caring for the less dependent could have positive attractions for a cost conscious proprietor.

All types of home have some residents who are heavily dependent and, perhaps more interestingly, many who are of minimal dependency. While there are differences, there are also considerable overlaps. There were considerable variations between individual homes in all sectors. The Social Services Division with the highest degree of dependency in homes was the one with the lowest level of N.H.S. geriatric residential care. Interestingly, this did not apply to the private and voluntary homes in the Division since their catchment is not so local. Also, the converted local authority homes in Suffolk had a lower degree of dependency amongst their residents than did the purpose built homes, putting their average dependency level far nearer the private and voluntary home level, in which sector nearly all the homes are converted.

Table 2 Regional Growth of Non Public Residential Homes 1972-1981

Voluntary Homes	Region	Private
97	London Inner/Outer	90
118	East Midlands	107
100	Northern	127
120	Yorks/Humberside	130
117	London North	134
106	South	143
111	South West	162
101	North West	169
108	West Midlands	169
107	TOTAL	139

Sources: DHSS "Feedback" Tables 1972 & 1981. BSGT Table 2

Further Comments

The findings of this research project in Suffolk highlight real differences between sectors of residential care for the elderly. They also demonstrate that the differences are primarily a result of the differing objectives and responsibilities of the agencies that run them. The local authority has a duty to provide a continuum of services to local areas, with the general aim of promoting the welfare of elderly people. The long-stay beds of a residential home form just one part of this, and such homes are more and more being seen as an integral but flexible part of the total packages of care. Long-term care is generally used only after alternative community solutions have been found wanting. By contrast, organisations and individuals running a private home are usually in the business of providing only residential care, and the same is true of the majority of voluntary homes. In such a situation, the appropriateness or cost effectiveness of a community placement is not a relevant question for the admitting agency. These differences between thetypes of home argue for far greater caution in policy statements about 'privatisation' since it has been shown that there is a great danger of treating different situations and types of home as if they were alike, which, it is demonstrated, they are not. How is such a policy consistent with a coherent, planned, comprehensive provision of care for social work clients?

The local authority homes fulfil a far more comunity-oriented role than do the private and voluntary homes and any comparisons must be made carefully. It is ironic that the growth of the private sector and the current Government-led thrust toward privatisation, when linked to the above facts, are directly at odds with a major policy objective of this (and other) governments - to provide a community, even family based, care with the State playing a supporting, i.e. day care, rather than total, i.e. residential care, role. Given the rapid rate of recent growth, as well as the emotive overtones of privatisation, it is perhaps surprising to find little published research on this topic.

A recent symposium at the Centre for Policy on Ageing brought together researchers with direct experience in this area and Homes Advice practitioners and other staff from the Centre to look at future policy for voluntary and private homes for the elderly, at which several important points were raised, which go beyond the statistical bones I have used so far.

The major point was the quality of care in these homes. A number of researchers spoke highly of the quality of care that they had witnessed (rather than measured) during interviews with proprietors in the private sector. The Homes Advice Officers were rather less sanguine, because of their long practical experience assisting proprietors and staff with their problems. Donovan (1983) commented on the "highly routinised and predominantly functional nature of the work of care staff in both private and vountary homes". How many managers of local authority homes can put their hands on their hearts and say that all their homes are of such high quality that, should they need to, they themselves would spend their last years there? Current research cannot answer even the most basic questions about the quality of care in the different types of home.

Another contentious point was 'value for money'. While some homes, particularly voluntary ones, can offer places at a lower charge to residents than the full charge of a local authority place, this was only one aspect of the question. In addition to the difficulties of not comparing like with like, it was also argued that a low charge for the resident in private homes was often achieved by paying the junior staff low rates for the job. It was agreed that further analysis, of the type that Knapp had so ably done, to compare public and non-public day care services for elderly people was needed before an informed opinion could be put forward on inter-sectoral cost comparisons. The role of DHSS in financially supporting residents in private homes, undoubtedly a factor in the rise of placements, was seen as useful for residents, but also as an important state intervention in an area sometimes felt to be purely privately financed. A recent estimate found this to be £100m a year - see Johnson (this volume). The symposium did reach general agreement on some issues. It was imperative for all agencies to respond positively, unhindered by any prior ideological view of the growth rates demonstrated in Figure 1. The establishment by DHSS of a working Party to draw up a code of practice for such homes was welcomed, but it was felt that local authorities need to take an interest greater than merely that of efficient registration in this growing area of provision. As might be expected from such a gathering further research was called for, particularly to examine the process of admission and how people came to be in care in one sector or another.

Conclusions

The facts shown by this study have clear implications for the debate on privatisation. Firstly, since like is not being compared with like, the question to be asked is how do the private and voluntary sectors complement rather than replace the local authority homes? Secondly, a more rigorous cost comparison needs to be done before extravagant claims about value for money can be evaluated. Finally, the area of great concern should be the quality of life (not just care) of elderly residents in all sectors. Observation in the private sector shows some examples of high standards, particularly in regard to privacy, the retention of personal possessions and flexibility of daily living patterns, as well as the converse. Research in the local authority sector gives no reason for complacency on this topic. While the national data show that the private sector lives, and indeed grows, in the field of residential care for the elderly, perhaps a more pressing issue should be the quality (or lack of it) of the private lives of elderly people in all forms of care, particularly residential care. It is quite understandable that politicians on both sides of the privatisation argument should give priority to rhetoric rather than research and do not welcome a gang of ugly facts mugging their beautiful theories. The responsibility of service providers to their elderly clients demands a more rigorous and disciplined approach to data and to issues, in order to make the best of all relevant and available resources.

REFERENCES

Boldy, D. (1983) 'When the Doors Close on the Dependent', Health and Social Service Journal, May 26th

D.H.S.S. (1983) Personal Social Services Local Authority Statistics RA/82/1, January, H.M.S.O., London

Donovan, T. (1983) Staffing Needs and Conditions in Private and Voluntary Homes : Summary of Progress, Centre for Policy on Ageing, London

Judge, K. Knapp, M., Smith J. (1983) The Comparative Costs of Public and Private Residential Homes for the Elderly, P.S.S.R.U. Discussion paper 289, University of Kent, August

McCoy, (1980) Census of Residential Accommodation, Suffolk County Council

Social Work Today (1983) Vol. 14, No. 37, June 7th, p.6

PART THREE : EVALUATION OF SERVICES

Chapter Ten

THE EVALUATION OF INTENSIVE DOMICILIARY CARE FOR THE ELDERLY MENTALLY ILL

C. Crosby, R. C. Stevenson and J. R. M. Copeland

Introduction

The Intensive Domiciliary Care Scheme (IDCS) for the Elderly Mentally Ill (EMI) started in Liverpool in May 1981. It is administered by Age Concern under joint finance arrangements with the Liverpool City Council and the Health Authority. This paper is an interim report on the DHSS financed research project to evaluate the scheme.

The scheme provides a flexible and comprehensive package of care in their own homes to patients who would otherwise be likely to be heavily dependent on social services or hospital care. The issue at stake is whether by these means it is possible to improve the quality of care and delay or avoid costs elsewhere in the public sector. Also notable in this pilot scheme is the central role of Age Concern which provides the opportunity to assess the quality of service and the cost-effectiveness of a voluntary agency working in close collaboration with the statutory bodies.

The scheme cares for up to 16 patients at a time, all of whom suffer from dementia (as diagnosed by a consultant psychiatrist using the Geriatric Mental State Procedure - (Copeland et al (1976)), are over 60 and live alone with a single helper (usually an elderly spouse). Most are highly dependent and would be likely candidates for admission to Part III accommodation or long-term hospital care as their dementia develops. They were selected from referrals from a variety of sources in two central Liverpool social service districts.

The scheme is organised by a full-time co-ordinator with support from Age Concern and an Advisory Group which reviews the general progress of the project. The co-ordinator recruits, trains and monitors the performance of 48 male and female aides. Most are women between 30-60 who have experience of caring for the elderly or who may be former auxiliary nurses. The aides receive training specific to the problems of the EMI and attend weekly meetings with the co-ordinator who takes pains to match the personalities of aides and patients. A full-time psychiatric community nurse, employed by the Health Authority, provides additional support and is responsible for conducting assessments of potential clients' mental states and for monitoring changes in their mental and physical conditions. Three aides are allocated to each patient. Each aide has one week off in three and works part-time. EMI patients could be unsettled by this rotation system but, in general, they have accepted it well.

The scheme is intended to be flexible. The amount of care can be varied according to need. Cover can be provided between 8 a.m. and 10 p.m. but in practice this flexibility has not been fully tested. Most of the patients are highly dependent and need the normal maximum amount of care which is five hours a day, seven days a week. Typically, the aides work between 9 a.m. - 1 p.m. and from 5-6 p.m., although they have worked longer hours in emergencies.

The aides are encouraged to use considerable personal intitiative in carrying out their duties. Their training stresses the importance of stimulating the patients mentally and socially with a view to maintaining independent functioning. Amongst the services provided most commonly are: preparation and serving of meals; dressing and putting to bed; assistance in the lavatory; shopping; money management; laundry and cleaning; escorting clients outside the home; monitoring the safety of the home; supervision of self-medication; liaison with family, neighbours and medical and social services.

The aides receive £1.96 an hour (June, 1983), travel expenses and £10 a month clothing allowance. This is seen as reasonable remuneration rather than an enabling device to overcome inertia, as in the Kent Community Care Project - Challis and Davies (1980). Nevertheless many of the aides are activated by more than financial incentives. Although the work is highly demanding, many go well beyond their nominal duties even to the extent of raising private funds to provide holidays for clients.

Intensive domiciliary care was not intended to replace other services entirely but clients are limited to a maximum of one day a week in local authority day-care. They do not use home-helps or 'Meals on Wheels'; they do not receive attendance allowances. Although the full range of other social services is available to the clients, in practice the IDCS has replaced almost all non-medical services.

Research Procedures

The experimental nature of the IDCS and its potential importance as an example which might be followed in other areas made it desirable that an independent research project be set up to evaluate the scheme. The prime aim of the research is to compare the costs and benefits of the IDCS with those of conventional community care. The this end, a control group was established consisting of patients who would have qualified for admission to the scheme and were roughly matched in mental state, age and social isolation with the IDC group. The control group received the normal range of community services and the attendance allowance.

The Clifton Assessment Procedures for the Elderly (CAPE) have been used as a measure of mental and physical disabililty - Pattie and Gilleard (1979). CAPE comprises a simple cognitive test of 12 items, a brief mental ability test, a psychomotor test and a behavioural rating scale which includes the common activities of daily living such as bathing, dressing and helping about the house. From these procedures a single combined score of mental and behavioural impairment is derived which enables the patient to be allocated to a dependency grade on a five-point scale. The tests were administered to all patients in the IDC and the control groups upon admission to the study and were repeated at three monthly intervals.

For the economic evaluation, all contacts with the social and medical services were monitored so that it will be possible to compare the costs of treatment for the two groups and to analyse their impact on several budgets involved.

An important qualification to the statistical findings is that since this is a pilot project, the sample sizes are necessarily small. Only 23 clients are, or have been, members of the IDCS (five have died; two have withdrawn) and the control group has 17 members. Up to the end of June 1983, the scheme has provided 1344 weeks of care and this is compared with 924 weeks for the control group. It follows that the statistical tests are unlikely to be very robust but, in defence of the study, it can be said that the researchers know the patients individually and have a good grasp of the fine grain of the data. Since large medical aggregates can mask a wide variety of experience, a small study may have advantages over larger ones which seem to have superior statistical properties.

The Evaluation Problem

An ideal evaluation requires a comparison of all the pecuniary and non-pecuniary benefits and costs of care to the patients and society at large. This would require an assessment of at least the following:

1. The mental and physical health of the patients.
2. The quality of their domiciliary environment.
3. The opportunity cost of resources used by family and friends in caring for the EMI. These may be pecuniary (income foregone) or non-pecuniary (leisure time foregone, psychic wear and tear, physical strain) and not all of these may be regarded as costs by those who incur them.
4. The opportunity cost of resources used by the caring agencies in the public sector and Age Concern.

If it were possible to quantify and aggregate these incommensurate streams of benefits and costs, their ratios could be calculated for each group of patients. If the IDCS generated a higher benefit-cost ratio than the control, it could be said to be superior to conventional community care.

The measurement of costs is never easy or uncontroversial but, as is well known, the central problem in health economics, and medicine generally, arises in the measurement of benefits. This difficulty is nowhere more pronounced than in the care of the EMI for the following reasons:

1. There is no possibility of measuring the benefits of treatment in terms of rehabilitation to employment.
2. It is not likely that treatment can increase life expectation.
3. Methods of constructing utility values from patient interviews are unlikely to be effective because these patients cannot be assumed to be the best judge of their own welfare and, in any case, society may wish to overule their revealed preferences.
4. In practice, professional and other interest groups make welfare judgments on behalf of patients. The hospital consultants, family practitioners, social workers and relations who make these judgements are likely to have different preferences for alternative configurations of costs and benefits. Even if their separate utility functions were known, there would be no generally agreed method of aggregating them into a social welfare function.

It would be premature to conclude that the problem of directly measuring the output of programmes for the care of the EMI is intractable. Not all demented patients can be assumed to be incapable of providing a transitive ordering of alternative care packages and there is a body of painstaking work which attempts to combine the several dimensions of output into a general measure of effectiveness - Wright (1978). Detailed psychiatric testing of the IDCS and control groups is continuing and it is possible that this will result in more refined measures of output but, at this stage, the direct measurement of output has been avoided by an approach akin to cost-effectiveness analysis.

Cost-effectiveness analysis aims to find the least-cost method of achieving a well-defined objective. In simpler situations, this amounts to asking, for instance, what is the cheapest way of producing one month's renal dialysis where patient welfare is assumed to be independent of the mode of treatment. A major obstacle to the application of cost-effectiveness analysis to the care of the EMI is the absence of an objective which is sufficiently well-defined. Therefore, for the purposes of this interim report, it is argued that if the outcome of care (measured in terms of mental and physical state, domestic environment and pressure on friends and relatives) is at least as good in the IDCS as in the control group, the scheme can be evaluated solely in terms of its economic implications.

Measuring the Outputs

Mental and Physical Health

CAPE scores have been used as the principal measure of levels and changes in mental and physical well-being. Although senile dementia is a progressive disease, the decline of patients' health can be irregular and may be related to social factors. If the IDCS were superior to conventional community care, the rate of the patients' decline might be reduced. To test this possibililty, changes in CAPE scores over three monthly periods were analysed in terms of their means and variances. At this stage, there seems to be no statistically significant difference between the two groups so that medical outcome does not appear to be influenced by the choice of care scheme.

Physical Environment and Costs to Helpers

Work is proceeding to build a systematic picture of these aspects of care in the two groups but there exists a large body of case notes which suggest that some patients are more responsive and less violent than when they were admitted to the IDCS. Much of the work of the aides is concerned to improve the domestic environment. Anecdotal evidence suggests that strain on helpers has been reduced, as would seem likely if only because most clients are in the care of the scheme for 35 hours a week.

It seems most unlikely that further work will show that the output of the IDCS is not at least as good as conventional community care, in which case an approximate evaluation in terms of its economic implications seems justified.

Measuring the Costs

The conceptual and practical problems of costing care for the elderly are explained and applied by Wright, Cairns and Snell (1981). Economists have a strong preference for the opportunity cost approach over the simpler measure of public expenditure costs because they are concerned to value all costs, private and public, to society at large. The opportunity cost measure also deals explicitly with capital costs which are not always treated systematically and are sometimes omitted in health service costings. This study aims to provide an opportunity cost comparison between the IDCS and the control group but is also concerned with the allocation of costs between different budgets in the public sector.

Average costs have been calculated for the two groups and estimates are provided of marginal costs for small expansions of the scheme. The major question of whether the scheme should be replicated in Liverpool or elsewhere requires a judgement on the likely magnitude of long-run costs and this is discussed briefly.

In this interim report, it is not possible to give final costings but sufficient work has been done to give some idea of their relative magnitudes and those elements which are likely to be decisive in the final evaluation.

Intensive Domiciliary Care

Cost of the Scheme. 1. The average cost of intensive domiciliary care per client in 1983 prices was approximately £110-£120 per week. The maximum capacity with one full-time administrator, a full-time psychiatric nurse and a part-time secretary is estimated at 25 clients. The average variable cost amounts to little more than the cost of employing extra aides and can be taken as a good approximation to marginal costs for a small expansion of the scheme. They were approximately £80 per week.

2. Using Local and Health Authority figures, the cost of all health and social services was calculated at about £15 per week on average which gives a total cost in the region of £125-£135 per patient week.

3. To this should be added an allowance for the opportunity cost of housing and personal consumption. The opportunity cost of housing is common to both groups and is unlikely to differ between them.

<u>The Control Group.</u> The striking difference between the two groups is that the control group patients were much more likely to resort to care in Part II accommodation, hospitals and psychiatric units. the average control group patient spent 40 percent of the period studied in hospital or residential care and only 60 percent of the time in the community. Using standard costings for Local and Health Authority services, the average cost of care in the control group was at least as high as the top of the range estimate for the IDCS group. This finding is subject to at least two qualifications:

1. It is possible that standard costings for hospital care overstate the true cost of caring for an elderly patient in an acute hospital. Against this, mentally ill patients require more than the average amount of attention in Part III accommodation and all standard residential and hospital costings are underestimates to the extent that they omit capital costs.

2. It is in this area that the small sample problems of the study are most acute. The control group included several patients who spent a large part of the study period in residential accommodation. Others spent several months in acute hospitals. The costs of maintaining even a single patient for a lengthy stay in a fully staffed hospital will have a large impact on total costs when the groups are so small.

Two further modifications need to be made to the costing of the control group. During the 60 percent of the time which they spent in the community they were in receipt of the attendance allowance; to the extent that this was used to purchase care, it should be added to the costs. Against this, the allowance for personal expenditure to be made for the IDCS group has to be reduced for the 40 percent of the period which the control group spent in hospital or residential care.

Observations on the Preliminary Costings

1. It seems most likely that on cost savings alone, the IDCS is superior to conventional community care if the small samples are representative. Any other advantages which may be claimed in the quality of output can be regarded as a bonus.

2. It might be argued that this study is not a fair comparison of alternative forms of community care since the control group patients spent 40 percent of the study period in hospitals and residential accommodation. Against this, the findings are broadly consistent with those of Bergmann et. al. who have demonstrated the very low viability of demented patients in the community - Bergman et. al. (1978).

3. It might be though that all community based schemes are likely to offer capital savings if the alternative is some form of residential accommodation even when due allowance is made for the opportunity cost of housing. If the study's control group is representative, conventional 'community care' includes a high proportion of hospital and residential care which implies heavy capital costs if the provision of care of the EMI is to be increased.

The Role of Age Concern

If, as seems probable, it can be shown that the IDCS has improved the quality of community care for the EMI and is cost-effective, the next question is whether it can and should be replicated. This raises questions about the long-run costs and benefits of the scheme, the role of Age Concern and important issues for health care policy.

A voluntary agency such as Age Conern consists of a stock of good will which confers certain advantages over the NHS and the local authorities in the provision of some sorts of care. A voluntary agency attracts charitable donations which represent additions to the resources available for care, unless those resources are perfectly inelastically supplied or government anticipate charitable donations and make offsetting reductions in the public sector.

On the basis of good will and past performance, voluntary agencies also attract grants from the public sector as in the case of the IDC scheme. To the extent that the voluntary agency contracts to provide services which would otherwise have been provided by the statutory bodies, this is a transfer from the public to the voluntary sector and does not increase the quantity of care unless the voluntary sector is more efficient than the statutory bodies.

If voluntary agencies are to receive public funds, the presumption must be that they can use them more effectively than other bodies in both the public and private sectors. If they are able to do this, it must be because they are able to avoid some of the rigidities in the labour markets which raise the cost of labour to otheremployers and because they are able to tap a fund of good will which is not available to public or private employers. This seems to have been the case in the IDCS. The overhead costs of employing labour were low and the wages paid were probably insufficient to explain the high level of enthusiasm and commitment which the scheme generated. Enthusiasm and good will were factors of production to the scheme and these have an opportunity cost to Age Concern and to society in general. The cost is not readily quantifiable but it consists of the value of other projects which Age Concern might have undertaken. This should be added to the rest of the costs of the IDCS.

It seems safe to suppose that the scheme could be replicated at least a few times with similar costs and benefits but the success of a large scale expansion of IDCS administered by voluntary agencies is likely to depend on the following considerations:

1. Would a large number of schemes of this sort be able to avoid the overhead costs which are borne by public and private sector employers?

2. What is the nature and likely size of the stock of good will which is available to Age Concern for the care of the EMI? Is it a fixed stock or, if it is augmentable, is it augmentable only at the expense of other voluntary agencies? It would also be interesting to know whether its size is influenced by conditions in local and national labour markets.

3. A more general point concerns the nature of pilot schemes. Are they always successful and, if so, is it likely that if IDC schemes were to become conventional, the pioneering spirit would move elsewhere and problems might emerge which have not been encountered in this project?

Acknowlegements

The project is directed by Professor J. R. M. Copeland in the Department of Psychiatry and the Institute of Human Aging. The authors are indebted to Mr J. A. Flynn for helpful comments, to Mrs E. Diamond and other members of the staff of the scheme for their co-operation and to Mr A. Black and the Department of Economics, Liverpool University for research assistance.

Bibliography

Bergmann, K. Foster E. M., Justice, A. W., Mathews V. (1978) 'Management of the Demented Elderly Patient in the Community', British Journal of Psychiatry 132, pp. 441-449

Challis D. and Davies, B. (1980) 'Care for the Elderly', British Journal of Social Work, 10, 1, pp. 1-18

Copeland, J. R. M. et al. (1976) 'A Semi-structured Clinical Interview for the Assessment of Diagnosis and Mental State in the Elderly. The Geriatric Mental State Schedule', Psychological Medicine, 6, pp. 439-449

Pattie A. H. and Gilleard C. J. (1979) Manual of the Clifton Assessment Procedures for the Elderly (CAPE), Hodder and Stoughton, Sevenoaks

Wright, K. G. (1978) 'Output Measurement in Practice' in A. J. Culyer and K. G. Wright (eds) Economic Aspects of Health Services, pp. 46-64, Martin Robertson, London

Wright, K. G., Cairns, J. A., Snell, M. C. (1981) Costing Care, Joint Unit for Social Services Research, Sheffield University

Chapter Eleven

EVALUATION OF LONG-STAY ACCOMMODATION FOR ELDERLY PEOPLE

J. Bond

Introduction

This paper describes an evaluation of long-stay accommodation for old people commissioned by the Department of Health and Social Security. In the summer of 1983 the first of three NHS nursing homes set up by DHSS in collaboration with three health authorities was opened in Chapeltown, Sheffield. Homes in Cosham, Portsmouth and Fleetwood admitted their first residents in the summer of 1984.

There are at least two concepts of a nursing home (Evans 1981). First, an additional continuing care facility combining in effect the conventional functions of the residential home and the long-stay hospital which is run administratively and clinically by nurses. Second, an alternative continuing care facility to the long-stay hospital which is run administratively and clinically by nurses. Although past Government statements about the experimental NHS nursing homes have confused the two concepts (DHSS, 1981; House of Commons Parliamentary Debates, 1982), the most recent statement has clearly defined that the experimental scheme will provide an alternative facility to long-stay geriatric hospital:

> "The experimental schemes will care for these patients who need continuous, non-psychiatric nursing to a degree which cannot be provided through the community health services, but who do not need the full range of hospital facilities or active medical treatment. The great majority of such patients are at present in long-stay geriatric wards." (DHSS, 1983, para. 1.3)

Background to Study

It has been recognised for a number of years that many long-stay hospitals and other residential institutions for the elderly and chronic sick exhibit the characteristics of what Goffman (1961) has termed total institutions. The essential feature of the total institution which distinguishes it from other forms of organisation is that, unlike life outside, there is no separation between the three central spheres of modern life: work, leisure and the family. All aspects of life are conducted within the boundaries of the institution and under the control of a single authority. Each phase of daily activities is shared with a large number of other people, all of whom are treated alike and are required to do the same thing together. These activities normally follow a strict routine imposed from above by a system of explicit formal rulings and a body of officials. The routine of daily activities comprises a single rational plan which has been designed to fulfil the official aims of the institution (Goffman, 1961, p.6).

British studies of residential homes for the elderly (Townsend, 1962), of residential homes for the physically disabled and young chronic sick (Miller and Gwynne, 1972), and of long-stay geriatric hospitals (Baker, 1983; Evers, 1981) exemplify Goffman's model, although these studies show that the concept is not relevant to all long-stay institutions. The contrast between the kinds of care provided in the different organisations being studied was described as the warehousing and horticultural models of care by Miller and Gwynne (1972). In geriatric hospitals Evers (1981) recently identified two kinds of warehousing: minimal warehousing where patients' care is organised in order to achieve the primary tasks of prolonging life, and personalised warehousing where some attempt is made to provide a personalised service to patients. The horticultural model, in contrast, aims to develop an individual's capacities by encouraging independence. It is a relatively recent development, which is more an aspiration than a reality.

Three groups of factors have been identified as influencing the quality of life in long-stay institutions: the physical environment, the social environment and the attitudes of care providers (Hughes and Wilkin, 1979).

The Physical Environment

The physical environment has been shown to affect elderly people in two general areas (Hall, 1966; Lipman, 1968). First, the structure and layout of buildings have considerable implication for functional ability. Second, the immediate surroundings of the institution can exert specific influences on residents or patients. By 'deinstitutionalising' the environment the process of normalisation can be assisted.

The Social Environment

The principle of normalisation is the principle that people living in institutions should be able to follow a lifestyle similar to the patterns followed in the community. Even though general and recreational activity of the elderly living in the community is reported to be low (Hunt, 1978) a number of writers have argued that the social isolation and the low level of activity experienced by the elderly living in institutions is due to the effects of institutionalisation. (Townsend,

1962; Meacher, 1972, DHSS, 1979).

The increasing use of remedial therapy in institutions has probably increased the activities undertaken by residents and patients. However, in some of the residential homes included in a London study outings and activities were compulsory (DHSS, 1979). As George (1978) points out compulsory activity may have no benefit since organised activity may well aggravate the problem by setting activities within the same rigidity of routine and staff control that characterises other features of institutional life.

The Care Providers

A number of writers have indicated the importance of the effects of the attitudes of care staff in the process of institutionalisation (Goffman, 1961; Miller and Gwynne, 1972). Data from studies of long-stay wards suggest that the traditional medical and nursing roles are inappropriate to the process of normalisation (Baker, 1983; Evers, 1981). In this context the importance of the head of the institution in influencing the development of a particular type of environment has been identified (Burrage, 1975; DHSS, 1979).

Aspects of Evaluation

Illsley (1980) has indicated the breadth of meaning given to the term evaluation. First is the experimental study in which randomisation is the essential feature. Second is the quasi-experimental study in which a new service is compared with existing services. Randomisation may be impossible for practical or ethical reasons. Third is the descriptive study in which existing services are described. Intervention of any kind is unacceptable.

Evaluation by any of these three kinds of study can yield two kinds of information for policy makers: 'process data' on the way the service is being provided and 'outcome data' on the effects of the service on patients. Only the experimental study will adequately inform the policy maker of the effect of a service on patient outcome. Less rigid forms of evaluation cannot be expected to provide more than information about the process of patient care.

The Experimental Design

One particular form of experimental design, the randomised controlled trial, has been widely used in medicine (Cochrane, 1972). The basic principle of this method is the randomised allocation of subjects to alternative modes of care. Effectiveness is assessed by comparing outputs.

A number of problems have been identified concerning the application of experimental designs in health care evaluation (Cochrane, 1972; Adler et al, 1974; Bennett, 1974a and 1974b; Garraway and Prescott, 1977; Illsley, 1980). Such problems include the choice of sample size and the recruitment of subjects to the trial, the choice and validity of measures of outcome, the evaluation of outcomes and the replicability of findings. Most of these problems are effectively dealt with in the seminal article by Schwartz and Lellouch (1967) who identify two kinds of randomised controlled trial according to the objectives of the experiment. The first is called the explanatory model because it aims at understanding: to discover whether a differences exists between two clearly defined treatments. The second, called the pragmatic model, aims at informing the decision about which alternative treatment is to be used. In health care research we are usually concerned with deciding between two modes of care and therefore the pragmatic model would appear more appropriate.

However, elements of the explanatory model would normally be included because the evaluation would be used not only to decide between two modes of care in one centre but also to assist other centres in making similar decisions.

The Definitions of the Modes of Care. Under the pragmatic model the two modes of care can be flexible and undertaken under normal conditions. Thus in this experimental scheme the management of patients may differ in the three nursing homes being evaluated. Similarly we would expect the management of patients in the long-stay hospitals to differ. Pragmatic analysis will therefore be of direct application in the three areas concerned. An important aspect of evaluation is, therefore, a detailed description of the modes of care being provided in the experimental and non-experimental settings.

The Assessment of Results. With the explanatory model multiple criteria may be used in the assessment of the results of the experiment. With the pragmatic model a single criterion must be used since a decision must be reached. This single criterion however may be a weighted combination of several criteria such as patient satisfaction, clinical effectiveness and cost. The weights for each criterion will be difficult to identify but should be clearly specified in advance.

Choice of Subjects. The initial choice of subjects for the experiment should be undertaken according to specific criteria laid down in advance and adhered to throughout the study. If patients satisfying the criteria are excluded by nursing or medical staff prior to randomisation, they should still be followed up. The explanatory model requires that strict selection be employed, and withdrawals (after randomisation) should be excluded from analysis, whereas with the pragmatic model withdrawals are acceptable as long as these are retained in the analysis.

Methods of Comparison. Schwartz and Lellouch (1967) show that two modes of care can be compared in radically different ways. With the explanatory model we would wish to know whether the difference in care is theoretically significant. We would want to avoid reaching the conclusion that a population difference exists when it does not. We would also wish to avoid wrongly concluding that the two modes of care are not significantly different when they actually differ by an amount of some practical importance.

With the pragmatic model we would be concerned with choosing the better mode of care and not with measuring a theoretical difference. We would aim to avoid chosing the mode of care which is in fact the inferior mode. The present evaluation retains elements of both the explanatory and pragmatic approaches and therefore takes account of all three types of error in the design of the experiment.

Ethics of Experimental Designs. The ethics of experimental designs and, in particular, the ethics of randomisation have been specified by both the World Medical Assembly and the British Medical Research Council (Hill, 1977). Two principles have emerged. First, patients can only be randomised to alternative modes of care when we are ignorant of the relative value of each. There is no consensus about the relative value of NHS nursing homes and long-stay geriatric wards. Second, the patient must give informed consent before being invited to take part except in exceptional circumstances when patient psychology indicates otherwise.

Design of Evaluation

The focus of this evaluation is an experimental design in which patients, identified as long-stay geriatric patients requiring nursing care, are randomised between two modes of care: existing long-stay geriatric wards and the experimental nursing homes. In addition to the experimental design, however, two other components to this evaluation are needed. There are three separate research activities:

A. A randomised controlled trial comparing patients in the experimental nursing home with patients in associated long-stay geriatric wards. This will provide policy makers with information about the relative value of each mode of care.

B. A descriptive study of the alternative modes of care provided in the experimental and non-experimental settings. This will inform policy makers about the process of care in each setting. The experimental design will only evaluate the modes of care as a whole whereas patient outcomes may be determined by certain elements of the process of care. This descriptive study will help policy makers identify these elements and will also provide descriptions of the organisation of care so that they might be replicated in other centres. This study will also identify changes in the process of care as they occur in the experimental and non-experimental settings.

C. A baseline and follow up survey of all long-stay institutions used by elderly people within the catchment area of the experimental nursing home. It will describe the facilities available in each institution and the dependency characteristics of all elderly patients and residents before and after the commissioning of the experimental nursing homes. Any changes occurring during the experimental period will thus be identified. This study will inform the policy makers about some of the effects that the experimental nursing homes might have on the geriatric services in each centre.

Study A Randomised Controlled Trial

Objectives.

(A1) To compare the clinical effectiveness of two modes of care - NHS nursing home and long-stay geriatric ward.
(A2) To compare patient satisfaction with the two modes of care.
(A3) To compare staff satisfaction with the two modes of care.
(A4) To compare costs of the two modes of care.
(A5) Thus to provide a sound basis for judging the social efficiency of the two modes of care.

Method. We are undertaking an essentially pragmatic randomised controlled trial in each of the three centres. Patients normally cared for in long-stay geriatric wards are randomly allocated to the two alternative modes of care. We will pool the results from the three trials if appropriate in order to inform about overall efficiency of the experimental NHS nursing homes.

Selection of Patients. New patients living within a defined catchment area of the NHS nursing home, who, following assessment by the local multi-disciplinary team would normally be cared for in long-stay geriatric wards, are eligible for inclusion in the study. All referrals to the trial are assessed by a fieldworker prior to random allocation to one or other mode.

Assessment of Results.

1. Clinical effectiveness. We will compare the clinical effectiveness of the alternative modes of care using data on dependency - functional capacity, mental state and incontinence - discharge and referral, changes in diagnosis, changes in general health status and mortality.

2. Patient satisfaction. We will compare the satisfaction of patients with the alternative modes of care using data on life satisfaction and their views about various aspects of the physical and social environment.

3. Staff satisfaction. We will compare the satisfaction of staff with the alternative modes of care using data on job satisfaction and their views about various aspects of their job.

Cost. We will compare the costs and benefits of each mode of care from at least two angles. We shall take a patient-based view, which will entail building up a profile of the resources consumed by each patient in the trial. Such data would include length of stay, number of GP consultations, number of hospital referrals or visits, and the quantity and type of drugs prescribed. This approach will help us to identify the sources of cost differences both within and between alternative modes of care. However, since decision-makers are concerned not only with the allocation of patients at the margin between the different modes, but also with the question of whether to provide a new nursing home at all, it would be desirable also to take an institution-based view: to examine the setting-up costs, as well as the running costs, of a new home compared with existing facilties.

Methods of Comparison. Altman (1980) has emphasised that it would be unethical to undertake a randomised controlled trial in which the sample size was too small to detect important therapeutic effects. Freiman et al. (1978) catalogue a number of clinical trials in which the sample size was too small to offer a reasonable chance of rejecting the null hypothesis. Using estimates dervied by Clark and Downie (1966) we judge that at the five per cent significance level 100 controls and 100 propositi, i.e. subjects in the experimental group, will be required in each centre in order that we will have an 80 per cent chance of detecting real differences of at least 20 per cent between controls and propositi. We estimate that it will take about three years to reach this target group size.

Methods of Data Collection. Data are being collected from a variety of sources using different methods.

1. Residents Interview Schedule - Dependency Characteristics. This schedule is used by the fieldworker in structured interviews with patients and residents. After an initial interview with all referred subjects each propositus and control are reinterviewed at six monthly intervals. The schedule comprises measures of functional ability, continence and mental state and is based on instruments used successfully in earlier studies. (Bond et al., 1980; Bond and Carstairs, 1982).

2. Residents Interview Schedule - Social Characteristics. This schedule is used by the fieldworker in semi-structured interviews with propositi and controls approximately three months after selection and subsequently at six monthly intervals. The schedule comprises questions on family structure, visitors, friends, the views of subjects toward food, washing, bathing and toileting arrangements, social activities, costs to the resident and their family and a modified version of the Neugarten Life Satisfaction Index - A (Luker, 1982).

3. Residents Dependency Schedule. This schedule is used by the fieldworker in structured interviews with qualified nursing staff about the dependency characteristics of the residents and patients. After an initial inteview with all referred subjects,

interviews about each propositus and control are held with a member of nursing staff at three monthly intervals. This schedule consists of the modified Crichton Royal Behavioural Rating Scale (Wilkin and Jolley, 1979) and questions about drug use, reasons for admission and nursing problems.

4. Clinical record. This record is kept by the fieldworker and completed with the help of medical staff every three months. Data are also abstracted from nursing notes. The record comprises sections about diagnosis, treatment, discharge and services and facilities used.

5. Staff Attitude Questionnaire. This questionnaire is self-completed by all qualified and unqualified nursing staff in both settings six months after the opening of the home and subsequently at twelve monthly intervals. A sample of staff are followed up with a series of focused interviews. The questionnaire comprises questions on nursing careers and a measure of job satisfaction (Brayfield, 1951).

Study B The Descriptive Study of Alternative Modes of Care

Objectives.

(B1) To provide an analytical description of the alternative modes of care given in the experimental and non-experimental settings.

(B2) To validate measures of patient and staff satisfaction.

Method. In order to describe the modes of care given in the different settings, we are using various forms of participant observation. This is a combination of sociological techniques often used in studying the interactions between members of complex organisations, for example, between doctors, nurses and patients in hospitals. Techniques used include direct observation, formal and informal interviewing, systematic counting, and systematic analysis of records and documents. The aim of the investigation is to provide an analytical description of a complex social organisation. An analytical description is more than a journalistic description. It employs the concepts, propositions and empirical generalisations of a body of theory as the basic guides in analysis and reporting; it provides a thorough and systematic method of collecting, classifying and reporting data; and it generates new empirical generalisations based on these data (McCall and Simmons, 1969).

An important reason for the insistence on analytical description in this evaluation is that we expect organisational differences both between and within the experimental and non-experimental settings. We also expect features of these complex social organisations to change during the period of the evaluation. Many of the changing features of these organisations will not be recognised by patients and staff even when carefully questioned by a skilled interviewer.

Consequently, in order to obtain an analytical description of the experimental and non-experimental settings we must undertake direct observations of the alternative modes of care. Even to the trained participant observer many of the features of the organisations will not be readily apparent and will only emerge through systematic classification, enumeration and comparison of facts.

In order to validate measures of patient and staff satisfaction the participant observer is focusing on some of these aspects during interviews with staff and patients. For this purpose it is essential that the fieldworker does not have knowledge of the results of the data collected as part of the randomised controlled trial.

Methods of Data Collection.

1. Observation. Gold (1956) examined four roles which the participant observer might adopt while collecting data: complete participant, participant as observer, observer as participant, and complete observer. The participant observer in this study will employ the third of these roles. In this situation the fieldworker and those being observed are aware of their research relationship. Data collection is overt and the observer is not actively engaged in the activities of those being observed.

2. Formal and informal interviewing. Direct observation alone will not be sufficient to obtain a thorough analytical description. The observer can neither be available in the organisation continuously nor when available observe all possible interactions. Direct observations must, therefore, be supplemented with indirect observations provided by other persons, called "informants". We will collect data from these "informants" through informal and formal interviewing. Informal interviewing will consist of asking "informants" to describe events which occurred during the observers' absence. Formal interviewing will be undertaken to identify "informant's" interpretations of events and their overall attitudes towards the mode of care provided in the experimental and non-experimental settings.

3. Records and documents. Data are being abstracted by the fieldworker from nursing notes and other organisational records to ascertain facts and events which are not directly observed.

Data Analysis. In participant observation, data collection goes hand in hand with data analysis. This limits the collection of unnecessary data. Spradley (1980) describes the process as circular - collect data, analyse data, generate new hypotheses, and collect new data. Data collection is organised by first making descriptive observations from all sources of data - observations, interviews and records. This provides the fieldworker with an overview of the situation. After analysing these initial data more focused observations are made. Finally, after more analysis, the investigation will be narrowed even further by making selective observations. However, even while focused observations are being made the investigator will continue to make descriptive observations throughout the period of the study in order to record notable changes. Theoretical sampling (Glaser and Strauss, 1967) and analytical induction (Robinson, 1951 ; Denzin, 1978) will be employed as methods of focusing and selecting observations.

Study C The Baseline And Follow Up Surveys

The baseline survey will provide the research team with relevant information about each of the study areas in preparation for mounting the randomised controlled trial. The follow up survey will identify changes which have occurred in the areas during the experimental period.

Objectives.

(C1) To describe the facilities and residential accommodation available for long-stay geriatric patients and residents in the catchment areas of the three experimental nursing homes before and after the introduction of these homes, and in three control areas in neighbouring health authorities.

(C2) To describe the dependency characteristics of elderly occupants in these institutions before and after this introduction.

Method. We are undertaking surveys before and after the randomised controlled trial of the hospitals, residential homes and private nursing homes within the area from which patients are admitted to the experimental nursing homes, and in three control areas in neighbouring health authorities. Two self-completed questionnaires will be used.

1. Institutional Environment Questionnaire. This questionnaire is being completed by heads of homes and ward sisters. The questionnaire consists of questions about the physical and social environments of the ward.

2. Residents Dependency Questionnaire. This questionnaire is being completed by an appropriate member of the caring or nursing staff about the dependency characteristics of patients and residents. The questionnaire is a self-completed version of the Resident Dependency Schedule being used in Study A.

Health Care Evaluation

The basis of this evaluation is a randomised controlled trial. The desirability of using this method in health care evaluation has been persuasively argued by Cochrane (1972). However, as he and other writers have pointed out the application of the method is not without snags. The design of the evaluation attempts to take account of many of these by undertaking three separate but related studies in each centre. Thus we are following the procedures for a pragmatic trial in Study A, but are additionally undertaking a descriptive study of the two modes of care (Study B) and a baseline and follow-up survey of other long-stay institutional care for old people in each of the three centres (Study C).

In practice the evaluation requires three pragmatic trials, one in each of the three centres. Each trial should provide information about differences in patient outcomes between the two modes of care. There are differences in the way that long-stay care is provided in the three centres and therefore the results of the three trials may also differ. However, each trial should provide policy makers with information about the relative value of each mode of care.

One problem which policy makers face when interpreting the results of randomised controlled trials in health care settings is how to identify those characteristics of the experimental mode which contribute to the 'success' of the mode. Study B will provide descriptions of the modes of care studied in each of the three trials. This will inform policy makers about the process of care in each setting and assist in the identification of the essential characteristics of the experimental modes. This study will also provide data which will help explain differences in outcomes between the different modes of care and changes in the modes of care during the evaluation period.

Study C will provide a description of all the services available to old people requiring long-term care in the three centres and will also identify changes to these services during the period of the evaluation. This study will help explain any differences in the dependency characteristics of long-stay patients entering the three trials.

No single research project can answer every question necessary for the implementation of health care innovations in other districts. Thus this evaluation should be seen as the essential first step in the continuing evalution of long-term institutional care for old people. Future NHS nursing homes may differ in many respects from the three experimental nursing homes, which have been set up as 'model institutions' and may, therefore, have a number of advantages such as idealistic staff and strong local support.

From a research perspective it will be difficult to generalise from the experience of the three centres. Some data will be difficult to collect and to interpret. We judge that clinical outcomes can be measured and used to judge the relative effectiveness, in clinical terms, of the two modes of care. Data about patient and staff satisfaction will be more difficult to collect and to interpret. However, we judge that it is the collection and interpretation of valid and reliable economic data which will provide least reward for our efforts.

Whatever the outcome of this evaluation it will provide some basis for judging the efficiency of the three experimental nursing homes, provide some indication of whether NHS nursing homes should be established in other centres as an alternative to long-stay geriatric wards and provide a basis for the future re-evaluation of the nursing home concept. This evaluation will also provide a basis for judging the acceptability, effectiveness and feasibility of future evaluations in health care settings using this kind of pluralistic research design.

Acknowledgements. I am grateful for financial support from DHSS and to colleagures in the Health Care Research Unit, particularly members of the project team: Eva Brown, Senga Bond, Ann Charlesworth, Joyce Crawley, Gillian Donkin, Barbara Gregson, Margaret Hally, Graham Loomes, David Newell and Lesley Speakman for their help in the design of this evaluation and in the preparation of this paper.

Bibliography

Adler, M.W., Waller, J.J., Day, I. et al. (1974) 'A Randomised Controlled Trial of Early Discharge for Inguinal Hernia and Varicose Veins: Some Problems of Methodology', Medical Care, XII, 541-547

Altman, D.G. (1980) 'Statistics and Ethics in Medical Research. III - How Large a Sample?' British Medical Journal, 281, 1336-1338

Baker, D. (1983) '"Care" in the Geriatric Ward: An Account of Two Styles of Nursing', in Wilson - Barnett, J. (ed.), Nursing Research: Ten Studies in Patient Care, pp.101-117, John Wiley and Sons, Chichester

Bennett, A.E. (1974a) 'Evaluating the Role of the Community Hospital', British Medical Bulletin, 30, 223-227

Bennet, A.E. (1974b) The Reliability of a Survey Psychiatric Assessment Schedule for the Elderly', British Journal of Psychiatry, 137, 148-162

Bond, J., Brooks, P., Carstairs, V. and Giles, L. (1980) 'The Reliability of a Survey Psychiatric Assessment Schedule for the Elderly', British Journal of Psychiatry, 137, 148-162

Bond, J. and Carstairs, V. (1982) 'Services for the Elderly: a Survey of the Requirements for Health and Personal Social Services for 5000 Old People', Scottish Health Service Study, No 42, SHHD, Edinburgh

Brayfield, A.H. and Rothe, H.F. (1951) 'An Index of Job Satisfaction', Journal of Applied Psychology, 35, 307-311

Burrage, M. (1975) 'Nine Homes in a London Borough: a Summary', Clearing House for Local Authority Social Services Research, 1, 43-71

Clark, C.J. and Downie, C.C. (1966)'A Method for the Rapid Determination of the Number of Patients to include in a Controlled Clinical Trial', Lancet, ii, 1357-1358

Cochrane, A.L. (1972) 'Effectiveness and Efficiency. Random Reflections on Health Services', Oxford University Press for the Nuffield Provincial Hospitals Trust, London

Denzin, N.K. (1978) 'The Research: A Theoretical Introduction to Sociological Methods' (2nd Ed), McGraw-Hill, New York

Department of Health and Social Security (1979) 'Residential Care for the Elderly in London', DHSS, London

Department of Health and Social Security (1981) Growing Older, Cmnd. 8173, HMSO, London

Department of Health and Social Security (1983) The Experimental National Health Service Nursing Homes for Elderly People - An Outline, DHSS, London

Evans, J. G. (1981) 'Hospital Care for the Elderly', in Shegog, R.F.A. (ed.) The Impending Crisis of Old Age: A Challenge to Ingenuity, pp.133-146, Oxford University Press for the Nuffield Provincial Hospitals Trust, London

Evers, H. (1981) 'The Creation of Patient Careers in Geriatric Wards: Aspects of Policy and Practice', Social Science and Medicine, 15A, 581-588

Freiman J.A., Chalmers, T.C., Smith H. and Kuebler, R.R. (1978) 'The Importance of Beta, the Type II Error and Sample Size in the Design and Interpretation of the Randomised Control Trial', The New England Journal of Medicine, 299, 690-694

Garraway, W. and Prescott, R. (1977) 'Limitations of the Controlled Trial in Health Care', Health Bulletin, 35, 131-134

George, L.K. (1978) 'The Impact of Personality and Social Status Factors upon Levels of Activity and Psychological Well Being', Journal of Gerontology, 33, 840-847

Glaser, B.G. and Strauss, A.L. (1967) The Discovery of Grounded Theory: Strategies for Qualitative Research, Aldine, New York

Goffman, E. (1961) Asylums: Essays on the Social Situation of Mental Patients and Other Inmates, Anchor, New York

Gold R.L. (1956) 'Roles in Sociological Field Observations', American Journal of Sociology, 62, 210-212

Hall, E.T. (1966) The Hidden Dimension, Bodley Head, London

Hill, Sir, A.B. (1977) A Short Text Book of Medical Statistics, London, Hodder and Stoughton

House of Commons Parliamentary Debates (1982) Weekly Hansard, 1230, HMSO, London

Hughes, B. and Wilkin, D. (1979) Residential Care of the Elderly: a Review of the Literature, Research Report No. 2, Department of Psychiatry and Community Medicine, University of Manchester

Hunt, A. (1978) The Elderly at Home. A Study of People Aged 65 and Over Living in the Community in England in 1976, HMSO, London

Illsley, R. (1980) Professional or Public Health? Sociology in Health and Medicine, Oxford University Press for the Nuffield Provincial Hospitals Trust, London

Luker, K. (1982) Evaluating Health Visiting Practice, Royal College of Nursing, London

Lipman, A. (1968) 'A Socio-architectural View of Life in Three Homes for Old People', Gerontologia Clinica, 10, 88-101

McCall, G.J. and Simmons, J.L. (1969) Issues in Participant Observation: a Text and Reader, Addison-Wesley Publishing Company, Reading, Massachusetts

Meacher, M. (1972) Taken For a Ride, Longman, London

Miller, E.J. and Gwynne, G.V. (1972) A Life Apart: a Pilot Study of Residential Institutions for the Physically Handicapped and the Young Chronic Sick, Tavistock, London

Robinson, W.S. (1951) 'The Logical Structure of Analytical Induction', American Sociological Review, 16, 812-818

Schwartz, D. and Lellouch, J. (1967) 'Explanatory and Pragmatic Attitudes in Therapeutical Trials', Journal of Chronic Diseases, 20, 637-648

Spradley, J.P. (1980) Participant Observation, Holt Rinehart and Winston, New York

Townsend, P. (1962) The Last Refuge - a Survey of Residential Institutions and Homes for the Aged in England and Wales, Routledge and Kegan Paul, London

Wilkin, D. and Jolley, D.J. (1979) Behavioural Problems Among Old People in Geriatric Wards. 1976-1978, Research Report No. 1, Manchester, Department of Psychiatry and Community Medicine, University of Manchester

Chapter Twelve

THE EFFECTIVENESS OF SOCIAL CARE FOR THE ELDERLY

E. M. Goldberg

Introduction

Recently my colleague Naomi Connelly and I explored the state of the art in evaluating social care for old people - Goldberg and Connelly (1982). The picture that emerged was somewhat patchy, but by no means discouraging.

Many local *ad hoc* enquiries into the working of services carried out largely by research officers in Social Service Departments revealed much satisfaction on the part of users, especially with domiciliary services. But these surveys also threw up some negative aspects of social care routines: mismatch between needs and distribution of resources, inadequacy of initial assessment and lack of monitoring and review procedures leading to even greater discrepancies between needs and provision of services. Lack of co-ordination between the various services was evident, not only at field level, but also at the organisational and policy levels.

The relatively few experimental and cross-sectional studies carried out by outside researchers were able to throw a sharper light on the effects that specific types of social care have on the well-being of clients and those closest to them and on the satisfaction of care givers and occasionally also at what cost.

In the community care field the Thanet experiment - Challis and Davies (in preparation), which devolved budgetary responsibility to field level and allowed social workers to 'buy in' services and help from sources other than the local authority, has shown most encouraging results. They indicate that packages of service, imaginatively tailored to individual needs and carefully monitored, not only 'keep very vulnerable old people out of institutional care', but significantly improve the quality of their lives and apparently also prolong life compared with a similar control group receiving conventional services. Perhaps most important, these researchers are well on the way to answering one of the most vital questions which group comparisons often mask: to which clients under what circumstances is a particular scheme of intervention more beneficial and cost effective than existing provision?

Promising beginnings have also been made in controlled activity experiments in residential settings - Felce and Jenkins (1979). Much more needs to be learned, however, about the optimal balance between engagement and disengagement among different types of residents in varying social environments. The mere measurement of activity rates does not tell us nearly enough about their meaning for particular people.

Valuable pilot experiments have also begun to assess the impact of different types of social arrangements, e.g. group living which can further social interaction among residents, mutual help and preservation of self-care. Again, more comprehensive cross-sectional studies now need to assess the effect of different patterns of living and their effect on the social functioning and well-being of different kinds of residents and staff.

Finally the national consumer study - Willcocks et al. (1982) was able to highlight some simple consumer choices among residents of Old People's Homes: for more privacy and for more individual control over their environment, such as being able to open and shut doors and windows and turn radiators on and off.

In our exploration of evaluative studies we also came across many encouraging attempts at clarifying concepts, forging research and practice tools and refining methods of surveying, monitoring and evaluating different aspects of social care in community and residential settings. Some theoretical and practical issues relating to the effectiveness of social care for old people now and in the future kept recurring either overtly or covertly in our explorations and subsequent seminar discussions to which I want to devote the rest of this paper.

Contradictory Views on Problems of Ageing and Their Solution

Negative stereotypes about old age as a period of decline, alienation, non-participation and passive reception of 'services' are often deplored and criticised by sociologists and social care personnel who at times appear to deny the realities of physical and mental deterioration. Medical scientists and practitioners on the other hand are often so preoccupied with deterioration of function that they are almost blind to the compensating social mechanisms that can be called into play. One might wish that the optimism of the social scientists who recognise the 'social construction' of many current stereotypes and beliefs about old age could be merged with the biological realism of the medical profession. In other words more cross-fertilisation and multi-disciplinary research and practice are badly needed for medico/social care to become more effective.

Many social service professionals tend to see negative and positive aspects of ageing largely in individual terms. They argue that if only older people could be encouraged to be more self-reliant, and stand up for their rights, if more opportunities could be created for their social participation and for the cultivation of interests and mutual help, then old age could become as rewarding as other phases in the life cycle. Such views tend to ignore some dominant characteristics of Western society in which people are recognised by their status and by what they do, rather than what they are, and where participation in the production process is considered paramount and wisdom derived from experience has low currency. It is also a world of rapid changes in fashions, technology, and customs - in marriage for example - which render out-of-date, if not redundant, many contributions older retired people might usefully make in a more slow-moving society.

The growing literature on the social care of the elderly is mainly concerned with the problems and crises created by the physical and mental decline and mounting dependency of advanced old age. Much less is known about the concomitants of successful adaptation to ageing, and how the discomforts of the 'pre-death phase' - Isaacs et al. (1983) - could be, if not avoided, at least postponed and shortened. We do know one important fact: that good material conditions tend to reduce morbidity and prolong life - Black et al. (1982). Many researchers propound the need for longitudinal studies. However, such investigations will have to allow for many variants of adaptation within different social contexts over long periods of time; they will be very expensive and require long-term institutional support. The attrition rate would probably be very large, as other longitudinal studies have shown. Also, the possibility of rapid social changes could render any results obsolete or irrelevant within a comparatively short time. For example, if within the next decade an answer were to be found to coronary heart disease or lung cancer in men, this would transform the social experience of old age as we know it. There would be fewer lonely and depressed widows, but the greater longevity of men would pose formidable additional social and medical care problems. One solution to the impracticability of longitudinal studies might be to devote more resources to medium term studies of 'good risk' groups among older people. Power in his volunteer experiment among old people over 75 in Weston-super-Mare observed that 20 percent were healthy, well-adjusted and mobile when first assessed; two-thirds of them were still living healthy and independent lives on follow-up two years later - Power and Kelly (1981). This 'sparkling' group contributed three percent to the mortality of this sample after two years, whereas those who were initially the least mobile contributed forty percent to the mortality. What are the associated physical, social and personal characteristics and contributes to the continuing health and mobility of an appreciable minority of very old people?

Another way of learning more about 'ordinary' and succesful ageing is to engage in locality studies of an anthropological type such as those carried out by Wenger (1984) in rural settlements in North Wales. Important and informative though the increasing studies of <u>organised</u> neighbourhood care are, we also need to know more about naturally occuring neighbouring and friendship patterns and what the unspoken norms of mutual help and support are in different geographical neighbourhoods and in different ethnic groups and social classes. Leat (1983) and Ball and Ball (1982) have made stimulating contributions in this direction.

Finally there is general awareness that major changes are taking place in family structure and in working patterns and pension arrangements which will affect the nature and effectiveness of social care for old people. It is commonly assumed that increased mobility, shrinking families, fewer spinsters, the fuller participation of older women in the labour market and their growing rejection of the 'taken for granted' caring role may reduce the scope of family support in the future. Perhaps most important: how will the increasing divorce and separation rate among younger and middle aged couples affect the care of parents and grand-parents? The basic question is whether the loosening of marriage ties will inevitably be accompanied by a loosening of parent/child ties. Hence extensive as well as intensive studies of these profound changes in family life and their consequences not only for children but also for elders are urgently needed.

Implementation of Research Findings

In contrast to the broader social trends just discussed, which pose baffling problems and demand much further exploration, there are a number of practical issues emerging from cumulative research findings which call for changes in policy and practice rather than further extensive study. I can indicate only some of the areas here.

In the field of domiciliary care, sufficient evidence has been produced by a variety of studies - Goldberg and Connelly (1982), and innovative schemes - Ferlie (1982) to consider functional and structural change in the home help and meals services. For instance, it has been suggested that their closer integration into area social work teams of social services departments could eliminate unnecessary separate hierarchies and barriers to communication and ensure a more unified approach to the problem of matching care to need. Extensive studies by Butler and his colleagues - Butler et al. (1983), Tinker (in preparation) and others in this country and by Lawton (1980) in the United States, have given us sufficient information about developments in housing old people and about their own preferences to formulate appropriate local housing policies.

I wonder how many more surveys will need to be carried out to confirm that a large proportion of general practitioners are unaware of the prevalence of psychiatric disorders among their elderly patients and to point to the seriousness of this state of affairs, since general practitioners are the principal gate-keepers to specialist medical and social services. Action rather than further research seems to be indicated. For example, crash courses could be planned for general practitioners and social service personnel which would at least enable them to recognise early cases of dementia and other forms of psychiatric disorder where intervention can still lead to alleviation of symptoms and to a considerable easing of the burden on informal carers.

Enough is now known about the plights and attitudes of families who look after mentally and physically frail old people to initiate an overhaul of the criteria for obtaining attendance allowances, to extend the right to claim invalid care allowances to married offspring and to consider possibilities of tax relief for family carers. Evidence is forthcoming - Levin et al. (1983) - that domiciliary support to carers of old people suffering from severe dementia can substantially delay admission to residential care and measurably improve the mental health of the carers. These findings stengthen the case of early discovery of dementia and strain on carers and the timely provision of domiciliary support.

Finally, sufficient evidence has accumulated to suggest that more attention to and investment in systematic problem-oriented assessment and monitoring procedures is essential if help is to be matched to individual need and optimal use is to be made of scarce resources.

Intervention Research

Many questions thrown up by recent evaluative research however require further applied research. Tools are being developed to monitor flows of clients in and out of the caring system, recording their social characteristics, and pinpointing (a) those who get minimal help and consume few resources and (b) those who consume many resources and become almost permanent fixtures in the welfare system - Goldberg and Warburton (1979). It is also pssible to describe more succinctly what the carers are up to, whether in fieldwork or day care or residential settings, and to arrive at some crude judgements of outcome. At present these instruments are freely adapted by different groups of researchers and practitioners for various specific purposes. But, if policy-makers are to take serious notice of the ensuing results and if comparisons between areas and regions are not to be misleading, there is an urgent need to carry out reliability and validity studies of these instruments.

In the evaluation of social work practice we have experienced great leaps from case descriptions with over-optimistic interpretative generalisations through tight field experiments using random allocation designs and inappropriate measurements leading to disappointingly negative results, to experimental research based on more specific hypotheses and using at least partially tested tools. More attention is now paid to the different factors that determine entry into the welfare net, to differentiated descriptions of input and to operational definitions of outcome. For example, the care givers' satisfaction and their interpretation of outcomes is distinguished from evaluation by consumers and independent assessments of outside observers.

In the residential field, casual impressionistic observations are giving way to time-sampled, carefully recorded observations. The many ingredients that make up 'residential care' - physical environment, regime, client/staff interaction, client satisfaction and staff attitudes - are being disentangled. It is, however, proving very difficult to arrive at the configurations of all these interactive forces that offer the optimal chance for a reasonably satisfying life to residents and staff, as Smith and his colleagues are showing clearly in their evaluative study of a psychiatric Day Hospital - Smith et al.

(1983).

Many issues concerning the relative effectiveness in different situations of voluntary, semi-voluntary and statutory help, their interweaving and co-ordination, await further exploration, as do many questions surrounding decentralisation of services, in particular the claims that are being made for the success of patch organised service delivery.

Meanwhile, so-called experiments of opportunity should be exploited wherever they offer themselves. For example a variety of statutory and voluntary agencies are embarking on innovatory schemes providing intensive support for very old frail people in the community. The situations are being tackled by very different methods in different areas - the Kent Community Care scheme with its emphasis on case management through delegated budgets for specific clients, different ways of expanding home help and community nursing services, local resources centres with residential facilities, informal voluntary neighbourhood schemes - Ferlie, (1982). Even rough comparisons of methods, outcomes and costs of these different approaches could pay high dividends at the current rather fluid stage of development.

However, before the effectiveness of various types and mixes of intervention can be validly and reliably assessed, more research needs to be done on relevant, acceptable and reliable operational definitions of all the three essential elements in the evaluation process: problem or need definitions, descriptions of input, and outcome criteria. Succinct problem categories have to be developed in terms of social functioning and situational problems rather than by reference to disabilities or to psychiatric labels. We need clearer descriptions of methods of intervention supported by tape or video recordings, supplemented in institutional contexts by systematic observations. The mediating roles of social workers between formal agencies and informal networks are important ingredients of input that need further exploration. In day care or residential situations, regime, daily practices and client/staff interactions form complex patterns of input. Finally, the characteristics of helpers need to be fed into the equation of input in all settings. The hardest task of all is to develop specific operational criteria of outcome which are, at the same time, sensitive and appropriate. Improvements in the material environment and in physical functioning are relatively easy to capture, but even in this area there is no agreement on the common use of well-validated measures of physical functioning and of dependency. Adequate criteria of social functioning pose greater difficulties, although in this sphere some good measures of psychiatric disturbance, for example, are available. Subjective feelings of well-being and life-satisfaction present the greatest challenge. Do the morale and life-satisfaction scales in use actually measure what they purport to measure? In order to be convincing they need to be validated by careful observation and unstructured interviews. In what circumstances can they be applied as measures of success and failure of specific methods of intervention? These and similar tough and relevant methodological questions need to be tackled.

Promising beginnings have been made in all the areas discussed in some recent descriptive, monitoring and experimental studies, (especially in the area of residential care), but so far practitioners and researchers in this country have contributed comparatively little to the development of these essential measuring devices. As already indicated, insufficient work has been done to test the reliability and validity of any measurements that are being used. Unless time, skill and money are invested in developing appropriate theoretical and practical tools, we cannot tackle the evaluative jobs that confront us with confidence.

Bibliography

Ball, C. and Ball, M. (1982) What the Neighbours Say, A Report on a Study of Neighbours, The Volunteer Centre, Berkhamsted.

Black, D. et al (1982) in P. Townsend, and N. Davidson (eds), Inequalities in Health, Penguin, Harmondsworth

Butler, A., Oldman, C and Greve, J. (1983) Sheltered Housing for the Elderly Policy Practice and Consumer, George Allen and Unwin, London

Challis, D. and Davies, B. (in preparation) Matching Resources to Needs in Community Care

Felce, D. and Jenkins, J. (1979) 'Engagement in Activities by Old People in Residential Care', Health and Social Service Journal, 2, November

Ferlie, E. (1982) Source Book of Initiatives in the Community Care of the Elderly, Personal Social Services Research Unit, University of Kent at Canterbury

Goldberg, E. M. and Warburton, R. W. (1979) Ends and Means in Social Work: A Case Review System for Social Workers, George Allen and Unwin, London

Goldberg, E. M. and Connelly, N. (1982) The Effectiveness of Social Care for the Elderly: an overview of recent and current evaluative research, Heinemann Educational Books, London

Isaacs, B., Pike, L. A. and Williamson, J. (1983) 'The Process of Ageing: Medical Dimensions' in DHSS Elderly People in the Community: Their Service Needs, HMSO, London

Lawton, M. P. (1980) Evironment and Aging, Brooks Cole, California

Leat, D. (1983) Getting to Know the Neighbours, Policy Studies Institute, London

Levin, E., Sinclair, I.A.C. and Gorbach, P. (1983) The Supporters of Confused Elderly Persons at Home, Unpublished Report to DHSS

Power, M. and Kelly, S. (1981) 'Evaluating Domiciliary Volunteer Care of the Very Old: Possibilities and Problems' in Goldberg, E.M. and Connelly, N. (eds), Evaluative Research in Social Care, Heinemann Educational Books, London

Smith, G. and Cantley, C. (1983) Pluralistic Evaluation: A Study in Day Care for the Elderly Mentally Infirm, Department of Social Administration, University of Hull

Tinker, A. (in preparation) Housing the Elderly in the Community. HMSO, London

Wenger, G. C. (1984) Getting On: Support Networks in Old Age. George Allen and Unwin, London

Willcocks, D., Peace, S. and Kellaher, L. (1982) The Residential Life of Old People: A Study in 100 Local Authority Homes. Department of Applied Social Studies, Polytechnic of North London

Chapter Thirteen

EXPLORING SERVICE VARIATIONS IN THE CARE OF THE ELDERLY. A VOYAGE INTO THE INTERIOR

D. J. Hunter and C. Cantley

Introduction

The paper reports on an attempt to examine the operation of a selected group of interrelated services for the elderly in a predominantly rural area of Scotland as part of a wider study aimed at accounting for variations in service patterns and pathways. Findings are not reported here because they have not begun to emerge though they will do so shortly. The research study comrises three main stages the second of which - entry-exit studies - forms the basis of the paper. The other stages are described briefly in the next section. The remainder of the paper then describes the approach adopted in studying decision-making and service interaction.

The Research Project

The project, which is funded by the Chief Scientist's Office, Scottish Home and Health Department, seeks to examine and compare, in three locations in Scotland over five years, the interaction between services and people with problems associated with ageing. The main aim is to document and attempt to understand this interaction and not, in the first instance, to prescribe changes.

Variations in service levels and mixes are a feature of all types of provision for the elderly. They occur at all levels of health and social services although their causes and consequences remain unexplored and unaccounted for. It is not known, for instance, to what extent services have tended to develop as much for accidental as for rational, planned reasons. Several possible explanations have been advanced: historical influences, organisational factors, personality factors, variations in family and neighbourhood networks, but they have been subjected to only limited testing, if any, of their validity in particular locations - see Moseley (1968) and Davies _et al_ (1971). Moreover, the work that has been completed pre-dates major reorganisations of health and personal social services. For instance, in the case of the 1974 NHS reorganisation its primary _raison d'etre_ was to facilitate the planning and delivery of integrated care to groups like the elderly.

Some of the explanations for service variations are being explored in the research project. It is proceeding in three linked stages and employing a variety of methodologies and data-gathering techniques which distinguishes it from previous work in this area:

Stage One Charting patterns of provision and pathways of a 'flagged' sample of patients/clients.

Stage Two Monitoring contacts, referrals, admissions and discharges at selected service points (entry-exit service point studies) and linking actual practice with policy development at higher levels.

Stage Three Surveys of the elderly population living at home.

Stage Two forms the core of this paper. Stages One and Three are described briefly below. Throughout, the focus is on those aged 75 and over who make the heaviest demands on services for elderly people.

To implement Stage One we have drawn a sample of some 500 patients/clients aged 75+ at four sources: sheltered housing, residential homes, district nursing and home help service. We have established those in the sample who are in contact with more than one service, i.e. a person in sheltered housing who may also be getting a home help. The exercise began in February, 1983 and will run for approximately three years with checks at approximately three monthly intervals to monitor any movements. At each check all new referrals to the four sources mentioned, as well as those to hospitals, day care and occupational therapy, will be checked against the sample. For various reasons we have had to exclude meals-on-wheels and chiropody services. One of purposes of Stage One is to provide a more general picture of patient/client flows and pathways against which to locate our entry-exit studies (Stage Two) since these will not yield sufficient numbers for the purpose of determining whether our particular case studies seem reasonably representative of service pathways in the area.

Stage Three comprises two surveys of the elderly at home which have been conducted in two of the locations. A set questionnaire was used covering living conditions, family contacts, personal functional ability and use of help from formal and/or informal sources. The achieved sample is approximately 1000 subjects, 500 approximately in each location. The purpose of the surveys is to tap the 'need' of the elderly as perceived by them, i.e. expressions of 'felt need', in order that these expressions of need can be set alongside the definitions of need, and the criteria for determining priorities, that service providers employ in their assessment, referral, allocation and discharge decisions (which it is the purpose of Stage Two to illuminate). The surveys might well raise questions about, for instance, referral, assessment and allocation policies and procedures if it emerges that some people with observable and self-acknowledged needs for services are receiving them while others with similar characteristics are not. The contact/no contact frontier is of major interest. A re-survey of the population in one of the locations has just been completed, seven months after the initial survey. Its purpose has been to record any changes in circumstances that may have occurred in the intervening period and the ways in which individuals have coped with them. The re-survey will enrich the contextual background against which the entry-exit studies will be located, in particular by picking up individuals who do not seek, or require, assistance from services when problems occur.

The Selected Territories

The three territories have been chosen to reflect the broad mix of services for the elderly in Scotland. Two are located in the North-East of the country and a third is in the West Central belt. Of the two in the North-East, one is primarily rural with several modest townships centred on agriculture, fishing and oil-related activities while the other is chiefly urban-industrial. The West Central territory provides a fairly evenly balanced urban-rural mix. The three territories may be said to be reasonably representative of a diverse Scottish landscape with its sparsely populated rural tracts in the Highlands and Islands, its fertile agricultural areas in the North-East and the lowlands, and it industrial areas in the Wast Central belt where multiple deprivation is most prevalent, although pockets exist elsewhere, for example, parts of the North-East. Just as there are differences between health districts and social work divisions within health board areas and local government regions, so there are differences within districts/divisions.

Entry-Exit Studies

This section of the paper is divided into two subsections: (1) Research Agenda and Conceptual Issues, and (2) Towards a Preferred Research Design.

(1) Research Agenda and Conceptual Issues

The approach envisaged for the analysis of entry-exit studies is a qualitative, inductive one. Essentially it occupies the middle zone between grounded theory and logico-deductive theorising - Glaser and Strauss (1967). Rather than systematically deducing a set of hypotheses from a well articulated body of theory and then seeking to test them by attempting to disprove them, we are engaging in a process of generating propositions and theories from observed phenomena. Of course, there is no completely inductive approach, for a researcher will inevitably start with some body of theory or set of concepts in order to select what to observe. This, therefore, is the middle ground. Analysis proceeds in an iterative, cyclical fashion moving from data to theory and back again. The inductive approach precedes the generation of a formal theory or set of propositions but, at the same time, is loosely informed and guided by a set of theories, concepts and assumptions. These are considered below.

The whole process of who gets what, why, where, when and how from health and social services can be depicted as a multiplicity of rationing devices which stretch from central government to individual GPs, social workers, home helps and many other front-line operators. Rationing is an inevitable by-product of finite resources coupled with infinite demand. Most rationing occurs through resource (financial or manpower) allocation decisions which take place in the continuous flow of day-to-day work with patients/clients undertaken by various professional groups.

The starting point for the entry-exit studies is a concern with understanding these rationing devices and, in particular, notions of blockages, discontinuities and gaps in the availability and accessibility of services. It is by no means certain that all service providers agree upon what may constitute blockages, discontinuities or gaps. In order to unscramble these notions, and the meanings different actors ascribe to them, the aim in this main stage of the research is to explore the 'assumptive worlds' - Young (1977) - of service providers as well as of patients/clients and primary carers. The technique permits events to be interpreted in the light of the meaning which the actors involved attach to their actions rather than to interpret these in terms of stated motives, interests or goals which may bear no relation to actual practice. The aim is to understand the ways in which decision-makers construe the situations confronting them in their daily work. Our activities at the entry-exit service points may be seen as constituting a loose form of 'administrative anthropology', though there will be constraints on how far we shall be able to go at any one entry-exit point. Essentially, the approach adopted will be a localist, bottom-up one in contrast to the more common centralist, top-down approach found in the literature on service planning and delivery. The latter approach interprets local differences, or departures from central policy or guidelines, as deviations or recalcitrant behaviour giving rise, on occasion, to blockages, discontinuities and gaps. Our concern in the entry-exit studies is to look at service provision from the other end: to look up rather than down by penetrating to some degree the service jungle surrounding, and confronting, the elderly in receipt, or in need, of care.

The notion of a 'continuum of care' is usually employed by policy-makers and planners to convey a system of care with people enjoying maximum independence at one extreme and people who are totally dependent at the other. The assumption underlying the continuum of care is that individuals move from one form of provision to another as their dependency state alters. A second assumption perceives the movement by people from independence to dependence as they grow older as an inevitable progression that can actually be anticipated and planned for. A further assumption is that in general terms people move to care rather than care to people. The latter may occur in the early stages of minimal dependency but thereafter a series of insitutional moves may be expected. The continuum of care offers a logical model for understanding the care delivery process. But care takes place far less systematically and is certainly less linear than depicted by the model.

The continuum of care concept has been criticised for its

inflexibility, its simplistic and mechanistic view of human behaviour and its stress upon people moving progressively and inevitably from one form of provision to another as their circumstances and state of dependency change. The concept makes no allowance for individuals moving into and out of care at different points along the continuum. Many people do not follow a linear progression from minimum to maximum dependence. They recover and either require different services, or none at all or seek them at a later stage in their lives. Individuals, then, do not necessarily move sequentially from service A to B to C and so on but may only need A and B. At a later stage they may enter care again but at point C. Such varied requirements cannot be encapsulated in the continuum of care concept and problems are created in the attempt to do so. For instance, an inflexible policy of care is at risk of smothering people with more help than they need and with fostering the very dependency which such intervention is intended to manage or even forestall. It is argued in consequence that what is needed is a much more flexible approach which tailors provision to individual needs and avoids a situation whereby people are, with increasing rapidity, moved from one form of care to another as they get older with all the psychological stress and organisational problems that are likely to ensue.

The perception of blockages, gaps, discontinuities of care and mismatch between people and provision is an integral feature of the continuum of care concept as it has been conceived and outlined in the paragraphs above. An alternative approach which is gaining ground among some policy-makers is not to make rigid distinctions between care settings, i.e. the basis of the concept of continuum of care, but to accept that <u>all</u> degrees of disability and dependency may be looked after in <u>every</u> setting. In other words, whether or not individuals are in the 'right' setting is not at issue. the task facing policy-makers is to provide effective support to elderly people <u>wherever</u> they happen to be. Accoding to this view, a continuum of care means something rather different from the orthodox, logical use of the term. It means mobilising services as appropriate and tailoring them round individual needs wherever that person is currently placed. The emphasis is on flexibility and on the production of individual care plans.

These competing notions of the continuum of care underlie our study of pathways through services. It is possible that the discontinuities and contradictions associated with the term which have been documented in some of the literature are a product of the concept itself. It has been directed towards the construction of a rational system of care delivery that is both unattainable given the building materials available and the infrastrcuture of services already <u>in situ</u> and in some forms also undesirable. A continuum of care cannot be abstracted from reality and viewed <u>in vacuo</u>. For instance it is known that:

1. There is discontinuity at many levels from the national arena to provider-patient/client interactions.

2. Planning is piecemeal and divided both vertically between levels of organisation within a service and horizontally between separate, but related, agencies.

3. There exists a multiplicity of agencies and professions responsible to different authorities and employing different decision criteria in respect of the needs of old people.

4. Administrative complexity makes it difficult for both professionals and consumers to know what services exist and how they may be mobilised.

As mentioned earlier, the focus of the reserch study as a whole is an attempt to account for variations in service levels and mixes in care of the elderly. In the production of such an account our primary interest is in the dynamic interactions between services. The entry-exit studies are intended to capture whole systems, or more precisely whole sub-systems, in action rather than detach individual bits of the care 'system' for scrutiny as discrete entities. While research has been conducted in regard to the latter, the former has received scant attention. Moreover what little research has been completed has been at the level of statistical analyses aimed at identifying correlates, for example, Moseley (1968), Davies et al (1971), Gorbach and Sinclair (1982). The 'assumptive worlds' of participants in these service interactions have not been considered in any detail. This omission seems surprising since, of the many possible explanations in common currency to account for service variations, the influence of service providers, and their organisation, must figure among them. Services are divided within professions, like the medical profession and its divisions: clinicians, geriatricians and psychiatrists. As Goda (1982, p. 42) reminds us, 'we know little about the ways in which the provision of one service influences demand for or provision of another'. If the Macdonald report on services for the elderly in Scotland is correct - SHHD (1980), what is notable is the apparent absence of inter-service relationships whereby a low level of, say, domiciliary provision may be compensated for by a high level of institutional provision. The relationships, or rather lack of them, depend, as Goda asserts, 'not only upon need but also.... upon criteria for access to each service, which in turn depend upon demand and provision'. The scope for discretion is wide and is likely to have an impact on service levels and use. The evidence available from Moseley's (1968) study of service variations for the elderly on Tyneside did not support his 'compensatory hypothesis', i.e. areas providing one service at a relatively low level compensate by providing at a relatively high level in some other service. He cites statements made by officers in interviews, i.e. 'we do not provide as many places in Part III accommodation as our neighbours but then we have a good home help service' or 'we have to provide rather generously in Part III because there are not enough hospital beds in the area'. This implies that an explanation of service variations must take account of the fact that each individual service belongs to a system (or systems) of substitutes and complements, the providers of which might well adapt their supply to the availability of other services in the system. But in the case of various domiciliary services and the activities of various domiciliary workers and admissions to Part III accommodation, the hypothesis was not supported by the data.

Davies et al (1971, p.15) argue that there exists 'abundant evidence that the roles played by services do in fact differ between areas because of the supply (and expressed demand) situation of other services in the chain of substitutes'. They found that the provision of places in residential homes affected expenditure on home helps thereby providing some support for the hypothesis that domiciliary services may respond to a deflection of demand (or an awareness of need) arising from a scarcity of provision of institutional services. Davies et al go on to state the need 'to assess whether the level of provision of institutional substitutes affect (sic) domiciliary services as well as assess the impact on the level of provision of all substitutes'. In their view, institutional services are less likely to be influenced by the level of provision of substitutes than domiciliary provision.

Unfortunately, data currently available are not particularly helpful in enabling us to comprehend the rationales behind different levels of provision. Rates of provision, like the number of health visitors and district nurses per head of population, tell us nothing about the actual service they are providing or in what ways they may be improving the quality of life of old people. The Macdonald report notes 'with interest the increasing proportion of professional time of health visitors which is now devoted to work with the elderly' and recommends that the service 'be substantially expanded' (para. 3.44, p. 30). There is an assumption that quantity may be equated with effectiveness, i.e. that more visits can only be 'a good thing'. Questions concerning health visitors' criteria for selecting clients and the tasks they seem themselves as performing are not raised. Much the same comment can be made of other services like home helps.

The scope for discretion in service delivery extends across the whole range of services for the elderly. For instance, in the provision of home helps no criteria are offered for the purpose of assessment and eligibility for the service. 'The output is defined by input - to provide home help' - Hedley and Norman (1982, para. 1.5, p.6). The provision of meals-on-wheels is greatly determined by discretionary powers exercised at various points from policy formation to implementation. The really significant determinants of policy are the personal preferences of those who deliver meals - Hill (1981). Research comparing elderly people of similar dependency in receipt of residential and hospital care shows 'that the same needs are being met in a variety of different settings' - Charlesworth and Wilkin (1982, 5:7). Studies of residential home placement reveal the allocation process to be seemingly arbitrary, random and unbalanced - Marshal and Boaden (1978), Spackman (1981), Mitchell and Earwicker (1982). Research suggests that sheltered housing is becoming like residential accommodation because of the way in which health service providers in particular operate allocation processes and fill vacancies - James

(1978). Priority is given to urgent cases and, as a result, fewer allocations are being made to the young old and many more to the frail elderly.

These brief examples have been cited to show that within a variety of service settings those providing services possess the potential for exercising considerable discretion within permissive legislative policy frameworks laid down nationally and/or by health and local authorities. These 'street level bureaucrats' are able to shape the way in which a service operates and also to decide who should, and who should not, receive it - Lipsky (1980). Studies of decision processes - see, inter alia, Bloor and Venters (1978) - in regard to particular medical services and medical interventions show that variations in service provision appear to correlate strongly with differences arising from the characteristics of populations or geography (though providers' views will be shaped to some extent by local policies and patterns of services as well as by patient/client perceptions and circumstances). A study of the general practictioner referral process shows that doctors had different preferences about specialities and consultants which resulted in marked variations in referral practices - Dowie (1981). Dowie's research was aimed in part at learning more about the referral process, which has received little documentation.

Discretion by front-line operators is frequently examined in the context of its giving rise to implementation problems. The focus of attention is on bringing a recalcitrant periphery into line or in some way improving the grip of central policy-makers on local activity. Use of the terms 'central' or 'centre' in the present context embraces both the national and local policy levels. Both may be regarded as the centre by front line staff. A more valuable perspective may be to see implementation problems as referring to the centre's failure to comprehend the values, perceptions, motivations and definitions of a situation held by peripheral actors. There are practical implications here for policy analysis given the proclivities of central policy-makers for stressing the importance of statutory requirements, rules, guidelines and advice all aimed at securing compliance.

It is important not to regard front-line operators as mere functionaries faithfully and passively implementing policy initiatives from above. They are but one factor in a whole web of demands and pressures which peripheral actors have to manage. In conceptualising this activity we have employed the terms 'assumptive worlds' and 'discretion'. Most decision-making, and certainly all in human service settings, is discretionary though the scope will vary among services and participants. Paradoxically, too, what may begin as discretionary activity may be mediated by providers into a set of routines or standard operating procedures - Edwards III and Sharkansky (1978, pp. 138-141, 313-317). Therefore, the routinisation of discretionary professional decisions will be an important part of our inquiry. Moreover, as we have pointed out, it is not only providers who exercise discretion. Patients/clients and informal carers also exercise discretion and contribute, implicitly or explicitly, to the decisions affecting their futures.

Our contention is that much operational research and other work designed to foster more rational approaches to meeting need fall into the trap of ignoring the realities of the supply and demand situation at local level which affect directly both definitions of, and the ability to meet, need. At issue here is whether need can be abstracted as a fixed state or whether it is more often an expression of demand which is dependent both upon the level of information and knowledge possessed by patients/clients and the availability of provision. In a study of decision-making and service provision it is necessary to embrace the realities of what is actually happening rather than attempt to superimpose a rational, normative approach upon local practice, e.g. the admission procedures to old people's homes, which may make little sense and may even by counter-productive.

So far we have considered (1) the importance of the 'assumptive worlds' of front-line operators, patients/clients and informal carers, and (2) the importance of discretionary decision-making. Given the focus of the entry-exit studies upon a mix of services in health and social work, and in institutional and community settings, a third concept should be introduced - 'jointness'. Our concern in the entry-exit service point studies is essentially with two types of joint activity: co-operative service provision, i.e. different services devising joint solutions to specific problems on a one-off basis as problems arise, and joint working, i.e. instances where individual professionals come together to tackle specific cases involving individual patients/clients. Joint activity at the level of strategic social planning is not a major concern of this particular component of the research.

The thrust of national policy for the elderly, as already noted, is a stress upon community care provision. The expectation is that an increase in domiciliary services will lead to reduced pressures upon, and a consequent decrease in the level of, in-patient hospital provision - DHSS (1981). Of course a quite different scenario may be put forward. Increased levels of community provision could lead to greater pressure upon institutional provision because services like residential homes will increasingly be required to accept a more dependent clientele - Gorbach and Sinclair (1982). Expanding amounts of sheltered housing may already be having such an effect, as Gorbach and Sinclair report. It seems likely that inter-service variations in levels of provision may be linked to the presence or absence of joint arrangements between agencies and between professionals.

From the catalogue of service variations presented it appears that joint planning is generally either absent or ineffective at the level of planning services in relation to each other. This is not so say that joint efforts may not be successful in specific cases in regard to particular developments. Nor is it to dismiss the possibility in some places of positive associations occurring between services. What may be questioned is whether these associations are implicit or explicit, that is, whether they are merely an inevitable by-product of certain constellations of services, or the product of conscious cross-boundary planning. Also, it is not clear which factors may account for the occurrence of these asociations on the one hand and for their absence on the other. Furthermore, not all associations between services may be desired: some may create additional pressure on other parts of the social care system rather than ease it thereby shifting blockages, discontinuities and gaps and resolving them only temporarily. Gorbach and Sinclair cite their finding of a systematic connection between residential homes, geriatric hospitals and home helps: 'the degree of priority given by one service to the more elderly was reflected in the age structure of the users of others' (p.19). They note that this effect may be present since a high proportion of admissions to residential homes emanates from hospitals and home helps. This suggests that joint planning in this sector needs to be sensitive to these dynamics of service delivery and to the possibility of 'knock on' effects between services.

Whether such awareness currently exists is unknown, though doubtful, and is in any case likely to be clouded by the complexity, and highly discretionary nature, of the operating environment. Compartmentalised budgeting, planning and administrative arrangements and professional practices are all likely to militate against achieving a connected response. What is also currently unclear is whether the associations are health-service led or social-service led, or whether inter-service pressures have their origins in health or social services or both. The entry-exit point studies are intended to shed much-needed light on these service interactions at a micro level, that is, at the level of front-line operators like GPs, social workers, home helps and others.

From a scan of the literature on obstacles and issues in health and social services linkages it is possible to identify five problem components:

1. Inadequate services (insufficient resources: financial, manpower).

2. Inaccessible services (bureaurcratic complexity, regulations).

3. Under-utilised services (insufficient knowledge about available services).

4. Fragmented services (poor communication, loosely developed referral procedures, conflicting goals).

5. Discontinuous services (limited inter-professional collaboration, inadequate follow-up).

We propose to employ some such set of criteria in studying 'jointness' at the chosen entry-exit service points. For instance, inadequate services through lack of resources may contribute to the establishment of particular regulations and allocative procedures, i.e. rationing devices. Also, if services are under-utilised, this may be a consequence of their fragmentation.

Understanding the interaction between the five components of service linkage will be at the heart of the entry-exit exercise together with an exploration of the 'assumptive worlds' of participants in the cases selected, and the use of 'discretion' in their decision-making. Our framework for analysis, to be loosely deployed, comprises the following elements through which we propose to examine participants' 'assumptive worlds', 'discretion' and 'jointness':

1. The complexity of the environment: multi-professional, multi-institutional, giving rise to boundary/frontier problems.

2. Resources: availability, distribution, substitutability, i.e. flexibility, of all resources (financial, manpower, hierarchical, political, information).

3. Process of exchange, rules of the game and strategies: adopted by participants as they interact and, possibly, negotiate.

4. Discretion: its scope and management, types, constraints upon it.

We appreciate that the study of entry-exit service points is unlikely to display the completeness or comprehensiveness implied by the framework, the main purpose of which is to help illuminate the sorts of factors governing service provision and interaction which such a study should aim to explore.

(2) Towards a Preferred Research Design

In setting up the entry-exit studies it was necessary to keep several aims in mind. Ideally the entry-exit studies should:

1. Provide information on patient/client flows throughout the system of services and relate the pattern of provision in the area to the occurrence of perceived blockages, discontinuities and gaps in the availability and accessibility of services.

2. Focus on the dynamic interactions between services rather than the operation of isolated services set apart from their organisational context.

3. Aim to understand service operation in terms of the ways in which service providers and clients construe the situations they face.

4. Attempt to illuminate the relationship between the micro level of service operation and the meso level of policy and planning.

These aims immediately raised a number of methodological problems. On the one hand the study of 'flow' in the system would require comprehensive coverage of services, involving large numbers of cases. On the other hand the second and third aims, which would involve in-depth studies of individual cases, would, given existing research resources, necessitate small samples and restricted numbers of entry-exit points.

Our compromise was an approach which would permit the compilation of a background picture of flow in the system from a comprehensive but retrospective and simple records analysis of movements during the period of the case studies. Against this background we would set selected, detailed entry-exit studies, chosen on the basis of service providers' views about the relative importance of various service points. Our entry-exit studies would not concentrate simply on the allocation decisions of the selected services. Rather, they would focus on the ways in which the ideologies and actions of the various service providers, clients and their relatives interact to produce various outcomes at particular points in the service system.

The methods chosen for the entry-exit studies again involved an element of compromise. Ideally our intention of trying to understand the assumptions underlying 'decisions' would have involved observation of provider/client interactions and the interactions of the various service providers. But 'decisions' in service provision for the elderly frequently cannot be tied down to specific times, locations or personnel. Because of the practical difficulties of observing the numerous events which in the end constitute 'decision-making', we decided that, while we would observe any formal case conferences or allocation meetings, the main approach to entry-exit studies would be retrospective interviewing of as many as possible of the actors involved: patient/client, supporters, referral agents, service provider receiving referral and other service providers involved in each case. Although we wanted to elicit the respondents' own construction of events we also wanted to ensure comparability between cases. A focused interview technique was chosen as the best way of coping with what, in many ways, were conflicting requirements. The topics covered in the interviews are listed in the Appendix.

Additionally in the interviews with patients/clients, we decided to incorporate part of our survey questionnaire. We hoped this would facilitate comparisons between cases and also some generalisations about the nature of the entry-exit samples as compared with the population of elderly in the area as a whole. So while our approach is essentially qualitative we hope to combine this with some quantitative analysis of our data. As well as detailed case discussions with service providers we plan, towards the end of the fieldwork period, to include some general discussion of their views about service provision and policy. This is intended to go some way towards meeting thefourth aim noted above.

In summary, in order to try to capture the complexity of the processes at each entry-exit point, we decided to adopt an approach which combines triangulation of data sources (records, focused and structured interviews, some observation) with triangulation of actor perspectives in each case.

In the rest of the paper we describe our experiences of setting up entry-exit studies in the first of our research areas. We outline the methods we used to select service points and geographical locations for the studies, and describe some the difficulties we encountered and attempts to resolve them.

In line with the methods previously outlined, our first step in devising a research design was to try to obtain a fairly detailed picture of service provision and operation in North Grampian by interviewing a number of professionals involved in each service. The interviews focused on descriptions of the day-to-day operation of the service and relationships with other agencies. We also sought respondents' views about levels of provision and their involvement in, or awareness of, broader policy at both local and national levels. From these interviews we were able to identify a number of features of service provision which were significant to providers, some of which were particularly characteristic of the area, or parts of the area. However, if we simply based our selection of services for study on the point of view of service providers, there seemed to be a case for the inclusion of almost every service: geriatric, psychogeriatric, local authority residential, GP beds, home help, health visiting, day care, sheltered housing, acute hospital discharges. Given the practical constraints of available staff and research time it was essential that we were rather more selective. This initial wide range of possibilities had to be narrowed down to form a more coherent and manageable research design.

Our concern to focus on the dynamic interaction between services rather than the functioning of individual services demanded that we attempt to study services which are interrelated at an operational level. In the initial interviews with service providers we identified major concern with the problems of misplacement and bed blocking in geriatric, psychogeriatric, local authority residential, and GP hospital provision. This suggested that these services were linked and that a study of movement in this 'institutional sector' might be fruitful. Such an approach was also in line with the emphasis in national policy on joint planning of hospital and residential provision. Furthermore while previous research has been concerned with identifying 'misplaced patients' and quantifying the problem, little attention has been paid to the interrelationships between the services at referral and admission.

In the institutional sector we decided to pick up all cases referred for admission or admitted to each of the services involved, i.e. psychogeriatric, geriatric, residential, GP beds. By doing this we include patients in their own homes, in acute hospital beds, and those already in long-term institutional care but awaiting transfer to another facility. For each case we propose where possible to contact the patient, a caring relative, the referral agent and other services involved to discuss: why the patient has been referred to a particular service and why the 'community subsystem' is no longer able to maintain the person at home. We will also look in each case at the outcome of a particular episode, the reasons for this and the implications this has for the various services involved in the case (especially those community services which may be required to continue supporting a client who is not admitted to institutional care). We have deliberately avoided following up discharges from acute hospitals because of the difficulty in separating those with problems of ageing from those with acute conditions and because of limited research resources. Finally, where possible, we will observe allocation meetings and case discussions.

Having decided on entry-exit studies of this 'institutional sector' we then considered how we might incorporate entry-exit points which would centre on domiciliary services and which would be less concerned with the highly dependent elderly. We opted for entry-exit studies based on the home help service for two reasons. First, this service is very much the backbone of domiciliary support and works very closely with the community nursing services and general practitioners. Second, the lack of reported pressure on the service in this District, despite low levels of provision, suggested that a study of the interrelationship of this service with other domiciliary services might reveal some of the characteristics of the functioning of the 'community sector' as a whole. Although, we have referred to the 'institutional sector' and the 'community sector' we are in no way suggesting that these operate indepenently. Indeed, the methods chosen for our entry-exit studies are intended to capture the interactions both within and between these sectors.

Much previous research on the home help service has concentrated on allocation criteria and procedures. This would necessarily form only one aspect of our entry-exit studies which would be attempting to answer the question: 'Why is it that in an area of low provision service providers do not feel under pressure as a result of shortages of resources?' It was evident from our general interviews in the District that home help supervisors very seldom refuse to provide a service. It therefore seems that decisions about 'suitability' for service are effectively being taken elsewhere. As most referrals come from GPs and community nurses our hypothesis is that these services are playing an important part in defining 'need' and regulating demand. So although the entry-exit studies will look at the rationing devices used by the home help supervisors, they will pay attention to the interaction of these other services with the home help service as manifested in the referral process. Entry-exit studies at the home help service, as with the 'institutional' entry-exit points, involve interviewing clients, their relatives, referral agents and other service providers involved in each case.

Another point which emerged from our general interviews in relation to home help provision is that an increase in the number of hours of home help service forms one of the main avenues of intensifying community support. Yet this important means of altering service provision does not involve any entry or exit. This highlighted the desirability of studying home help supervisors' reviews of cases, especially of a sample where service level is being significantly increased. Our research resources would not permit the inclusion of a specific sample of these cases. However, we still hope to be able to address this issue through data gathered at some of our entry-exit points.

Although we have throughout been referring to 'the system', in practice it is difficult to identify self-contained systems of services. In so far as these do exist they comprise very large areas, more often

Regions rather than Districts or smaller areas. Certainly the North District of Grampian does not itself constitute a self-contained system because the geriatric, psychiatric and most acute hopsital services operate on a regional basis, centred outwith the District. Therefore it seemed that the best we could achieve would be the identification of small geographical areas which could be considered as semi-autonomous subsystems with identifiable links with the wider system of services. In these smaller areas it would be realistic to study the services we had selected in the 'institutional' and 'community' sectors in settings where the range of options open to service providers could be delineated. The use of limited geographical areas for the entry-exit studies would also facilitate the epidemiological component, i.e. the detailed reconstruction of flow patterns over the period of fieldwork. This would be extremely difficult to carry out district-wide because of the very large numbers involved.

One of the prime considerations in choosing geographical areas was that the numbers of cases arising in the selected services should be sufficient without being excessive for the purposes of the study. We estimated, using the available, somewhat crude statistics on services, that we could achieve adequate case numbers if we based the entry-exit studies in two of the several towns in the District. In addition, we thought that our selection of areas should take into account some of the variation in the structure of services within the District. Having decided on this approach we embarked upon a lengthy and complex process of negotiating access to each of the services in two areas. This proved to be a major undertaking because it involved contacting both a large number of professional groups and individual practitioners within each group. In one of the two towns we initially chose we were unsuccessful in gaining access to all services. However an alternative was selected and we eventually obtained full co-operation from all service in two areas.

The focus of attention in each of the two sites in North Grampian is on selected statutory services, which leaves us open to the charge that by omitting other statutory services, voluntary services, and possibly also private provision, we are presenting an incomplete and distorted picture of what is happening. While accepting the charge of incompleteness we do not believe we shall be presenting a distorted view of services. In striking contrast to coastal communities in the South-East of England, private provision in the coastal towns in the North East of Scotland is negligible. Voluntary services are in evidence but not to such an extent that their omission from the study is likely seriously to distort our analysis of the grouping of services we have assembled. In individual cases where they are of obvious significance we shall be alerted to this, though only in those cases where our selected statutory services become actively involved. Much the same argument holds where other statutory services are concerned.

We are confident that, between them, the two sites in North Grampian should yield sufficient numbers of cases at most, if not all, of the selected service points to enable us to comment with reasonable authority on service interactions and decision processes. We were unable in advance to estimate with any degree of precision the overall number of cases we expected to collect. Hazarding a guess, we thought it could be upwards of 70 over the six month period. In practice this turned out to be a significant underestimate. We eventually studied some 170 entry-exit decisions involving approximately 135 patients/clients. We estimate that the majority of cases will each give rise to an average of seven separate interviews with all active participants. We shall, of course, be repeating a similar exercise in each of the other two research locations over the next two years or so, over roughly the same period, that is, August to January.

Conclusions

A study of pathways through services for the elderly contains implications for future service provision. Recalling the earlier discussion of the 'continuum of care', the data from the study of pathways might go some way towards showing the extent to which such a notion is useful for policy planning purposes or whether a more flexible strategy would better accord with actual practice. Knowledge of blockages, discontinuities and gaps from the perspectives of providers and patients/clients is needed in furthering and understanding both of these notions and of the interaction between services and in planning future provision. Such understanding has a bearing on both the effective and efficient management of services. Presently there is too much planning by hunch or on the basis of wisdom handed down from high levels. A 'bottom-up' perspective grounded in actual events is lacking. The material to emerge from the entry-exit studies may also be expected to illuminate a number of wider issues in social care.

First, there is the notion of need which is contingent upon the perceptions of service providers and of patients/clients as well as upon organisational and resource constraints. Differential definitions of need are particularly evident in relation to conditions, like problems of old age, which involve social, economic and moral criteria as well as strictly medical ones. In some cases it may not be the actual needs of patients/clients which are uppermost but those of relatives who are under extreme pressure and can no longer cope. There is presently a lack of empirical data about these and other pressures.

Second, there is the matter of service availability and the relevance of service provision to patients/clients' self-perceived needs. This is important in services for the elderly because in many cases they are either non-existent or limited. Certain pathways, then, might not be seen as options which, in turn, will distort the logical sequential notion of a 'continuum of care'. Yet, if alternative arrangements are acceptable does a rigid adherence to a continuum of care matter?

Third, rather than depicting a steady progression of care for old people starting with services which are least restrictive and culminating in those which are most restrictive, pathways through services are determined not only by availability but also by alternatives. Action taken depends upon alternative options and, in particular, upon whether they are regarded as such if available and if deemed acceptable or relevant. Apart from selective criteria for access and their selective application by service providers, certain options may be rejected by old people for a variety of reasons. For example, residential care may have no appeal.

Fourth, a study of pathways of the type we have outlined will show a variety of organisational, managerial and professional features which have a direct effect upon service delivery. Individual patient/client pathways will be affected by rules, standard operating procedures and routines, by professional knowledge and beliefs and by the views of each patient/client, and where applicable, his/her relatives.

Fifth, a study of pathways will show whether or not there is participation in decision-making between service provider and patient/client and the form this takes. In the case of old people, there is considerable scope for the exercise of judgement on the part of a service provider deciding upon an appropriate referral route and, in turn, much of what is decided will depend upon each old person who, implicitly if not explicitly, will be participating in his/her future.

All five issues briefly reviewed above have potentially profound policy implications but probably never more so than at a time of demographic change, which is resulting in a larger number of very old people, coupled with moves by all governments to contain costs by improving efficiency. Compounding these issues is the occurrence of rapid change which is resulting in new service developments the necessity and efficacy of which may remain unproven.

Policy development is frequently predicated on the assumption that formal rules and 'objective' measures of need and outcome govern service provision and the activities of service planners and providers. All too often the processes involved in actually providing services are overlooked or are subordinated to more 'rational' concerns. It is hardly surprising, then, if policy-makers at governmental level worry about under-performance, delay and have doubts that government can make things work. A more informed view of what is actually taking place at the interface between providers and patients/clients must surely be to the advantage of policy-makers intent upon improving service provision.

There is no such thing as a representative or typical locality, health authority or social work department and we do not claim that the results of the study, when they emerge, or the conclusions drawn from them will necessarily hold good across Scotland or even across our three locations. Nevertheless, taken together, the three locations should reveal a broad span of issues, problems and opportunities which are likely to be similar to those found elsewhere in Scotland and beyond.

Appendix

The main topics covered in interviews with service providers in Scotland are listed below for illustrative purposes. The range of topics and details of questions vary considerably depending on the professionals involved, the circumstances of individual cases, the particular service or entry-exit point being studied and the relationship of the entry-exit point to other key components of a health system.

1. Knowledge of patient/client prior to referral.

2. Contact with the patient/client, relatives and other services in relation to the referral.

3. Outcome of the referral.

4. Views about reasons for the referral and for the particular outcome. Relevant factors might include: accommodation, or financial problems, physical and/or mental condition of the patient/client, problems experienced by the patient/client's family, isolation, adequacy of support from relatives and/or existing services, notion of 'risk', precipitating events, views of patient/client, relatives, neighbours or other services, pressure exerted by the patient/client, relatives, neighbours or other services.

5. Alternatives and/or options considered and why rejected. Reasons might include: patient/client needs, family needs, shortage of resources, management constraints, lack of provision.

6. Views about outcome as a solution to the patient/client's problems, the family's problems, also from the service provider's own standpoint.

The interviews with patient/clients and relatives are similarly varied according to circumstances but the main topics covered are:

1. The circumstances leading up to the referral. Relevant factors might include: changes in the physical or mental condition of the patient/client, changes in family circumstances, precipitating events, changing attitudes towards service involvement, pressure from family members, neighbours or professionals.

2. Contact with services prior to referral.

3. The part played by the patient/client, relative and various service providers in initiating the referral and determining the outcome.

4. Alternative options considered or preferred and why not obtained. Reasons might include: different services, changed living arrangements.

5. Views about the outcome as a response to patient/client and family needs as they see them.

Bibliography

Bloor, M. and Venters G. (1978) An Epidemiological and Sociological Study of Variations in the Incidence of Operations on the Tonsils and Adenoids, Occasional Paper No 2, Institute of Medical Sociology, University of Aberdeen

Charlesworth, A. and Wilkin D. (1982) Dependency Among Old People in Geriatric Wards, Psychogeriatric Wards and Residential Homes 1977-81, Research Report No 6, Research Section, Psychogeriatric Unit, University Hospital of South Manchester, Manchester

Davies, B. P. et al. (1971) Variations in Services for the Aged, Occasional Papers on Social Administration, No. 40, Bell, London

Department of Health and Social Security (1981) Report of a Study on Community Care, DHSS, London

Dowie, R. (1981) The Referral Process and Outpatient System. Report no. 45, Health Services Research Unit, University of Kent at Canterbury

Edwards III, G. and Sharkansky I. (1978) The Policy Predicament, Freeman, San Francisco

Glaser, B. and Strauss A. (1967) The Discovery of Grounded Theory, Aldine Publishing, New York

Goda, D. (1982) 'Relevant Statistics' in Research Highlights No. 3 Developing Services for the Elderly, Department of Social Work, University of Aberdeen

Gorbach, P. and Sinclair I. (1982) Pressure on Health and Social Services for for the Elderly, unpublished working paper, National Institute for Social Work Research Unit, London

Hedley R. and Norman A. (1982) Home Help: Key Issues in Service Provision, Centre for Policy on Ageing, London

Hill, M. (1981) 'The Policy-Implementation Distinction: a Quest for Rational Control?' in S. Barrett and C. Fudge (eds), Policy and Action, Methuen, London

James, L. (1978) '"Geriatric Ghettos" in the Making', General Practitioner, 17 November

Lipsky, M. (1980) Street Level Bureaucracy, Russell Sage, New York

Marshall, M. and Boaden N. (1978) 'Residential Care: How Can We Make Admission Less Haphazard?' Modern Geriatrics, 8, 1

Mitchell, S. and Earwicker J. (1982) Getting People Placed: The Allocation of Residential (Part III) Home Places in Hammersmith and Fulham, Research Project on the Needs of the Elderly, London Borough of Hammersmith and Fulham Social Services Department, London

Moseley, L. G. (1968) 'Variations in Socio-Medical Services for the Aged', Social and Economic and Administration, 2

Scottish Home and Health Department (1980) Changing Patterns of Care, Report on Services for the Elderly in Scotland (MacDonald Report), HMSO, Edinburgh

Spackman, A. (1980) The Allocation of Part III Places to the Elderly, (mimeo) prepared for DHSS, University of Southampton

Young, K. (1977) 'Values in the Policy Process', Policy and Politics, 5, 3

Chapter Fourteen

THE USE OF SERVICES BY THE ELDERLY THREE AND TWELVE MONTHS AFTER DISCHARGE FROM HOSPITAL

C. R. Victor

Introduction

The elderly are the largest client group of the NHS occupying approximately half of all acute beds. Given the projected increases in the size of the elderly population it is expected that the demands made by the elderly for hospital care will increase. To cater for this increase in demand, without significantly increasing resources, it has been proposed that the length of stay in hospital, for the elderly, should be reduced. See DHSS (1981).

This intention to increase discharge rates for the elderly may well have important consequences for the provision of care in the community. A study of patients discharged after treatment from a geriatrics unit found that their service use was considerably in excess of that described for ordinary populations of elderly - see Brocklehurst and Shergold (1969). More recently a survey in Oxford compared use of services by a cross-section of elderly before admission and after discharge - Hirst (1975). This survey demonstrated that service use by the elderly did not increase significantly after discharge from hospital. Given this conflicting evidence the present study set out to investigate whether the provision of services to elderly patients increases after discharge from hospital and if so whether this increase is long- or short-term. The data would then enable us to identify what the consequences would be, for the provision of community services, of increasing the discharge rate of the elderly from hospital.

Method

The study group consisted of 2711 people aged 65 and over discharged from NHS non-psychiatric hospitals throughout Wales in 1981. This represented a 4% sample of total discharges for that year from the seven Area Health Authorities participating in the study (Powys was excluded from the study as it lacked a district general hospital). Entry into the study was restricted to those elderly who had spent at least 48 hours in hospital. The sample was collected monthly for one calendar year to exclude the influence of seasonal variations in admission patterns.

Given the wide geographical spread of the study population the cost of employing interviewers was prohibitive. Thus the data were collected from subjects using a postal questionnaire. This method of data collection is not usually recommended for use with the elderly - see Bennett and Ritchie (1975). Consequently before the main study pilot studies were undertaken to find the most acceptable method of question presentation and to test the reliability of the answers provided. A sample of 50 subjects were sent postal questionnaires. They were subsequently interviewed by a fieldworker, using the same schedule, between three and four weeks later and the responses compared. Little evidence of subjects changing responses was found. Additionally where subjects reported receiving a service such as home help or meals on wheels or reported being re-admitted to hospital as an in-patient this was checked against administrative records. In all cases it was demonstrated that the elderly were extremely reliable reporters of the services which they had received. Further details about the pilot study are reported in Victor (1983).

The postal questionnaire was sent to subjects three and 12 months after discharge. The first interview time was selected to provide extra data about early rehabilitation whilst the one-year follow-up provided long-term data.

The first interview contained 127 questions and was eight pages long. Included in this interview were 24 questions which asked patients about the use of services in the month prior to their admission to hospital and in the three months since discharge. The second interview asked about service use in the month prior to the interview.

Both interview schedules recorded patients' disability using the nine item index described by Townsend (1979). This index defines disability as difficulty with or inability to perform tasks which are considered to be essential to independent life in the community such as washing, housework and preparing and cooking a meal. For each task subjects are asked if they can perform it unaided, which scores zero, if they require assistance to perform the task, which scores 1, or if they cannot perform the task, which carries a score of 2. Thus the score ranges from 0 to 18. Townsend classifies patients with a score of zero as not disabled; 1 to 6 as mildly disabled; 7 to 11 as moderately disabled and 12 or more as severely disabled.

Standard background demographic data such as age, sex, social class and civil status were also collected. Data about patients' stay in hospital such as admission type, i.e. waiting list or emergency, diagnosis and speciality of treatment were derived from the HAA (Hospital Activity Analysis) form.

Results

Response

Completed interviews were returned by 1930 (71%); 328 (12%) were dead 3 months after discharge, giving an overall response rate of 83%. No reply was received from 341 (13%); 62 (2%) refused the interview. Thirty-seven (1%) were in hospital and 13 (<1%) were in residential homes and considered unfit to reply by the officer in charge. The response rate to the second interview was 84%.

Use of Services After Discharge

Compared with before admission, service use increased markedly three months after discharge (Table 1). These increases were statistically significant, at the 5% level, for all services except attendance at OAP/lunch clubs and occupational therapy.

The increase in the proportions receiving support varied between the services, as did the total coverage. The use of medical services such as GP contact and visits from district nurses and health visitors increased the most and had the largest coverage. Social services use, such as meals on wheels, increased less and, interestingly, covered a lower proportion of the population.

Service use for survivors at 12 months is described in Table 2. Usage levels before admission and at three months were similar for this group of survivors and the total study group. However service usage at 12 months showed some substantial changes from the pattern observed at three months. Social service use, such as meals on wheels and home helps, showed very little change between three and 12 months post-discharge. Medical service use, however, such as GP, health visitors or district nurse contacts, decreased markedly during this period.

Changes in Service Use Between Admission and Discharge

Concern has been expressed that admission to hospital can result in elderly subjects losing contact with the services. Table 3, however, shows that only a small proportion of elderly who were receiving services before admission lost them after discharge.

More importantly this table serves to emphasise the very limited coverage of most of the community services. With the exception of GP contacts, where only 19% had not seen their family doctor since discharge, services were being received by only a minority of patients. The vast majority were not receiving either domiciliary medical or social services, suggesting that the family is bearing the greater burden of caring for the elderly after discharge.

Who Gets Services After Discharge?

The characteristics of patients receiving services after discharge were examined to identify if certain groups of elderly were being under-provided with services. Use of services was related to patients' demographic characteristics. There was a significant trend for the use of most services to be related to age (Table 4). The proportions receiving domiciliary health and social services, such as district nurse or home help visits, increased significantly with age as did contact with GP and therapeutic services. Outpatient visits to hospital decreased significantly with age and attendance at day hospitals showed no relationship with age.

The use of the two domiciliary social services of home helps and meals on wheels was significantly higher amongst females and those living alone. Additionally these groups were also more likely to have seen a social worker than were males or those living in larger households. There were, however, no differences between the sexes or household composition groups in the proportions receiving medical services after discharge.

Service use after discharge also varied with social class (Table 5). Subjects in classes IV and V had a significantly greater use of meals on wheels, home helps and visits from social workers/health visitors. GP contacts illustrated the reverse trend - subjects in classes I and II having a significantly higher level of GP contact. No social class variations in contact with district nurses, therapists or visits to day hospitals were noted.

Disability and service use is shown in Table 6. Consistently, the use of services, especially the domiciliary social services, such as meals on wheels and home helps, was highest amongst the most disabled members of the study group.

Use of services after discharge was also examined in relation to patients' treatment in hospital. No statistically significant relationships were observed between the type of admission to hospital, i.e. emergency, booked or waiting list and post-discharge service use. However, the use of services was related to both length of stay and the specialty in which patients were treated. There was a consistent trend for the use of all services, except visits to OAP clubs, to increase with the length of time patients stayed in hospital.

For all services, except physiotherapy and hospital outpatient visits, usage levels were significantly higher amongst patients treated in geriatrics units than in other specialties (Table 7). Comparing service use between specialties is difficult because of the different medical conditions seen in the various specialties. In this series there were no significant differences in the medical conditions of patients seen in general medical and geriatrics units - see Victor (1983). Patients seen in geriatrics units demonstrated a higher level of service use than their contemporaries treated in general medical wards. There were, however, age and disability differences in the demographic characteristics of patients treated in each of these two specialties. The use of services by patients seen in geriatrics units and general medical units was standardised to take into account age and disability differences between the two groups. In this instance disability was recorded using the Townsend index described earlier and the data were standardised using the indirect method - see Armitage

Table 1 Use of Services at Three Months (%)

Service	Before admission	At 3 months
GP	12	69
District Nurse	12	37
Health Visitor	3	15
Social Worker	4	23
Home Help	17	25
Meals on Wheels	6	8
OAP Club	6	7
Hospital Outpatient	-	64
Day Hospital	7	18
Physiotherapy	4	8
Occupational Therapy	1	3
Speech Therapy	-	1
N	1930	1930

Table 2 Use of Services by Survivors at 12 months (%)

Service	Before admission	3 months	12 months
GP	11	68	41
District Nurse	11	34	6
Health Visitor	3	15	7
Social Worker	4	21	8
Home Help	16	24	23
Meals on Wheels	5	8	7
OAP Club	6	7	6
Hospital Outpatient	-	66	20
Day Hospital	7	19	17
Physiotherapy	4	8	5
Occupational therapy	1	3	2
Speech therapy	-	1	-
N	1404	1404	1404

Table 3 Changes in Service Use Between Admission and Three Months Post-discharge (N = 1930)

Service	Gained Service	Lost Service	Retained Service	Did not Receive
GP	57	-	24	19
District Nurse	26	1	11	62
Health Visitor	13	-	2	85
Social Worker	19	-	3	78
Home Help	9	2	15	74
Meals on Wheels	4	2	4	90
OAP Club	2	3	4	91
Hospital Outpatient	64	-	-	36
Day Hospital	14	3	4	79
Physio-Therapy	2	2	2	94
Occupational Therapy	3	-	-	97
Speech Therapy	1	-	-	99

Table 4 Use of Services by Age (%)

Service	65	70	75	80	85+	Cox C
GP	67	67	70	71	72	2.4
District Nurse	27	32	37	46	55	8.2
Health Visitor	7	13	19	21	26	7.4
Social Worker	12	20	25	34	31	7.8
Home Help	13	20	31	39	33	8.9
Meals on Wheels	4	7	8	13	14	5.6
OAP Club	3	8	8	11	8	3.6
Hospital Outpatient	74	68	66	51	43	8.5
Day Hospital	19	20	18	15	18	0.8
Physiotherapy	6	8	9	8	12	2.3
Occupational Therapy	1	3	4	5	4	2.4
Speech Therapy	1	1	1	-	1	0.1
N	471	529	457	265	208	

Table 5 Use of Services by Social Class (%)

	Social Class			
Service	I & II	IIIN	IIIM	IV & V
GP	71	73	67	66
District Nurse	35	38	39	34
Health Visitor	11	15	17	19
Social Worker	17	24	23	24
Home Help	21	24	24	28
Meals on Wheels	6	6	8	10
OAP Club	3	6	8	9
Hospital Outpatient	67	62	68	61
Day Hospital	16	16	21	18
Physiotherapy	9	8	8	6
Occupational Therapy	3	3	4	3
Speech Therapy	-	-	1	-
N	322	195	514	636

Table 6 Use of Services by Disability (%)

Service	Disability			
	None	Mild	Moderate	Severe
GP	56	66	69	76
District Nurse	16	24	31	58
Health Visitor	5	9	14	26
Social Worker	6	11	26	38
Home Help	4	17	31	37
Meals on Wheels	3	6	8	13
OAP Club	4	5	9	10
Hospital Outpatient	75	70	68	54
Day Hospital	18	16	13	23
Physiotherapy	5	4	7	14
Occupational Therapy	1	2	2	6
Speech Therapy	-	1	-	1
N	284	530	363	685

Table 7 Use of Services by Specialty of Treatment (%)

Service	General Medicine	Geriatrics	General Surgery	T & O Surgery	Ophathal-mology	Others
GP	71	77	68	68	53	62
District Nurse	34	53	35	45	22	22
Health Visitor	15	30	9	10	9	9
Social Worker	23	40	14	26	14	15
Home Help	29	36	17	25	20	18
Meals on Wheels	10	11	5	14	5	7
OAP Club	8	11	4	5	10	6
Hospital Outpatient	64	48	72	74	90	69
Day Hospital	14	24	18	16	21	18
Physio-Therapy	9	14	1	28	1	3
Occupational Therapy	3	9	1	7	1	-
Speech Therapy	-	2	-	-	-	-
N	443	409	509	155	166	248

Table 8 Use of Services by Specialty Standardised by Age

Service	General Medicine	Geriatrics	General Surgery	T & O Surgery	Ophthal-mology	Others
GP	121	133	115	79	89	104
District Nurse	111	156	120	146	68	75
Health Visitor	116	201	79	118	66	81
Social Worker	122	184	80	135	69	86
Home Help	142	149	87	119	90	97
Meals on Wheels	141	133	76	201	73	113
OAP Club	138	157	73	74	148	103
Hospital Outpatient	99	98	123	138	159	119
Day Hospital	98	176	120	112	145	89
Physio-therapy	128	194	20	409	60	92
Occupational therapy	97	286	37	225	20	95
Speech therapy	111	308	67	0	0	69

Table 9 Use of Services by Speciality Standardised by Disability

Service	General Medicine	Geriatrics	General Surgery	T & O Surgery	Ophthal-mology	Others
GP	194	106	102	98	77	93
District Nurse	139	115	114	126	67	72
Health Visitor	88	151	76	93	66	76
Social Worker	91	136	78	110	69	86
Home Help	106	117	83	99	87	91
Meals on Wheels	107	106	69	172	72	100
OAP Club	81	129	62	61	140	90
Hospital Outpatient	88	79	106	115	137	104
Day Hospital	84	139	107	99	125	107
Physio-therapy	100	138	21	240	17	44
Occupational therapy	63	213	37	201	0	0
Speech therapy	30	244	110	0	0	89

Table 10 Use of Services by Movers and Non-movers for Treatment (%)

Service	Movers	Non-Movers
GP	72	68
District Nurse	26	37
Health Visitor	6	16
Social Worker	14	23
Home Help	11	26
Meals on Wheels	7	8
OAP Club	5	7
Hospital Outpatient	64	64
Day Hospital	17	18
Physiotherapy	3	9
Occupational Therapy	2	3
Speech Therapy	1	1
N	145	1785

Table 11 Use of Services by Movers and Non-movers Standardised by Age and Disability

Service	Movers	Non-Movers
GP	101	100
District Nurse	74	132
Health Visitor	43	154
Social Worker	65	133
Home Help	92	104
Meals on Wheels	91	108
OAP Club	98	101
Hospital Outpatient	99	100
Day Hospital	100	99
Physiotherapy	99	102
Occupational Therapy	89	109
Speech Therapy	101	99

(1971). This procedure did not alter the general pattern outlined above; patients treated in geriatrics wards continued to demonstrate a markedly higher level of service use than patients treated in general medical wards even when age (Table 8) and disability (Table 9) differences between the two groups were taken into account.

Service use by patients who lived in the county in which they received their medical treatment were compared with those who did not. Subjects who moved between counties for treatment were more likely to have seen their GP (Table 10). No differences were found between the two groups for contact with the hospital or therapeutic services. In contrast, patients who crossed between counties for treatment had a significantly lower level of home help use and were less likely to have seen a district nurse, health visitor or social worker. These observations could arise from differences in the characterisation of the two groups. For example patients who moved between counties could be less 'sick' and therefore need fewer services. To take this factor into account the data were standardised for age and disability. Table 11 demonstrates that this procedure did not alter the situation described above; patients crossing county boundaries to receive medical treatment were still less likely to receive domiciliary health and social services.

Further Need for Services

Defining need for services is a complex task. The data described above suggest that there is a relationship between service use post-discharge and 'need' as measured by the age and disability of patients.

Unmet need for services was investigated by asking patients not receiving the specific services of a home help or meals on wheels if they would like them. Four per cent of those without meals on wheels said they needed the service and 6% without a home help wanted the service. It was older subjects, females, those living alone and the disabled who expressed a consistently and significantly higher level of demand for these services. Thus although these groups were the main priority for receiving services some were still not receiving the help they felt they needed.

Discussion

Before admission to hospital the use of services by the study group was very similar to that which has been described for ordinary communities of the elderly living at home - Bond and Carstairs (1982). Three months after discharge, however, service use increased markedly. This contrasts with an earlier small study in Oxford which indicated that service use by the elderly did not increase after discharge - Hirst (1975). As that study was confined to the first 14 days after discharge it is possible that not all services had started to operate. The results of the present survey show that service use by the elderly increases after discharge and confirms the high levels of service use by ex-geriatrics unit patients described by Brocklehurst and Shergold (1969).

The high levels of service use noted as three months were not maintained at 12 months for the medical services but were for the social services. The need for medical services by the elderly after discharge may be confined to the short-term immediate post-discharge period whilst the need for social support may be more long-term. Alternatively, it may be that once social services are initiated they are not reviewed and terminated, where appropriate, as could be the case for medical services.

From the data collected by the study it is not possible to state with certainty which of these processes is operating. Several interesting hypotheses could be usefully tested and are of considerable importance if the discharge rates of the elderly from hospital are to be increased.

Whilst we cannot be certain of why the increase in social service use is maintained long-term after discharge, the data indicate that after discharge the elderly present an increased demand for services. Consequently any increases in discharge rates of the elderly from hospital will result in extra pressure upon community services, both medical and social, at a time when they are under particular financial pressure.

Service use varied between the sub-groups of the study population. A larger fraction of older subjects received services as compared with younger ones. Disabled subjects were also more likely to receive both health and social community services after discharge than were the non-disabled. However, only the social services saw those living alone, females or those in classes 4 and 5 as a priority group.

Use of services varied according to aspects of patients' hospital treatment. With increased length of stay in hospital service use increased. Service use varied between the specialties in which subjects were seen. Of the six major treatment specialties service, use was significantly higher amongst patients treated in geriatrics units, with the exception of meals on wheels (orthopaedics) and outpatient visits (ophthalmology). In particular, patients treated in geriatrics units illustrated a markedly higher level of service use compared with those seen in general medical wards even when age and disability differences in the characteristics of patients treated in these two specialties were accounted for. This could suggest that geriatrics departments have better links with community services than has general medicine, and that they are more aware of the availability and need for service by the newly discharged elderly patient. Alternatively, this might indicate that geriatricians 'over prescribe' services in comparison with other specialists treating elderly patients. The data do not make it possible to distinguish between these two processes. It is worth noting that the greater use of services by geriatricians results in a slightly more favourable outcome for their patients, particularly in comparison with the general medical patients -Victor (1983).

Patients who moved between counties for medical treatment had a significantly lower level of use of domiciliary services. Two factors may account for this. First, subjects moving between counties for treatment could be less 'ill' and therefore less in need of services than non-movers. Second, cross-boundary communications between health and social services departments may be poor. Given that standardising the data to take account of the differences in the characteristics of movers and non-movers did not alter the results, it seems that this difference is partly due to administrative deficiencies in the system of service provision.

The levels of felt need for service expressed by the sample were similar to that expressed by the elderly living in the community - see Bond and Carstairs (1982). The study indicated that older subjects and the disabled were considered 'top priority' for the receipt of services. Nevertheless, these groups were still the ones to express the highest levels of unmet demand for domiciliary social services, suggesting that many of the most vulnerable groups were not receiving the help they required. If the transfer from hospital to community is to be made more efficiently then some expansion of domiciliary services is required to take into account these levels of unmet need expressed by these very vulnerable groups who are often unlikely to have any other sources of care available to them - Victor (1983).

The survey has demonstrated that the use of both social and medical services by the elderly increases in the short term after discharge from hospital. Thus, increasing the discharge rates of the elderly from hospital will impose further strain upon the already stretched resources of the community. Failure to take this into account only highlights the separate identities of the two types of service when what is needed is a more integrated approach to the care of the elderly.

Bibliography

Armitage, P. (1971) Statistical Methods in Medical Research, Blackwell, Oxford

Bennett, A.E. and Ritchie, K. (1975) Questionnaires in Medicine, Oxford University Press, London

Bond, J. and Carstairs, V. (1982) 'The Elderly in Clackmannan', Scottish Health Service Studies, no. 82, Scottish Home and Health Department, Edinburgh

Brocklehurst, J. and Shergold, M. (1969) 'What Happens When Geriatric Patients Leave Hospital', Lancet, November 23, 1133 - 1135

DHSS (1981) Growing Older, HMSO, London

Hirst, J. (1975) 'Elderly Patients Discharged From Hospital', Social Work Department, John Radcliffe Infirmary, Oxford

Townsend, P. (1979) Poverty in the United Kingdom, Penguin Books, Harmondsworth

Victor, C.R. (1983) 'A Survey of the Elderly After Discharge From Hospitals in Wales', unpublished PhD thesis, University of Wales, Cardiff

Chapter Fifteen

IDENTIFYING EXCELLENCE IN THE CARE OF THE ELDERLY

P. P. Mayer

Introduction

This brief paper describes the first year of a project to identify 'centres of excellence' amongst National Health Services hospitals providing medical treatment for the elderly in the West Midlands.

Geriatric wards caring for the elderly present in many different ways, from the 'carpeted and bright' to those 'cluttered with unattractive furniture...where the apathy of the patients is matched by the frustration of the staff.' - Brocklehurst (1980).

Discussion groups based on a booklet published by the King Edwards Hospital Fund for London (1975) led to the formation of a multidisciplinary group discussing the problems of caring for the elderly in long-term care in the West Midlands under the auspices of the nurse training section of the West Midlands Regional Health Authority.

Competition and Prize

Examples of 'good' and 'bad' practice were disseminated through individual group members and through symposia on selected topics. The idea of a prize was conceived as a technique for identifying 'centres of excellence' whether in large or small centres in the Region.

The group felt that this should be supervised by an organisation outside the management structure of the Authority and for this purpose the West Midlands Institute of Geriatric Medicine and Gerontology was approached. The Institute had been founded in 1971, its prime activity being educational. It holds regular multidisciplinary courses, case conferences and symposia for those involved in the care of the elderly. It also has experience in conducting competitions for professional staff.

The Institute appointed a multidisciplinary panel including geriatricians, nurses, a clinical psychologist, a hospital administrator and a sociology researcher. Entries were invited from wards, groups of wards, or other small units within the Region. Those entering the competition had to complete an essay entitled 'Improving Geriatric

Care' in which they were asked to describe the unit from which the application came and the ways in which they used resources or ideas. They were also asked to identify how any prize money would be used. During this pilot year entries were deliberately limited by advertising only through line management.

Following receipt of the essays the panel achieved consensus on short-listing three of the units. These units were visited by panel members and asked to complete a short questionnaire designed to obtain detailed information about the resources in the unit and the way staff were trained and employed as well as more detailed information about their attitudes towards the patients in their care. In the event each judge developed personal criteria of assessment and used the questionnaire as a check list rather than as a means of judging the unit.

Fourteen units entered essays including eight geriatric medical inpatient units, two day units and four psychiatric units for the elderly. The essays varied from simple descriptions of the units concerned (eight essays) to descriptions which seemed to demonstrate ideas which were new or interesting (six essays) as judged by the panel.

Thirteen entries had come from members of the nursing staff and one from a geriatrician. We had asked for referees to support the applications from people outside the unit and again seventeen of a potential twenty-eight referees were nursing staff, four medical staff and seven from other sources including a Chairman of a Health Authority and a vicar.

Three units were short-listed. The unit which was eventually awarded the 'prize' described the use of reality orientation in poor circumstances which would have made most of us despair. The other two entries were from a psychiatric unit providing a short-stay support admission and a purpose built geriatric unit describing ward specialisms. The essays are published in the magazine Tripod (1983).

The size of the entry had been kept deliberately small for the 'pilot year' to assess both the technique and the Institute's ability to respond. Although an attempt was made to develop objective criteria through the standard essay and the use of check lists based on published scales, 'impact' criteria such as those described by Maxwell (1983) seemed the most important.

In retrospect our methods seemed, in principle at least, to be very similar to those used for accreditation of hospitals in the USA without attempting or indeed intending to be so detailed or comprehensive. Consensus was relatively easily achieved. The short-listed units expressed effective means of using resources and on visits there was a feeling of achievement not directly related to resources or overall organisation. The three units also expressed ideas of management which were thought to be exportable to other units without the necessity for a massive increase in their resources.

The competition is now underwritten by the Birmingham Hospital Saturday Fund for at least three further competitions in alternate years. The Institute intends to use the same structure and criteria to assess whether the units answer their clients' needs, how effectively they use their resources and how exportable the ideas will be in practice .

The method used seems to be a cost effective means of identifying units within the West Midlands practising a high standard of care and a means of publicising their ideas and methods.

Copies of the application form and questionnaires used may be obtained from Dr. P. P. Mayer at the West Midlands Institute of Geriatric Medicine and Gerontology, Moseley Hall Hospital, Alcester Road, Moseley, Birmingham B13 8JL.

Bibliography

Brocklehurst, J. (1980) 'Foreword' in T. J. Wells, Problems in Geriatric Nursing Care, Churchill Livingstone, Edinburgh

King Edwards Hospital Fund for London (1975) Living in Hospital - The Social Needs of People in Long Term Care, King Edwards Hospital Fund, London

Maxwell, R. (1983), 'Health Care - Seeking Quality', The Lancet, January 1/8, pp. 45-48.

Tripod (1983) No. 6, Winter Published by the West Midlands Institute of Geriatric Medicine, Birmingham

PART FOUR : CULTURAL FACTORS

Chapter Sixteen

SOCIAL CUSTOMS AFFECTING THE ROLE OF ELDERLY WOMEN IN INDIAN SOCIETY 1982

A. Merriman

Introduction

In 1982, the author became a student again after 19 years in order to take a Masters Degree in International Community Health at the Liverpool School of Tropical Medicine. She found herself with three other students of separate nationalities in Varanasi, North India, for three months attachment to Benares Hindu University, in order to write a dissertation necessary for the degree. Benares is the Holy City of Hinduism on the Banks of Ganges. Known today as Varanasi, in pre-Hindu times it was Kashi, the city of the sun god. Since the elderly had been my specialty and special interest in the NHS and Universities at Liverpool and Manchester for nine years, I chose a study of the elderly of India.

The study sample is shown in Table 1 and the site of interview indicated in small map of India.

Site of Interview in India in 1982

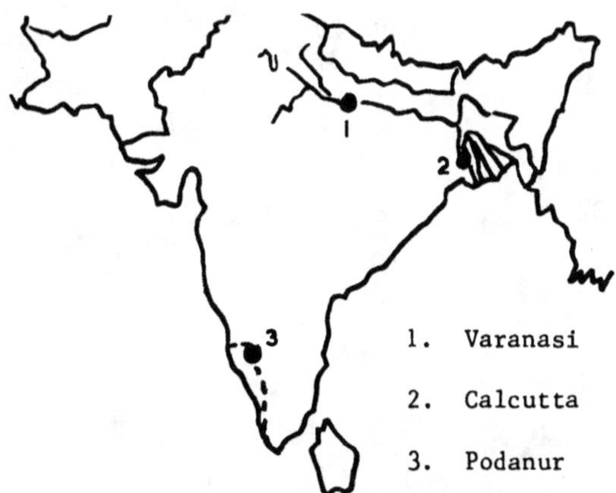

Table 1 (a) Study Population

Place	Sex M	Sex F
Varanasi		
Sunderpur Village	25	25
Widow (87) in service		1
Widows home Benares		6
Calcutta		
Prem Dam (OPH)	2	3
Kali Ghat (Home for Dying)	3	2
Tamil Nadu		
Podanur (OPH)	2	1
	32	38

Table 1 (b) Age Group of Respondents

	M	F	Total	%
60-69	10	10	20	28.5
70-79	17	14	31	44.3
80-89	4	11	15	21.5
90-99	1	3	4	5.7
Total	32	38	70	100

Table I (c) Religion of Respondents

	No.	%
Hindu	63	90
Muslim	1	1.5
Christian	6	8.5
	70	100

Table I (d) Caste Groupings of Hindu Respondents

	Total	%
*Upper	6	9.5
Middle	39	62.0
Lower	18	28.5
	63	100

* See section on Hindu Religion
Source: own study

Each interview took an average of one hour with the help of an interpreter. Only two interviews were held without an interpreter. The questionnaire covered living and financial conditions, family support, mental score test, attitudes to medical care, addictions, death, rebirth and after life. A full physical examination was carried out for each respondent. This paper draws on information gained from these interviews, and from a study of present day India, to give the reader a glimpse into social factors affecting the role of the elderly women in today's Indian Society.

Background Information

India in the second largest country in the world with a population approaching 700 million. India supports 15% of the world's population in 2.4% of the world's area. The population density is 221 per square kilometer - Census of India (1981).

The population pyramid of India can be described as "young"; the percentage of persons over the age of 64 is less than 4%.

From the population statistics, two factors reflect social attitudes to women: (1) At the age of 5 years, there are 2.5 million less girls than boys. Sex ratio approaches equality in old age as natural female longevity supersedes possible female prejudices - U.N. Statistical Yearbook for Asia and the Pacific (1981). (2) Overall sex ratio varies from state to state, the greatest difference occurring between Uttar Pradesh (the state where Benares is situated) and Kerala in the South - see Table 2.

Table 2 Females per 1,000 males

All India	950
Kerala	1034
Uttar Pradesh	886

Source: Census of India (1981)

"India", said Nehru, "is a bundle of centuries, in which the cow and the tractor march together." - Fodore (1981). This became very evident to me in my travels. Uttar Pradesh, the largest of India's 22 states, appeared as 19th century, and Kerala as 20th century (circa 1950) when compared to British milestones of time. Kerala is conquering many of the problems which the rest of India find insurmountable, e.g. population control, female education and reduced infant mortality. Travelling 3,000 miles alone by train across India, one was able to talk to people from many areas. I left India feeling that religious beliefs and consequent social customs had a major role to play in the development of India, and in particular, the circumstances of women today. Comparisons between Uttar Pradesh and Kerala supported my impressions.

Religions of India

Hinduism is the major religion, 82.7% of population being believers. However, in Uttah Pradesh, 95% are Hindu and for Kerala 50%; 11.2% of India's population are Muslim; Christianity is in third place with only 2.6%; in Uttar Pradesh there are less than 1% Christians whereas in Kerala there are 35% Christians. See Research and Reference Division (1981).

The Hindu Religion

The Hindu Religion was brought to India in 1500 BC when the Aryans invaded the Indus Valley from which India takes its name. They brought with them the epic hymns the "Vedas", which are passed from generation to generation by word of mouth. At that time, the Hindu caste system was established. This has has a great effect on religious thinking and in the development of India. Laws were made forbidding intermarriage between castes, because the fair skinned Aryans did not want intermarriage with the dark skinned races of the Southern

Table 3. Caste System.

(Caste System is related to status and not to economic grouping).

	Caste Order	Name	Origin	Function	Found Today	Notes
Upper:	1	Brahmins	Head of Brahma	Priests and Teachers	Priests Teachers Civil Servants	Boys have inauguration ceremony DWI-AJA. Twice-Born.
	2	Kshatriyas	Brahma's arms	Kings and Soldiers	Land Owners	Still use force to get education.
	3	Vaisyas	Brahma's thighs	Cattle-keepers Agriculture Trade	Businessmen and farmers	
Middle:	4	Sudras	Brahma's feet	House-keepers	Trade Craftsmen	Many Sub-castes today

Lower: Unclassed Harijans. Those unworthy of caste because of misdemeanour in past times. They perform menial tasks - removing night soil, sweeping streets, and so on. Today they can be found in any trade but are still shunned in the country - Thomas (1975). It is now an offence to call a person untouchable. Gandhi called them "children of God".

Peninsular.

Karma and Dharma

Hinduism is a loose confederation of beliefs bestowing a philosophy of life on the believer. This philosophy is based on Karma, Dharma and Rebirth.
Karma: one is born where one deserves to be, based on one's previous life.
Dharma: one does one's duty well within the state of life where one is born, never trying to move out of caste, but accepting any inconveniences.
Rebirth: if one follows Karma and Dharma, one will reach Mukti (union with God) or be reborn into a higher caste in the next life. If one lives a bad life, rebirth may be to a lower caste, or outside human life as animal or insect.

Beliefs Inhibiting Social Change Associated with Hinduism

The position of a woman in the Indian family is affected primarily by the dowry system. Women were equal to men in ancient India. However, the dowry system was introduced with the laws of Manu and its effect on the role of women can still be seen today. Girl children are economically disadvantageous to parents as money or goods have to be paid to the husband's family at marriage. Until recently all girls were married. On the other hand, boys bring in money and daughters-in-law at marriage and provide care in old age. If children are sick in a family, the best food and medicines will be given to the son. These attitudes are reflected in the female deficit at five years previously mentioned. Legislation has been brought in to suppress the dowry system, however it still continues with abuses such as bride deaths reported in papers even today.

If one follows the philosophy of Karma and Dharma, one does not promote social change or improvement for oneself or one's family and one discourages it in others.

Life Path of the Elderly Women of India 1982

Birth

The first female child is welcome but, because of future financial implications, girls become successively less welcome. One elderly man told me in front of an unmarried daughter that his life had been unhappy because he had four daughters before he had a son. A son would bring home a daughter-in-law and dowry to support them in their old age and to carry out death rituals. The sanskrit name for son is putra - पु त्र

पु = Pu = a particular hell

त्र = tra = to save

"He who saves the deceased from the hell called pu, by lighting the funeral pyre".

Childhood

Schooling was unusual for girls in India in the early 20th century - 96% of the women interviewed by me were illiterate, compared to 32% of the men. In Sunderpur Village (25 women interviewed) only one had been to primary school. Out of a total of 38 women interviewed, only three had been to school. The preference for educating sons must have become obvious to young girl children. In their responses to the mental test questionnaire - Isaacs and Walkey (1964) - the females scored poorly compared to males, showing little knowledge outside the domestic situation.

Childhood, however, appears to have been a happy time until arranged marriage cast its shadow, with thoughts of leaving parents.

Marriage

Betrothal took palce early - Thomas (1975), Gandhi (1927) - but consummation of marriage took place at puberty. Bethrothal was as good as marriage to this generation, for at least two of my respondents had been widowed before consummation, and were not allowed to marry again. Men are allowed to remarry if widowed, women are not. Until the 19th century, widows were burnt on the funeral pyre with their husbands - this custom was known as Sati. Gandhi (1927), a contemporary of my respondents, discusses child marriage in his autobiography.

Marriage was universal and I did not meet any single women amongst my respondents. Indeed they found it difficult to accept that I was single (they quizzed me too you see!). One old lady told me I was single because there are not enough men to go round in England.

I was present at Hindu marriages as I was in India during the "marriage season", which is after the harvesting and before the rainy season. The ceremony was geared towards the male who wore white, and was carried around the streets on horse-back or on an elephant, to the accompaniment of a band. The bride, dressed in red, awaited her betrothed inside, looking very miserable. This was understandable, as she was leaving the family she knew and loved, and going to strangers -particularly a strange mother-in-law who would rule her life. Divorce was allowed only by the husband if the wife did not produce a child.

Childbirth

During pregnancy, the woman is pampered with extra rest and special foods. She is allowed to return to her parents' home for the first delivery - after this she will deliver with her in-laws. If she does not produce male issue, family disharmony may result. She is usually blamed!

Mother-in-law

This lady rules the daughters-in-law. Each daughter-in-law joins the family in seniority according to the son she marries, the most junior having to obey the others. The new wife remains subservient to this system until she in turn becomes mother-in-law to daughters-in-law.

Widowhood

At the death of a husband, the wife cannot go to the funeral. Only men accompany the body to the Ganges for cremation. The eldest son takes responsibility for the funeral and ensures the Shraddah ceremonies are carried out. The widow remains with her in-laws and family and it is their responsibility to look after her. As all over the world, the affection and care varies with the previous relationships of the widow. One widowed respondent had been thrown out of her son's house by her daughter-in-law. She was extremely unhappy living alone.

In the widows' home at Varanasi, the widows had travelled from West Bengal in order to await death on the Ganges. It is believed that if one dies within the walls of old Kashi (Benares), one will attain Mukti or union with God. The Hindu widows wear a white sari and most shave their heads. To give alms to widows is recommended to all Hindus and many widows are seen along the banks of the Ganges seeking alms from pilgrims.

Further Personal Findings

Life Path

The life path for most of my respondents had taken the course described. However, those in institutions had been either widowed (usually early in life) or separated from families and were now left to face old age alone. They related their heartbreak and disillusionment. They missed their independence in Calcutta where they were institutionalised and their reduced circumstances in the widows' home in Benares.

Social Situation, Social Life and Personal Fulfilment

In the village of Sunderpur, most elderly lived in the bosom of the extended family where they played a major role in looking aftergrandchildren, who obviously loved their grandparents. There was hardly one interview without children present.

The elderly themselves, although illiterate, caught up on local news from their peers of the same sex, who they met daily at open field defaecation. Although this custom was to keep smells away from cooking areas and areas of worship, the social aspect of meeting together was obviously looked forward to. The young elderly helped the older elderly, as the distance could be as far as 600 yards. This custom replaced the daily newspaper among those who could not read!

Personal fulfilment at any age is often related to our usefulness to our family and community. Elderly women at home were happily engaged with domestic duties, looking after grandchildren and keeping cows and goats and other animals. They also taught life experiences to daughters-in-law and were obviously respected. Personal fulfilment was obviously lacking in institutions, except perhaps in cases where the old ladies were involved with work in the institution. In Podanur OPH, there was a farm where the elderly could be involved looking after animals. Most institutions, however, appeared to spend most of their energies in feeding and clothing the residents, and keeping them clean, rather than directing their efforts towards personal fulfilment.

Physical Health

Comparing my findings with my British experience:

(1) The following were noticeable by their absence in physical findings of 70 elderly - cardiac irregularities, poor peripheral circulation, organic brain disease, survivors of CVA, constipation, polypharmacy, Parkinsonism, hypertension, dental problems, foot problems.

(2) The following were present but in low percentage - hearing defects, diabetes, multiple pathology.

3. There was a higher incidence of cataract.

Mental Health, Dependence and Happiness

Mental fitness was defined for the study as absence of psychiatric disorder, obvious personality problem or inability to function in own environment. Seven to ten percent of the respondents manifested such disorders: one difficult personality, two agitated depression, one reactive depression, one neurotic depression, two poor memory associated with arteroisclerosis.

Physical Independence

This was defined as the ability to wash, dress, feed and go to latrine the without the help of another person. Except at Kali Ghat, the home for the dying, and one woman residing in Pre Dam, I did not meet any chronically chair or bedfast.

Two ladies in the study had sustained fractured femurs, neither of whom had had adequate treatment and therefore had a flail leg. In the government home, the lady was independent walking on three limbs and bringing the flail leg through. The lady in Prem Dam could do this, but mainly the Sisters and Helpers helped her to the latrine and to wash.

The lady who had become suddenly blind three weeks previously in Sunderpur was still trying to be independent. She had become blind from glaucoma as a result of the Benares Hindu University hospital strike. Her eye drops had run out and the clinic had closed and not renewed them. Both she and the dependent fractured femur lady were terribly upset about their loss of independence.

I was pleasantly surprised at the independence and physical fitness of this group. I now feel that the survivors over 60 in India (3.7%) are equivalent to that 25% of our 16% survivors in U.K. who are fit and remain so to the end. Those who survive in a developed country with chronic disability such as stroke or fractured femur, or severe arthritis, do not appear to survive in Indian society.

It is arguable that such a state of survival of the fittest could be envied by our own elderly. How many of our dependent, chronically ill elderly are impatient to die? Many times have such elderly admitted to me as their physician that they wish God would take them. They are not depressed or suicidal but realistic in feeling that dependence and real suffering are not a fair price to pay for an extended life.

Happiness in Life

At home in Sunderpur, 64% of the women and 88% of the men thought life had been happy. In institutions, 71% of the men and only 23% of the women said life had been happy. Happiness was associated with children being settled and good to them, being part of a joint family, being physically well, financially secure and keeping busy and useful. The respect of children and seeing great-grand-children also contributed. Unhappiness was associated with the death of sons and loss of independence. I suspect a similar group in UK would reveal similar statistics and reasons, especially among our 5% institutionalised elderly.

Of those who were living at home and glad to have lived to old age, 96% were men and 88% women. Of those who were living in institutions, 86% of the men and 42% of the women were glad.

Death and Happiness

In my experience, the majority of old people accept death as a natural progression of old age. However, although they accept and even welcome death, anxieties over funeral rites can cause anxiety. For centuries in Western countries, folk have worried about having a 'pauper's' funeral and schemes for saving for funerals, e.g. 'shilling a week schemes', have been started by the elderly themselves.

For the Hindu, who believes that safe passage to the next world depends on certain rituals in cremation and the Shraddah ceremonies, this can be a great anxiety.

The government in Britain gives an inadequate death grant (£30). In Uttar Pradesh the funeral grant is 20 rupees (£1.24). The cheapest funeral costs 200 rupees (£12). Many elderly women keep jewellery to be sold for their funerals and others put money aside. If they cannot do this they worry (as was observed in the study).

Beliefs in Life After Death

The question, 'What happens to your spirit after death?' brought the following replies:

	Male		Female	
	N	%	N	%
Heaven	9	27.3%	8	21.6%
Rebirth	18	54.5%	19	51.4%
Up to God	4	12.1%	9	24.3%
Other	2	6.1%	1	2.7%

Beliefs did not differ markedly between the sexes. The above sample included three Christians who wanted heaven after death and three who said it was up to God. Heaven to the Hindu is perceived as a waiting place for rebirth or union with God.

Conclusion

I have described some of the social and religious aspects of life in India and their effects on the life of elderly women. The vastness of this country necessitates great differences between the states and comparisons are made between Uttar Pradesh and Kerala.

The role of elderly women can be seen only in relation to general attitudes towards women. In old age, women who are fulfilled within their own family are obviously more appreciative of life than those who feel rejected and, by some misfortune, find themselves in institutions.

Until there is a change in social and religious practices, women, particularly the poor - the greater population of India - will continue to be regarded as inferior to men. The effects of these attitudes on women's lives were reflected in their answers to questions regarding happiness.

Bibliography

Census of India (1981) series I (i) Paper I of 1981; (ii) Paper 2 of 1981; (iii) Paper 3 of 1981. Registrar General and Census Commissioner, New Delhi

Fodore, E. (1981) India and Nepal, Hodder, London

Gandhi, M.K., (1929) An Autobiography or "The Story of My Experiments With Truth". The Navajivan Trust, Ahmedabad

Isaacs, B. and Walkey, F.A. (1964) 'A Simplified Paired Association Test for Elderly Hospital Patients', British Journal of Psychiatry, 110, 80-83

Research and Reference Division (1981) India. A Reference Annual, Director of Publication Division, University of Information and Broadcasting, Government of India, New Delhi

Thomas, P. (1975) Hindu Religion, Customs and Manners (6th ed.) D. B. Taraporevala, India

United Nations Statistical Year Book for Asia and the Pacific (1981) Economic and Social Commission for Asia and the Pacific, Bangkok, Thailand

Chapter Seventeen

COMMUNITY CARE IN THE UNITED STATES OF AMERICA: THE CHANNELING PROJECTS

D. R. Fabian

The Policy Problem

Traditionally in the United States most long-term care has been institutional in nature (that is, provided in chronic care hospitals or nursing homes), has been delivered largely to impaired elderly individuals and has been paid for out of public funds. Concern about this situation grew as the costs and the number of recipients of care expanded, and as increasingly critical examination of care, especially during the past decade, suggested appalling mismatches between the need exhibited and the services rendered.

It was difficult to reduce the institutional character of long-term care because of a pervasive medical bias in favour of nursing home treatment, because of the fragmentation of community care programs, with their overlapping and sometimes conflicting eligibility requirements and because reimbursement could be gained more easily for care within rather than outside a facility. Nevertheless, both Federal and private philanthropic support began to be given to projects designed to address long-term care problems at the client or system level. Some projects provided funding for community-based restorative services. In other efforts, organisations were developed to offer social and health maintenance services, and single entry systems and case management agencies were created.

All of these efforts generated excitement and most of them resulted in reforms in one or more aspects of care. However, the outcomes were not generalisable and therefore could not inform national policy because the interventions tested, the environments in which the interventions occurred, the populations served, and the scale of the various projects undertaken, had varied widely. Also, the findings about impacts on institutionalisation, costs, utilisation of community services, and client welfare were mixed. Certain features tested were thought to be useful: screening, comprehensive assessment, rational care planning, ongoing case management, as well as modifications in the availability of, cost controls on, and eligibility requirements for, community services. Clearly, a systematic approach to change was needed.

In 1978, planning began in Washington for a broad long-term care endeavor in which agencies would be created

> "to 'channel' all or part of the long-term care population, that is, to match those in need with appropriate long-term care service settings; to plan for the long-term care service system to ensure that sufficient supplies of needed services and settings would be available; and to coordinate directly or indirectly the provision of long-term care services." (Mathematica Policy Research, 1983)

Early during that initial planning, different organisational approaches, settings, and target populations were contemplated: channeling agencies to serve the elderly, health maintenance organisations for all ages, congregate living facilities, case management agencies in hospitals, and special community organisations to serve the mentally ill and mentally retarded. After exhaustive discussions and with due regard for program competition, the United States Congress appropriated funds only for a research and demonstration effort that was to test the feasibility and cost effectiveness of a community-based long-term care service delivery concept integrating health and social services for aged individuals who were otherwise likely to need care in nursing homes. This concept became the National Long Term Care Demonstration Program that for convenience came to be called 'Channeling'.

Overview of the Program

Overall management responsibility was lodged in the U.S. Department of Health, Education and Welfare (now Health and Human Services) Office of the Assistant Secretary for Planning and Evaluation, and funding for the effort was added to the research budgets of the Administration on Aging and the Health Care Financing Administration. Technical assistance was provided by the Temple University Institute on Aging, which became responsible for the development of clinical and administrative guidelines, for the training of all Channeling staff, and for ensuring that the Channeling functions would be carried out in accordance with the design of the demonstration and clinical practice standards. A research and consulting firm called Mathematica Policy Research became the national evaluation contractor, responsible for the research design and analysis, and for all data collection instruments and procedures.

Channeling was based on the assumption that a managed system of community-based long-term care could be developed that would produce more favourable outcomes for impaired elderly individuals than do conventional arrangements. The program was not designed to solve all the problems of the long-term care delivery system. There was to be no direct intervention in the professional practices of physicians, nurses, or therapists, and funding was not to be available for the establishment or expansion of major community service programs. The primary goals of Channeling were seen as good population targeting, improvement in the match of needs with services, better client outcomes, and efficient but low cost untilisation of services.

Interested states competed for inclusion in the demonstration, and twelve contracts were awarded. The number of participants was later reduced to ten. A major challenge for the program was how to ensure comparability of results while taking into account state and site specific geographic and organisational differences, as well as the fact that two models of the case management approach to the organisation of community-based long-term care for impaired elderly would be tested as an alternative to institutionalisation.

The program utilised a randomised treatment/control design, so that a comparison could be achieved of events in the presence of Channeling with what would have happened in its absence. A program-wide screen as well as an assessment instrument were developed, and personnel who were to adminster these instruments received uniform and intensive training. Training was also provided in care planning and case management to staff who would engage in those activities. Standardised client tracking and other documentation would provide information about utilisation of services, individual client outcomes, costs, and cost-effectiveness.

Participating states were permitted to determine whether site operation would be centralised, decentralised, or partially contracted out. In the last instance, outside agencies would be made responsible for the performance of certain Channeling functions. However, regardless of organisational arrangements, each site was to undertake the core Channeling functions of outreach, screening, assessment, care planning, service arrangement, monitoring and reassessment. The two models of Channeling are basic coordination, being tested in Maine, Maryland, New Jersey, Texas, and Kentucky, and a fiscal control variant under way in New York, Florida, Ohio, Pennsylvania, and Massachusetts. The five basic case management sites have to broker existing services but were awarded a limited amount of money with which to purchase gap-filling services. The five financial control sites enjoy expanded service coverage, an available pool of public funds (with upper limits set for caseload and individual client costs), cost sharing by clients with designated levels of resources, and case manager authorisation of the amount, scope, and duration of services provided to clients.

The Maine Experience

The sites differ not only according to the model of Channeling being implemented, but also in their geographic and demographic characteristics, as well as the identity of their lead and host agencies, and the mode of site organisation adopted. Maine and Kentucky, both basic co-ordinating sites, are the most rural of the participants. The project in new York, testing the more complex fiscal control model, is in Rensselaer County, much of which has a suburban character. The remaining sites are all urban.

In Maine, the signatory to the Channeling contract is the

Department of Human Services, which assigned responsibility for Federal and local liaison and general administration to the Bureau of Maine's Elderly. That Bureau hired the State Director of Channeling (the author) to oversee the research components of the project, to be responsible for its general administration, and to act as state liaison with the Federal government management team, the technical assistance and evaluation contractors, other state Departments and Bureaus, the host agency, and the site.

The catchment area for the project includes the two southernmost counties of the state, and comprises 1900 square miles, in which are located the city of Portland (population about 60,000), smaller cities, industrial towns, fishing and farming villages, and large areas and some islands which are very sparsely populated. The southern part of Maine was designated as the catchment area because of a perceived readiness for an increased emphasis on community rather than institutional care for the impaired elderly, and because of the expected availabillity of service resources (home health and homemaker agencies, a meals program, and a regional transportation program)

The host agency housing Channeling is southern Maine Senior Citizens, Inc., the local Area Agency on Aging (a private non-profit planning and coordinating body that recieves most of its funds from the Bureau of Maine's Elderly). Under a subcontract, Southern Maine Senior Citizens acts as a conduit for the state's Channeling funds and provides local administrative services to the site. Site staff are centralised, i.e. perform all of the Channeling functions, and consist of a Site Director, a screening unit, a case management unit, and an office service unit.

Historically, residents of Maine, the northernmost of the New England states, have wrested their livelihood from the sea, from forests, and less successfully, from a grudging and rocky soil. More recently, attempts have been made to promote tourism. Population clusters are to be found on the coast and along a somewhat inland corridor. Except within the larger cities, there is no public transportation. The harshly beautiful geographic environment has produced a people who are for the most part poor, conservative, independent, and both self-reliant and concerned about those who are close. Government, especially the Federal government, and in general people "from away", are not accepted easily. It was in this context the Channeling was introduced: a project that would impose research constraints on the time-limited (two years) co-ordination of the delivery of health and social services to a portion of the impaired elderly population.

It seemed clear that determined efforts would have to be made to create a reasonably favourable climate for the project so that it could recruit its imposed caseload target of 300 treatment group clients and an equal number of controls (Maine's portion of the national sample of 4900 to be observed by the evaluators for 12 to 18 months). The State Director of Channeling, the Site Director, the Director of the Bureau of Maine's Elderly, and the Director of Southern Main Senior Citizens engaged in extensive education of the general public about the goals of the project. Also, the State Director and the Site Director met frequently and at length with provider organisations: hospitals, welfare agencies, home health and homemaker providers, and fraternal, educational, union and church groups, to explain the Channeling processes and encourage referrals.

There were several deterrents to smooth caseload buildup. Perhaps the most difficult aspect of Channeling to gain acceptance for was randomisation. Randomisation was performed by the national evaluator after applicants had pased the screen, and did not mean that care would not be received. What randomisation did mean was that members of the treatment group would be assessed comprehensively and receive services through the efforts of the Channeling case management unit, and members of the control group would be referred back to the referral point (if that was a hospital or other organisation) or on to Southern Main Senior Citizens (if the original referral had come from applicants, families, friends, or other individuals) for the conventional delivery of services (usually, post-hospital discharge application for nursing home entrance or fairly short-term provision of services by home health and homemaker agencies).

Another problem Channeling had to overcome was the fact that it was not an emergency response endeavor. Since a major objective of the program was to test out a long-term alternative to institutional care, time was needed for the thorough assessment of clients, a process that took from one and one-half to two hours, for the development of a comprehensive care plan that would involve both formal (agency) and informal (family, friend, volunteer) providers in care, and for brokering and co-ordinating the necessary services.

Still another problem seemed to be caused by the stringency of the eligibility requirements of Channeling. In addition to age (65 or older) and residence (in one of the two selected counties), these included certain degrees of impairment in the performance of physical and/or instrumental activities of dailyliving, a fragile support system, residence in a community setting, and the likelihood that a need for two or more services would continue for at least six months.

A complicating factor was the establishment of a state-wide home based care program (gap-filling funds and case mangement services) on exactly the day Channeling began to process applications. Arrangements were made to dovetail the two programs in the catchment area, but intitially confusion was rife among providers and the public about which program would provide what.

While the fiscal control sites could authorise and purchase whatever services clients needed, the only real leverage available to the basic co-ordinating sites was Service Expansion Funds, a set amount awarded for the life of the project. Maine was one of the earliest sites to use this resource, mostly for unskilled personal care services and for objects such as egg-crate mattresses, bathroom grab bars, and wheelchair ramps that could not otherwise be paid for. In the absence of Service Expansion Funds, the project might have foundered. With the availability of the money, as well as with extraordinary outreach efforts on the part of all staff (public appearances, the canvassing of churches and physicians' offices, etc.), caseload build-up proceeded. However, it did not proceed at the rate expected, while the attrition rate from death or necessary nursing home placement soared. Finally, permission had to be granted by the Federal management team and the evaluation contractor for a reduction in the target caseload figure.

The Channeling Functions

After referrals have been received by the Channeling office, a member of the screening unit either administers a 10 to 15 minute screening interview on the telephone or, if that is not feasible, makes a visit to the applicant. Applicants who are in nursing homes must have been certified as capable of discharge within three months to be eligible.

Identifying numbers are assigned to appropriate applicants. By use of these numbers, Mathematica Policy Research makes a random assignment of membership in treatment group or control group. The Channeling screener then contacts the referral individual or agency with the information that the applicant will or will not become a Channeling client. Those who do not become Channeling clients are either not appropriate or members of the control group. This information is not given to the referring agent. Non-Channeling individuals then receive whatever services are usually available to impaired elderly. Controls are assessed and reassessed by the evaluation contractor.

Treatment clients are assigned to case managers on the basis of the currently existing size of that case manager's caseload and where the client lives. Where possible, attempts are made to minimise the distances that case managers have to drive. A visit, in some instances, could require two hours of driving time one way.

The case managers make appointments with applicants for the assessment interview, which may take place with the client alone or in the presence of a family member, who under certain circumstances may have to act as a proxy. On the basis of information gained during the assessment as well as from physicians and service providers if necessary, and when possible with the participation of clients and families, the case managers develop care plans which are time limited and have concrete expected outcomes. These care plans are reviewed by a supervisor, and upon approval clients and/or family members are asked to sign the care plans as an indication that what is proposed is understood and agreed to.

Costs of services are estimated. If a client can pay for needed services, he or she is expected to do so. Otherwise, public funds are used if eligibility is established. In cases where there are insufficient private resources, but eligibility for public funds does not yet exist, the Service Expansion Funds may be used temporarily.

Much case manager time is used in orchestrating the array of formal and informal service provision that constitutes implementation of a care plan, and in early monitoring to ensure that the care plan does not fall apart. Subsequent monitoring occurs both at regular intervals and as needed. Formal reassessment also occurs on a set periodic basis.

A great deal of case manager time is also occupied in the preparation of case notes and the plethora of documents required for research purposes. While the case managers understand and agree to the need for this, when given the chance they do not hesitate to point out that the endless paperwork constantly gets in the way of effective and sufficient case management.

Conclusion

Channeling clients began to be served in February 1982, and the national program will end in the spring of 1985. While the impact of Channeling on clients, families, and the service delivery system will not be known until the data are analysed and the reports appear, participation seems to suggest the value of precise population targeting, comprehensive care planning, and ongoing case management by carefully trained workers. Case managers differ in whether they concentrate on service arrangement or counseling. To some observers, the worker involvement, the intense and long-term case management that is characteristic of channeling, is a luxury that cannot be maintained outside of discretely funded demonstrations. But it seems clear that Channeling is helping to change the long-term care system. Channeling-like projects have been mounted in every state, and requests for information about Channeling forms, training, and procedures pour in to the Channeling sites. Nevertheless, of course, the full extent of Channeling-induced change remains to be seen.

Bibliography

Mathematica Policy Research (1983) 'The Planning and Implementation of Channeling: Early Experiences of the National Long-Term Care Demonstration', April 15, p. 15

Chapter Eighteen

THE DOUBLE JEOPARDY OF AGEISM AND SEXISM. MEDIA IMAGES OF WOMEN

C. Itzin

What the Images Are

Awareness of sexist images and attitudes in the media dates from the late sixties and early seventies: from the beginnings of the current Women's Movement - Embree (1970), White (1970), Courtney and Locheretz (1971), Nilsen (1971), Morgan (1970), Nightingale (1972 and 1977). Increased consciousness of women's exploitation and subordination during the seventies, and particularly the contributions of feminism to this understanding, produced increasing interest in the portrayal of women in advertising, magazines, television, children's books and romantic fiction - see Millum (1975), Tuchman, Daniels and Bennett (1978), Goffman (1979), Adams and Laurikietis (1980). The awarenss of sexism has now been popularised in the Guardian's weekly Naked Ape column (clippings from national newspapers and magazines sent in by readers) and put to practical test with a political view by the Equal Opportunities Commission in its survey of sexism and advertising -EOC (1982).

In a series of five pamphlets published between November 1981 and August 1983, the Women's Media Action Group (1981-1983) monitored the nation's press for images of women as sex-objects, as sex-role stereotypes and the willing or deserving victims of violence. Their findings, not suprisingly, confirmed the previous research and their observations provide a useful summary of the negative portrayal of women in the media. They found: (1) 'blatant depiction of naked or semi-naked women, generally in a seductive pose, suggestive of availability, purely for titillation' (as in pin-ups or on page three of the Sun), (2) 'wholly gratuitous and irrelevant use of female bodies' (as in advertising potato snacks or snooker), (3) 'unnecessarily frequent use of women, usually scantily clad, to advertise products used equally by men and women' (showers, cameras), (4) 'advertising of women's products using women in an unnecessarily titillating manner' (underwear), (5) 'trivialisation of women, emphasising their sexuality rather than achievements', (6) 'women as possessions, capable of being bought or portrayed as available', (7) 'blatantly sexual portrayal of women in cartoons', (8) 'art as an excuse for soft pornography',

(9) 'the use of parts of women's bodies, disembodied, therefore objectified and dehumanised, (10) 'the desirabililty of slimness, hairlessness, odourlessness, beauty, youth in the IDEAL WOMAN', (11) 'advertising of pornography in general magazines, with explicit pictures and descriptions of the sexual violence in them'. These were the ways women were portrayed as sex-objects. They also found the following sex-stereotypes: women at home, in the kitchen or in bed, or with children; at work in servicing jobs; as a fantasised ideal woman; as perfectly feminine (caring, nurturing, sensitive, home-loving and passive), incompetent at manual or technical jobs, in submissive or dependent relationships with men in jokes. They found women as victims of violence in video pornography ('nasties') and their advertisements in pornography, in movies, comics and detective fiction. In the reporting of violence against women, they found 'lurid headlines designed to catch the eye, rapes and sexual assults described in excessive detail, a pretence of moral indignation, with a real motivation to titillation, the whole issue manipulated with the aim of selling newspapers.' These were not just the predominant, but just about the only images of women to be found in the media - see Women's Media Action Group (1981-83).

The EOC (1982) report provided a summary of the research on images of women from a different angle. The statistics they found in various content analyses of advertisements in magazines showed that in 1971 only 3% of women were portrayed in working roles as compared to 45% of men; that between 1950 and 1971 there had been some increase in the depiction of women in working roles, but these were stereotypic and low status; that a content analysis between the period 1972 and 1978 revealed an 8.8% decline in the proportion of females shown in occupational roles; that the depiction of women in professional occupations was not found between 1958 and 1970, while in 1972 it rose to 4%, but then declined in 1978 to 2.2%. Results of a content analysis of women's roles in TV commercials showed that women are 'predominantly portrayed in the traditional roles of housewife and mother.' The report concluded that 'magazine and television advertising still tend very much to portray women in traditional and now largely out-of-date roles, as 'kitchen sink' caretakers reluctant to make (or incapable of making) important decisions - particularly outside the home, and as being essentially dependent or in need of men's protection or, of course, simply as sexual objects.'

While awareness of sexist images is almost taken for granted now, awareness of ageist images and attitudes is a more recent phenomenon. Alex Comfort (1977) deserves credit not just for making but popularising the distinction between biological ageing and what he called 'sociogenic ageing' - 'the role society imposes on people as they reach a certain chronological age'. He did not mean a positive role, either, but, for example, 'the abitrary rolelessness of retirement', the negative experience of poverty and the negative attitude of being regarded as redundant to life. More recently concern about ageism in the media has become an issue for organisations like Age Concern and the Centre for Policy on Ageing and has involved campaigns in the media against the ageist stereotypes of the media, particularly associated with poverty, uselessness and invisibility.

The specific combination of ageism and sexism, of ageist and sexist attitudes combining in media representations of women (the subject of this paper) has received little attention to date. Alex Comfort mentioned in his account of ageism the additional handicap of older women - 'the basic injustice which decrees that by tradition men of any age are sexually competitive while older women aren't.' The authors of The Gender Trap -Adams and Laurikietis (1980) - summarised the attitudes in their two page chapter entitled 'What a Drag it is Getting Old', as follows:

> 'Many of the trials surrounding growing older are ones that women feel more than men. Women are actually ashamed of growing older before they're anywhere near old age. Once they've reached their mid twenties, women are generally reluctant to reveal how old they are... Growing older for the vast majority of women purely and simply means becoming less attractive. Ageing in a woman is seen as making her not only unattractive but repulsive and almost obscene to the world. Sexually women are considered less desirable, which is reflected in their chances of marrying or remarrying after they are forty... Fame, money, power - all make a man more sexually attractive, and these often increase with age. But they don't make a women more attractive. What she has to do is keep young.'

The only documentation of age and sex role stereotyping, of ageism and sexism in the media, has been the most recent reports from the Women's Media Action Group - one on attitudes to young women, the other on attitudes to older women. They found advertisements such as these. This for a skin cream:

> 'Nobody minds if your husband looks his age. Men are lucky. They needn't look young to still be attractive. They often get better looking over the years. Unfortunately, the same can't be said for us women. From the first moment a tiny line appears, we need to take extra care of our skins, with the specialist moisturising treatment, Endocil.'

The picture with the text was of a middle-aged, moustached, wrinkled but handsome man in the foreground, smiling, and a woman, middle-aged or similar-aged in the background alarmed. As well she might, as 'her man' is talking to another, younger and 'more attractive' woman. Women's magazines are full of advertisements with headlines like: 'Look ten years younger, 'Free yourself of ugly stretch marks from preganancy, dieting, exercise, even ageing.' 'Ashamed of your appearance? Worried out wrinkles and lines, Worried by thinning hair? Lines around the mouth'. 'How to look younger longer'. 'Do some parts of your body look older than the rest? If so, physiology being what it is, the message is: buy this or that product, do this and do that in order to 'stay young and beautiful' (as the song goes).

Birthday card humour is even more crudely sexist and ageist. 'Here's to women over 40, and why men love 'em: They never yell, they never tell, they never swell and they're as grateful as hell.' Or 'To someone who looks 29, acts 29 and would like to be 29'. The authors of The Gender Trap found humour in general to be sexist and ageist and isolated the following stereotypes in jokes: the 'silly old moo - the missis' (the nagging wife), the mother-in-law (the wife's mother), the scatterbrain (stupid young woman); the dumb blonde (the young sex-object), and the Amazon (fantasised superwoman, a substitute man). They might have added the 'sour spinster'. In each case we have two sterotypes: an age stereotype and simultaneously a sex-stereotype. It is as if the sex-stereotyping and the age-stereotyping (the sex-objectification or sex-role stereotyping) do not exist independently of their age-role stereotypes - as if the age and sex stereotypes are inextricably inter-connected in communicating the negative images of and attitudes towards women.

Certainly, when young women, girls, are used, they are portrayed as sexualised and sex-role stereotyped. Age-graded birthday cards crudely present girls as feminine, boys as masculine, from baby's first birthday onwards: a five year old boy is digging in the sand, the five-year-old girl sweeping (yes!); the eight-year-old boy playing football, the eight-year-old girl reading demurely, the 12-year-old boy canoeing, the 12-year-old girl actually 'wearing adult style clothes and make-up reflecting the contradictory expectations of woman as seductress and innocent child.' - see WMAG (Report no. 4). Toy advertisements like Fisher Price Tool Kit - give him his own tool kit just like dad's, Fisher Price kitchen set - just the thing for the little miss', are the rule rather than the exception - Veitch (1981). The ageism is not just on the other, older, end of the life-span; it affects women from birth onwards, and is integral to the sex-stereotypes from the beginning.

When older women are portrayed - on the few occasions when they are not invisible by complete omission, they are exhorted to stay young and beautiful, to do things to their bodies to achieve this, and to wear make-up, hair products and clothes to conceal their real age. They - much more often than men - are shown as weak and helpless. They are used to sell mood-changing medicine - the anti-depressants and tranquillisers. A typical medical advertisement shows a haggard older woman before and after treatment. They are wholly categorised by exclusion in relation to romance, sex and leisure, excluded from many holiday package deals, shown as having fun only as part of a (heterosexual) couple on wedding anniversaries. They are excluded from work: any daily paper will be full of advertisements that specify ages, often of as young as 30 or 35, with a top limit of 40 or 45 for the employment of women. They are shown in dependent roles - as pensioners in clubs or dependent on a man. Or they are shown as victims of violent muggings, now of granny-bashing. Rarely are older women portrayed as capable and independent, never as sexually attractive.

The attitudes are obvious. Young women are prepared for their 'sexual' uses and their role (work) in the sexual division of labour. 'Adult' women exist sexually for the use (or abuse) of men, and the caring of men and children for reproduction, child-rearing and domestic labour (or what are usually referred to as female roles). Older women are deemed 'past it', good for nothing except possibly to be idealised as grandmothers. All women, at whatever age, are portrayed as subordinate to men: passive, submissive. This is the ageist/sexist message of the media images. It is part of an enormous apparatus of age-role and sex-role conditioning for women.

How The Stereotypes Function

To be aware of the images and attitudes begins to raise some important questions. What is the meaning of these representations, these negative attitudes? Are they real, or the advertiser's fantasy? What is reality anyway? How do they affect our lives, as women, indeed as men? What exactly is a stereotype and what is its function? Spender (1980) has defined a stereotype as 'bearing little resemblance to empirical reality, but serving a particular purpose.' If a stereotype is not true, and does not resemble reality, what does it do? What is its purpose?

A stereotype is a representation of an aspect of a human being, or rather a human being as a member of a group (women, children, old people, black people, Jewish people, people with disabilities), which suggests that it represents the whole of those people, which creates the impression that it is characterising those people in that group in an essential and significant way. As an aspect, however, a stereotype must be a distorted or exaggerated or misleading representation of a human being or a group of human beings. A stereotype is thus a source of partial information, at best, and thus of misinformation. A stereotype is less a representation of 'real' human beings (of the humaness of humans) than it is a representation of a particular idea about human beings. Basically a stereotype represents a set of ideas or a set of beliefs about people - an ideology - rather than people as they are. The term 'misrepresentation' would be more appropriate. Stereotypes are misleading, deliberately misleading. They perform the function of creating attitudes which, by their very nature, are negative attitudes. They function as a form of propaganda for an ideological view. Stereotypes are the language of ideology - the way it is communicated.

In one sense, stereotypes in advertisements (and other media of communication) are real. They are not, however, representations of real women, but rather representations of women's oppression. This - women's oppression - is real. The material conditions of oppression are real, as is the ideology (and its armoury of stereotypes) which sustain the oppression. The message of the media representations is thus a message about the oppression of women, not about women themselves. Stereotypes reflect the oppression and assist in the the construction of the oppression. They teach it, or rather they enable oppression to be learned - to be internalised.

The whole process of creating and communicating a set of beliefs that contradicts our real lived experience is deceptively simple, not too subtle, insidious and very effective. How the process works can be illustrated by looking at the ideology of the family which reveals the relationship of the 'reality' of ideology to 'real' lived experience: the relationship of the lie to the truth. It is, not coincidentally, an area in which women are subordinated as women and also according to age, so it is also an illustration of ageism and sexism in practice.

The ideology of the family and women's place in it is a powerful, pervasive and popular force in our culture. It is a set of beliefs fundamental to certain political views and to the maintenence of patriarchy. It is an ideology currently given status and substance by the Conservative government's Family Policy Unit and its programme for reaffirming and reinforcing the 'nuclear family' as the bulwark of free enterprise under the 'ideological direction' of Mount (1982). It is an ideology that is regularly offered a platform. Johnson (1982) defended 'the family' as a 'gentle ideology' and 'the stable monogomous marriage as one of the most fundamentally creative inventions of Judaic-Christian civilisation.' He blamed the Brixton riots on the breakdown of the nuclear family and single parents for a 'conspiracy of subversion to bring down in ruins the whole social security system.' His assumption: that the nuclear family is the norm and the ideal.

So powerful is this ideology of the family - happy ever after, husband at work, wife at home (where she does not work but has a role), children at school - that it persists in complete opposition to reality, to the facts that contradict it wholly. For example, 15% of households (in London) are single parents - National Council for One Parent Families (1983). Twenty percent of households have a sole female breadwinner - EOC (1982). Women are 40 percent of the workforce - EOC (1982). Sixty percent (or 73 percent depending on source) of married women work full or part time outside the home - EOC (1982). Women do 80 percent of the domestic work. Ninety-eight percent of men have never cleaned the lavatory. Men seldom scrub the kitchen floor, iron, spring-clean, or scour the cooker. And surveys in Britain, France and the USA all agree that in the vast majority of homes it is still women who take overall responsibility for running the household - even when each partner has a full time job - see Segal (1982) and Kenny (1983).

The inaccuracy of the ideology in reflecting reality could not be more revealed. The contradiction raises again questions of the relationship between the stereotypes to how we live, the reason for the stereotypes, the effectiveness of the propaganda. In whatever kind of family we live, whatever our domestic and employment circumstances, it is almost certain that we have internalised a very strong and powerful image of the nuclear family. There is a level at which we believe it, even if we do not live it. There is a profound irony. We know what we know. We know the stereotypes are lies. We know that it is not true, for example, that girls are stupid, that working class people are dull, that black people are inferior, that old people are useless and older women are repulsive. We know it and then we are surprised to find what we know as we know it proved : as for example in discovering that the education authorities at this very moment practice a system of upward adjustment of boy's scores on the secondary transfer exams to equalise them with the scores of girls which are much higher at the age 11. Those are the very girls stereotyped as less able. There is elaborate machinery to ensure that aspects of ideology and reality correspond. In any case, we know the stereotypes are untrue without being told. It takes a lot of pressure to make us give up on what we know and come to 'believe' the lies of the stereotypes, to give them credence on any level, let alone to live them.

What the stereotypes provide is an education for women (and men, on the other end of the oppression) about their place in the social structure. They are tools for teaching subordination (and to males, dominance). They inform women of what their uses are. The important new perception is that they also inform women of when they are useful and at what ages. There are two agendas, a double message: one of sex-stereotyping and control of sexuality, the other of age-stereotyping and age-control. Goffman (1979) noticed this, albeit in passing, 'Gender, in close connection with age-grades, more than class or other social divisions, lays down an understanding of what ultimate nature ought to be and how and where this nature ought to be exhibited.' The reality (however obscured) is that age-stereotypes and sex-stereotypes work together in constructing the oppression of women. The oppression has, up to now, been perceived simply as sexism. The age-factor in sexism - the combined effect of ageism and sexism - has not been as obvious as it deserves to be, or needs to be if one is to understand and counteract the oppression of women. Because of the extent to which we have internalised age-sex stereotypes we lead double lives. We live both our 'reality' and the 'reality' of the oppression. That is to say, we live what we know is true and we live the lie about us. We submit to the stereotypes and resist them simultaneously. This is the experience of the 45 women I have interviewed - Itzin (in preparation). One woman wrote:

> "What, fat, forty-three and I dare to think I'm still a person? No, I am an invisible lump. I belong in a category labelled a priori without interest to anyone. I am not even expected to interest myself. A middle-aged woman is comic by definition. The mass media tell us all day and all evening long that we are inadequate, mindless, ugly, disgusting in ourselves. Everything she reads, every comic strip, every song, every cartoon, every advertisement, every book and movie tells her that a woman over thirty is ugly and disgusting . She is a bag. She is to be escaped from. To be told when you have half your years still to wade through and when you don't feel inside much different than you did at 20 (you are still you! - you know that!), to be told then that you are cut off from expressing yourself sexually and often even in friendship, drives many women crazy - often literally so. I have insisted on using a

> pseudonym in writing this article because the cost of insisting I am not a cipher would be fatal. If I lost my job, I would have an incredible time finding another. Listen to me! Think what it is like to have most of your life ahead and be told you are obsolete. Think what it is like to feel attraction, desire, affection toward others, to want to tell them about yourself, to feel that assumption on which sel-respect is based, that you are worth something, surely he will be pleased to know that. To be, in other words, still a living woman, and to be told every day that you are not a woman but a tired object that should disappear. I am bitter and frustrated and wasted, but don't you pretend for a minute as you look at me, forty-three, fat and looking exactly my age, that I am not as alive as you are, and that I do not suffer from the category into which you are forcing me." Moss (1970, p. 188-196)

This woman - like all others in their different ways - testifies to the negative attitudes that have influenced her life, and how the attitudes are internalised - through fear in the oppressor and the oppressed. Stereotypes function to create fear and division, and even hatred between people. The images of older women are so overwhelmingly negative in their presentation of attitudes to wrinkles and greying that from an early age women fear what happens to their bodies. Younger women look at older women, and think 'yuk'. And in that 'yuk' is their fear of what is going to happen to them. This negative view of ageing is reinforced by the advertising put out by companies whose products are supposed to retard, diminish or disguise the affects of ageing.

The combined message of ageism and sexism is simple and devastating. Women have two functions: sexual and domestic. Each involves children; the first child-bearing and the second child-rearing. Each involves availability and services to men: sexual and domestic. Both functions begin for women from the 'age of marriage.' Both functions finish for women in their mid-forties: in <u>retirement</u> from reproduction and <u>retirement</u> from child-rearing. Neither of these rites of passage is marked by celebration. They are characterised by gloom and misery (the stereotype of the menopause) and categorised by loss (the empty nest syndrome of sociology). From the age of about forty when men are in the prime of life, women embark on the second half of their life with little status and almost no value. Is there anyone of less value in society than an old woman? This valuelessness is not inherent, but created, not biologically determined, but socially constructed - with the assistance of the media as illustrated above.

The Mating of Sexism and Ageism, of Capitalism and Patriarchy in WOMAN Magazine

Most research has been done on advertisements - Courtney and Lockeretz (1971), Wasner and Banos (1973), Sexton and Haberman

(1974), Venkatesan and Losco (1975). Some has been done specifically on women's magazines - Millum, (1975), Tuchman, Daniels and Benet (1978) and White (1970). What is revealing is the setting of the advertisements. Their editorial context reveals how the message of the advertising copy and the editorial copy merge and speak the same message.

A good example was a feature in Woman (1983) magazine described as a "Health Exclusive" and headlined in what sounded like a positive tone, 'The Good News About Growing Old.' On the credit side it provided some information that contradicted the myths - the sterotypes - of ageing: 'Society expects us all to behave in a certain way, and this is especially true when it comes to old age. We expect old people to be less creative, less capable of learning, less flexible. Physically we expect them to be bent, wrinkled and prone to illness. But it doesn't have to be so, and in reality often is not'.

The stereotypes of bad memory and slow learning were shown to be false. The article made clear that food, friends, and exercise would prolong good health and active life. All well and good, but the beginning of the article cunningly conjured up just the sterotypes it sought to banish, 'You thought growing old meant getting wrinkled, waving goobye to your bikini, watching your body - and maybe your mind - go slowly, sadly out of control? Well, now for the good news: the latest research reveals that this picture of ageing is totally wrong -if you really want it to be. Now none of us have to give in gracefully to growing older - and we can all cheat the ageing trap.' We recognise it all immediately, and we identify with it too. The article is premised on precisely that identification and the fear the stereotypes stimulate: if we were not terrified of the 'trap' we would not really 'want to cheat it'. We would not need exhortation to 'stay young and beautiful' which is implied the text.

The chrolonological checklist that accompanied the text - of what to expect between ages 20-30, 30-40, 40-50, - visually and textually reinforced the age-categories (the trap) and the age-stereotypes, assuming that at one end of the scale a woman would be young and beautiful and at the other old and unattractive (unless you were lucky or like the elderly celebrities interviewed and boxed along the bottom of the page, and had fame and fortune on your side). The illustration was of three women silhouetted, one young and beautiful (foreground), the second thickening and sagging (middle distance) and the third thickened and sagged (background). There was a quiz to test how well we 'adapt' to old age, implying that it is 'a slot that one has to fit into, adapt to.' But old age does not exist outside the person, it is a feature of the person. The concept of 'losing one's figure', seeing old age as somehow 'out there' contributes to our alienation from ouselves' - Women's Media Action Group (Report No. 5).

What is striking is the similarity of this editorial feature to an advertisement headed, 'How to Look Younger Longer' selling skin care advice and products for 'a youthful looking face and a youthful looking body' or even cruder advertisements exhorting us to buy something to 'free ourselves of ugly stretch marks', or some other product for lines and wrinkles around the mouth that mar our appearance and make us look older, or something else to 'prevent the grey from reappearing.' It is all saying that ageing is something to be feared; in short, it is dangerous to grow old. All this plays on the feelings we all have after years of being told that no part of us is acceptable or right. All of this conspires to create a context of acceptability and indeed necessity for advertisements for cosmetic surgery. The editorial feature in the July 1983 issue of Woman headlined 'Skin Shock' subheaded 'Latest and most extreme ways to uplift and deep cleanse your face include being skinned alive, pierced with needles and painted in paraffin wax' was illustrated with a truly shocking picture of a woman being treated with needles on her face and looking more like a hedgehog than a human being. She, obviously, like 'Fat and Forty-three' had got the message of the media and internalised it sufficiently to suffer considerable pain.

The EOC (1982) survey reported on a study by Scheibe (1979) which found that, 'consumers equate themselves with stereotypes, and some were likely to model themselves on the sterotype presented.' The Women's Media Action Group report summed it up by saying, 'The picture of older women is painted as fairly bleak; they are 'past it', uninterested in sex, incapable of having fun or of allowing others to have fun. Although we all know how unfair and unrealistic this is, these powerful images created by the media strongly influence the way we live our lives. If you are told (or read) often enough that you should know better than to do certain things, e.g. mountain-climbing at 65, 'at your age', then most of us will not do these things.'

The very small difference between the inventions of the advertisers and the inventions of the editors is significant. It is not surprising when the sources and functions of the material in relation to the prevailing ideology is considered. From the Gender Trap, 'In our society a great deal of value is placed on being young, because while you are young you are at your most productive. Also you have more money to spend and can therefore buy and consume more .... it is mostly women who decide how money is spent on consumer goods. So most advertisements are aimed at women. Women are bombarded with images of themselves with which they can identify. They think, 'I want to be like her.' Even though we are talking about advertising here, the same types of women appear constantly in all the media.' - Adams and Laurikietis (1980). The point is that the feature articles are as much an advertisement for the negative attitudes as the advertisements themselves. For the six month period from January to June 1983, I carried out a content analysis of Woman magazine. There was only one issue that did not have a major feature to do with women and age in some way, and most issues had at least two, many had up to four feature articles. In addition there were letters in almost every issue about ageing and attitudes to ageing, plus agony column letters.

There were many articles about 'stars': the famous - Petula Clark, Cilla Black, even men like Tom Jones; the royals - Countess Mountbatten, Princess Michael; the rich. The emphasis editorially would be on how good they still looked at 40 or over (how sexually attractive they still were even though they were supposed to be 'past it') or how long and happily they have been married. They were represented as ideal wives or mothers or widows, and it was implied that there was something unusual about them. In other words, ordinary people would have succumbed to ageing and unattractiveness and divorce. There were lots of articles on the theme of 'how to stay young and fit' (significantly, not just fit but young and fit) with the focus at different times on weight or hair or skin or health. There were single one-off features such as the one on five middle-aged (and fat) chorus girls who were making a success in their work, or the 'relatively youthful looking' 36-year-old top make-up artist who had decided, at 36, she would remain single for the rest of her life unless she met Mr. Right. Three 'serious' features were devoted to the issue of older women. One on the 'young image of the WI', one on the problem of 'granny-bashing' (Note the designation of female though the victims of the abuse were equally male and female), one on old people mistreated by their own children in the role of carers, and one on whether 'grandma and grandpa' should be put in old people's homes. However ostensibly 'serious', all three feature articles played on stereotypes of old people, and particularly of older women: for example, the sterotyped 'WI' woman is middle-aged and dull, and stereotyped happy old age is being surrounded by a devoted family.

The precise breadown of age references in editorial material was revealing. Out of 21 issues (Woman is a weekly) every one had significant editorial reference to age or ageing (usually reinforcing the stereotypes), eleven weeks had one major feature article, four weeks had two, one week had three, and two weeks had four. This was in addition to the column 'You and Us' at the front, the regular two pages devoted to readers' letters and anecdotes, and the Agony Column at the back, Virgina Ironside's problem page, which included such age-related dilemmas as what to do with nagging mothers-in-law, and should an older woman have a relationship with a younger man. Significantly, the only place where the sterotypes were questioned or contradicted was 'the readers' letters and the 'How I Coped' column within that section - about women acting powerfully and presenting a positive image.

Over fifty million women purchase a woman's magazine every month in the USA (1970 statistics). That is practically three quarters of the entire adult female population - Embree (1970). The money spent on advertising to this audience and that of the soap operas (whose purpose is to sell soap) was 16.5 billion dollars (in 1966). In one year, between July 1978 and June 1979 in the UK £121.5 million were spent on perfume, £58 million on make-up, £71 million on skin-care, £95 million on hair preparations, £42 million on shampoos, £37 million on other toiletries - Hogstan (1980). As the Magazine Publishers' Association in the USA advertised its products magazines to the advertisers:

> 'Magazines turned legs into a rainbow. Magazines convinced a gal she needed a flutter of fur where plain little eyelashes used to wink. Magazines have the power to make a girl forget her waist exists. And the very next year, make her buy a belt for every dress she owns. They

can move a fashion trend from Paris to the papa-mama store as fast as somebody can sew it up. Magazines help distressed damsels remake their wardrobes, faces, hair, body. And sometimes their whole way of being. And the ladies love it. And beg for more. When she gets involved with herself and fashion, in any magazine, she's a captive from cover to cover' - Embree (1970, p.207).

Is it really surprising then to find it difficult to see where an advertisement ends and an article begins? The very existence of the media is dependent on the income from advertising. Of course it will influence the content and message of the programming; of course one product will influence another. We would have to be naive to imagine that either the advertisers or editors were in business for altruistic motives. 'Revlon which manufactures cosmetics, also manufactures arming devices for army firebombs. The Lever Brothers Company, which penetrates the domestic market and produces enzyme cleaners to attack dirt biologically, has a Defense Department contract to study the 'Alteration of the Penetrability of Skin' for Edgewood Arsenal. Edgewood is the major chemical warfare center and the results of that study will most likely be used to penetrate Vietnamese skin with poisonous chemicals' - see Embree (1970, p.212). Yet we are naive to the extent that we suspend disbelief when we use the media. We take the lie at face value. What we have is a combination of capitalism and patriarchy operating in mutual self-interest; the ageist and sexist practices of each oppressive system combine. Fifty percent of the population and 75 percent of the market are consumers -women: victims of both systems.

Conclusions - Strategies

The EOC (1982) survey set out to examine the effectiveness of advertisements, to compare the effectiveness of using traditional stereotypes with using more modern and realistic images. They found that 'the treatment which incorporated a less restricted, modern female role-portrayal was consistently found to enhance the marketing-effectivenss of the brands' advertising'. Does this suggest that advertisers and the media will be enlightened and cease to use stereotyped images to sell to women? Can we expect to see, for example, healthy, active, attractive older women in positions of occupational power in the pages of women's magazines and television? At first sight it would seem to make sense, but that is only if we, naively, take the advertisements at face value, and assume that they are only selling us products and not images of ourselves.

In the long run, if the stereotypes do function as transmitters of oppressive attitudes on behalf of the oppressive system, then they are essential to the ends of the advertisers as well as the oppressive system. 'Real' women - women untainted by the ideology of patiarchy -would not have their faces cut and stitched or stuck with pins, or their breasts, bellies and buttocks butchered. They would not need make-up or high heels or restrictive clothing. If what the poet Honor

Moore has called the Male Approval Syndrome were not capitalised on, if 'real' women defined their 'needs', the needs created and catered for by the stereotypes would not exist. Or would they? We return again to the tricky question of whether the representation reflects the values of society or creates the values, or both. The stereotypes certainly function to keep the oppression operating by contributing to the 'construction of an identity', which is doubly jeopardising to women in relation to age and gender. With what force this propaganda operates, the fiction of George Orwell can illustrate. The slogan in Animal Farm after the coup in which the humans are despatched and the animals take over is 'Four legs good, two legs bad.' Is it very different for women in our society? 'Thin legs good, fat legs bad.' Or 'Young legs good, old legs bad'. You know it does not make sense. But if everyone acts as if they believe it, you have to give in and accept slimming pills, plastic surgery and self-hatred.

What has been the subject of some debate is whether the simple substitution of accurate information and real lived experience for the stereotypes would succeed in replacing the systems that seem to depend on the stereotypes. Is it enough to substitute positive images of women? Media images were used successfully during World War II to get women out of the home and into the factories and out of the need for cosmetics and expensive fashion. The subsequent shift to indoctrinate women with the idea that their place was in the home suggests that images in the media have the power to do precisely that: to change the system. But then the whole 'system' was behind the redefinition of women's role and attitudes to women; now it is 'just' feminism behind the push for positive images.

What is hopeful is that (1) we do know what is real and true about ourselves from our experience. However much the conditioning makes us mistrust this 'intuition', we never forget. (2) We can recognise lies. When this occurs the ideology has ceased to function. (3) To the extent that we come to believe the lies, we could believe anything, even the truth.

Bibliography

Adams, C. and Laurikietis, R. (eds) (1980) The Gender Trap, A Closer Look at Sex Roles 3: Messages and Images, Virago, London

Comfort, A. (1977) A Good Age, Mitchell Beazley, London

Courtney, A. and Lockeretz, S.W. (1971) 'A Woman's Place: An Analysis of the Roles Portrayed by Women in Magazine Advertisements', Journal of Marketing Research, 8 February

Embree, A. (1970) 'Media Images I: Madison Avenue Brainwashing -The Facts', in R. Morgan (ed.), Sisterhood is Powerful, pp. 198-207, Vintage, New York

Equal Opportunities Commission (1982) Adman and Eve. A Study of the Portrayal of Women in Advertising, carried out for the Equal Opportunities Commission by the Marketing Consultancy and Research Services, Department of Marketing, University of Lancaster

Goffman, E. (1979) Gender Advertisements, The Macmillan Press, London

Hogstan, J. (1980) 'Cosmetic and Toiletry Preparations Review, June 1979', in C. Adams, and R. Laurikietis (eds.), The Gender Trap, Virago, London

Itzin, C. (in preparation) Sexual and Age Divisions: A Study of Identity and Opportunity in Women, unpublished Ph.D. thesis (in preparation), University of Kent, Canterbury

Johnson, P. (1982) 'Family Reunion', Observer, 10 October, p.27

Kenny, M. (1983) She, August, p.6

Millum, T. (1975) Images of Women: Advertising in Women's Magazines, Rowman & Littlefield, New York

Morgan, R. (ed) (1970) Sisterhood is Powerful, An Anthology of Writings from the Women's Liberation Movement, Vintage, New York

Moss, Z. (1970) 'It Hurts to be Alive and Obsolete: The Ageing Woman', in R. Morgan, (ed.), Sisterhood is Powerful, Vintage, New York

Mount, F. (1982) The Subversive Family, Jonathan Cape, London

National Council for One Parent Families (1983), Annual Report, N.C.O.P.F., London

Nightingale, C. (1977) 'Boys Will Be Boys But What Will Girls Be?' in M. Moyles, (ed), The Politics of Literacy, Pluto Press, London

Nightingale, C. (1972) 'Sex Roles in Children's Literature', The Assistant Librarian, October

Nilsen, A. P. (1971) 'Women in Children's Literature', College English, 32, May

Scheibe, C. (1979) 'Sex Roles in TV Commercials', Journal of Advertising Research, 19, February

Segal, L. (1982) Unhappy Familes. New Socialist. July/August, p.16 (Figures from L. Rimmer, Families in Focus, Study Commission on the Family and Department of Employment, Manpower Paper No. 11)

Sexton, D. E. and Haberman, P. (1974) 'Women in Magazine Advertisements', Journal of Advertising Research, 14, August

Spender, D. (1980) 'Talking in Class', in D. Spender and S. Elizabeth, Learning to Lose, Sexism and Education, The Women's Press, London

Tuchman, G., Daniels, A. D. and J. Benet, (1978). Hearth and Home: Images of Women in the Mass Media, Oxford University Press, New York

Veitch, A. (1981) Naked Ape, An Anthology of Male Chauvinism from the Guardian, Duckworth, London

Venkatesan, M. and Losco, J. (1975) 'Women in Magazine Ads: 1959-1971', Journal of Advertising Research, 15, 4, August

Wasner, L. C. and Banos, J. B. (1973) 'A Woman's Place: A Follow-up Analysis of the Roles Portrayed by Women in Magazine Advertisements', Journal of Marketing Research, May

White, C. (1970) Women's Magazines, A Sociological Inquiry, Michael Joseph, London

Women's Media Action Group (WMAG) (1981-83) Sexism in the Media. Report No. 1. 'Women as Sex Objects'. Report No. 2. 'Violence Against Women'. Report No. 3. 'Stereotypes of Women', Report No. 4. 'Sugar and Spice'. Report No. 5. 'Women and Ageism'. Published by WMAG, Hungerford House, Victoria Embankment, London WC2

Chapter Nineteen

ELDERLY WOMEN AND THE CHALLENGE OF INEQUALITY

S. Clayton

Introduction

This paper raises the hypothesis that elderly women are in receipt of a lower level of welfare assistance, commensurate with their needs, than elderly men. It also suggests that if there is an imbalance it may pass unnoticed, partly because in absolute numbers more elderly women than men receive assistance. The paper does not set out to provide a detailed examination of the topic. It seeks only to raise the hypothesis in order to encourage people working in the field to study the position of elderly women carefully and to develop strategies and policies which will reduce any inequalities that are identified.

Any attempt to compare the position of women and men in our society is fraught with difficulties. This is all the more difficult when the women studied are elderly, and issues of both sexism and ageism may have to be taken into account. It is not possible in the space of this article to consider most of these difficulties, but a few basic issues are discussed as an indication of the problems faced by comparisons of the position of elderly women and men.

Comparisons by Age and Sex

Problems of comparison arise because women tend to live longer than men. In 1978 a women aged 60 could expect to live another 20.4 years while a men could expect only 15.8 years - Central Statistical Office (1982). Since it is the very elderly people in the population who especially experience illness and disabilities or require assistance with daily living - see Hunt (1978), DHSS (1982a) and Jolly (1983), it might be expected that more elderly women than men will require welfare assistance. Table I below illustrates the difference between the number of women and men at different ages.

Table 1 Elderly Women and Men in the Population Aged 65+

Age in Years	Women	Men	Women x 100 / Men
	000s	000s	
65-69	1374	1126	122
70-74	1247	900	139
75-79	959	566	169
80-84	604	261	231
85-89	288	94	306
90 and over	123	32	384

Source: OPCS, Population Estimates, England and Wales, HMSO, 1983.

Unfortunately, many people appear not to take these variations into account when considering the position of elderly women. It may well be, for example, that if people find twice as many women over the age of eighty-five as men in receipt of a service they assume women are more than adequately represented. In practice, if numbers alone are taken into account, there would need to be more than three times as many very elderly women as men. Most published statistics do not permit such analysis to be made. They give females and males by such age groupings as 65 years and over, 65 to 74 and 75 and over, or compare men aged 65 and over with women aged 60 and over (pensionable age). These crude groupings tend to conceal many important variations between elderly women and men.

Other problems arise because differences in the living circumstances of elderly women and men may influence the extent to which they require assistance from other people. Hunt (1978) found, for example, that fewer elderly women than men owned various items of household cleaning equipment, cars, refrigerators or telephones, objects which could lighten their load or increase their communication with others. However, a better example can be found by looking at statistics on elderly people living alone. Both Hunt (1978) and Abrams (1978) found four-fifths of elderly people living alone were women. Table 2 gives the proportion of women and men living alone by different age groupings.

Table 2 Proportion of Elderly People Living Alone, by Age and Sex

Age in Years	Women	Men	Women x 100 / Men
	%	%	
65-74	33.6	13.6	247
75-84	47.1	19.8	238
85 and over	50.0	27.3	183

Source: Hunt, A., The Elderly at Home, OPCS, HMSO, 1978.

Differences in need for assistance from statutory and informal services can occur as a result of variations in the proportion of elderly women and men who are married. This is relevant as researchers like Peace, Kellaher and Willcocks (1982) and Hunt (1978) found that most people requiring residential care, or assistance in their home, were without partners. Table 3 shows the proportion of elderly people who are married, as opposed to being single, widowed or divorced.

Table 3 Elderly People Who Are Married, By Age and Sex

Age in Years	Women	Men	Women x 100 / Men
	%	%	
65-69	57	81	70
70-74	43	76	57
75-79	29	68	43
80-84	17	56	30
85 and over	7	39	18

Source: DHSS, Health and Personal Social Services Statistics, England, HMSO, 1982.

A further issue in any comparison is the state of health of individuals. It is always difficult to measure the health or morbidity of elderly people, but more especially since elderly women and men experience slightly different disorders. However, Hunt (1978) found elderly women were more likely than men to lack personal mobility, to be bedbound or unable to perform self care tasks, and Tables 4 and 5 show the extent to which elderly people said that their health was not good in the preceeding year (as opposed to good or fairly good), or that they experienced chronic or acute sickness. If elderly women do have more illness then they might be expected to require more assistance than their numbers alone - Table 4 and 5 - would indicate.

Table 4 Self Report of Not Having Good Health in Year Before Interview

Age in Years	Women	Men	Women x 100 / Men
	%	%	
65-69	22	19	116
70-74	25	20	125
75-79	30	23	130
80-84	29	24	121
85 and over	32	16	200

Source: OPCS, General Household Survey, HMSO, 1982.

Table 5 Self Reported State of Health of Elderly Women and Men

	Women %	Men %	Women/Men x 100
65-74 years			
Longstanding illness	60	54	111
Limited longstanding illness	42	39	108
Acute sickness	17	14	121
75 years and over			
Longstanding illness	66	59	112
Limited longstanding illness	54	45	120
Acute sickness	21	17	124

Source: OPCS, General Household Survey, HMSO, 1982.

Even where sufficiently detailed factual information on subjects is available there are likely to be problems deciding which factors are relevant and how they should be weighted. Furthermore there are tremendous difficulties deciding what constitutes equality in any given circumstance. Terms like 'equality', 'social justice' and 'need' are fraught with difficulties of conceptualisation and assessment. Indeed there is no consensus that equality or equity are desirable objectives, or that services should be provided on a basis of need. It is not possible to discuss these in this article but interested readers might refer to Blowers and Thompson (1976), Bradshaw (1972), Weale (1978), the Black Report (DHSS, 1980), Le Grand (1982), and Clayton (1983). What is important here is to stress that there are very many practical and conceptual issues which have to be considered before any valid comparisons can be made.

While the author has not yet made a detailed study of the provision of services to elderly women and men a brief look at studies to hand suggest that this is a field worthy of consideration. It would appear that, in a number of medical specialisms, fewer elderly women than men are treated - DHSS (1982b), and Willcocks (1982) found that in residential homes elderly men were admitted at a much earlier point in the ageing process than women, were in a fitter condition and tended to receive more attention from staff. Social Trends (1982) shows that, when their health is taken into account, more men than women are probably in receipt of home helps and meals on wheels. Furthermore Abrams' work (1978) suggests that, rather than countering any inequaliites in the statutory sector, the informal sector may well also discriminate against women.

As far as income and wealth are concerned the Royal Commission on the Distribution of Income and Wealth (1978) noted, 'The elderly formed the largest group of family units with lower incomes. Family units where the head was aged seventy and over and lone women had a particularly high incidence of lower incomes, and widows the highest incidence' (paragraph 5.141). Table 6, which shows the proportion of people in Hunt's study who had a very low income, illustrates this point.

Table 6 Non-married Elderly People With a Total Annual Net Income of Less than £750

Age in Years	Women	Men	Women x 100 / Men
65-74	24.7	18.7	132
75-84	31.8	15.1	211
85 and over	35.2	20.0	176

Source: Hunt, A., The Elderly at Home, OPCS, HMSO, 1978.

Differences in income are very relevant to level of need for welfare assistance for, as the Black report (1980) noted, 'the relationship between income and capacity to protect personal health is strongest with elderly people than with any other age group'.

There may well be good reasons for the variation between women and men found in the above-mentioned studies and they are certainly open to many different interpretations. Similarly there are almost certainly many studies which show, at least on initial inspection, that elderly women receive more generous provision of services than men. In general it is difficult to assess the true position of elderly women in society as relatively little research focuses specifically on them and their requirements, even in the occasional studies which discuss the unequal position of elderly people vis-a-vis young people - for example, Age Concern (1983). Furthermore, even when data are available, various interpretations are possible. For example, many studies use longevity as an indicator of a healthy, advantaged life situation. It can therefore be argued that women are the fortunate sex, for they live longer and may be seen to be least in need of assistance, as measured by current use of services.

Conclusions

The situation is extremely complex and careful work has to be carried out to identify the true position of elderly women. However, the time has probably come to press for the type of attention that has focused in recent years on inequalities between different medical specialisms, geographical areas and social classes - for example, see DHSS (1976a 1976b), DHSS (1980), DHSS (1981) and Crombie (1984).

At this stage it can only be hypothesised that both the statutory and voluntary sectors treat elderly women less generously than men. It is surprising, despite a fairly careful literature search, to find how little attention has been focused on this topic despite the growth of interest in the overall position of women in society. The issue almost certainly deserves rigorous attention, especially as cut-backs in statutory services may be especially deterimental to elderly women, both as carers and potential clients. Furthermore, the move towards privatisation of services may also disadvantage women since on average they have lower incomes and fewer savings than men.

A careful watch needs to be kept on the position of elderly women for they may well in in a position of double jeopardy, experiencing the disadvantages of both their age and sex. The causes of their position, from both past and current experiences, needs to be considered carefullly. Policies and practices may also have to be developed to ensure that, when they require it, women receive equitable and satisfactory care from all sources of support.

Bibliography

Abrams, M. (1978) Beyond Three-Score and Ten, Age Concern, Mitcham

Age Concern Scotland (1983) Inequality and Older People, Age Concern Edinburgh

Blowers, A. and Thompson, G. (eds) (1976) Inequalities, Conflict and Change, Open University Press, Milton Keynes

Bradshaw, J. (1972) 'The Taxonomy of Need', New Society, 19:496, 640-2

Central Statistical Office (1982) Social Trends, HMSO, London

Clayton, S. (1983) 'Social Need Revisited', Journal of Social Policy, 12, 215-234

Crombie, D. L. (1984) Social Class and Health Status, Inequality or Difference, Occasional Paper 25, Royal College of General Practitioners, Exeter

Department of Health and Social Security (1976a) Priorities for Health and Personal Social Service in England, HMSO, London

Department of Health and Social Security (1976b) Sharing Resources For Health in England, Report of the Resources Allocation Working Party, HMSO, London

Department of Health and Social Security (1980) Inequalities in Health, (Black Report), HMSO, London

Department of Health and Social Security (1981) Care in Action, HMSO, London

Department of Health and Social Security (1982a) Health and Personal Social Services Statistics, HMSO, London

Department of Health and Social Security (1982b) Hospital In-Patient Enquiry, HMSO, London

Hunt, A. (1978) The Elderly at Home, Office of Population Censuses and Surveys, HMSO, London

Jolly, D. (1983) 'A National Aberfan: Dementia Denied: A Disaster in the Making in D. Jolly, A. Sheridan, N. Tutt and G. Jones Elderly People: Services for the Future, Department of Social Administration, Occasional Paper: Health and Welfare: No. 4, University of Lancaster

Le Grand, J. (1982) The Strategy of Equality, George Allen and Unwin, London

Office of Population Censuses and Surveys (1982) General Household Survey, HMSO, London

Office of Population Censuses and Surveys (1983) Population Estimates, England and Wales, HMSO, London

Peace, S. M., Kellaher, L. A. and Willcocks, D. M. (1982) A Balanced Life? School of Applied Social Studies and Sociology, Polytechnic of North London

Royal Commission on the Distribution of Income and Wealth (1978) Lower Incomes, Cmnd 7175, HMSO, London

Weale, A. (1978) Equality and Social Policy, Routledge and Kegan Paul, London

Willcocks, D. (1982) Gender and the Care of Elderly People in Part III Accommodation, Paper presented at the British Sociological Association, April, 1982

PART FIVE : INDIVIDUAL AND SOCIAL ISSUES

Chapter Twenty

THE VALUE OF REMINISCENCE IN ADAPTATION TO OLD AGE. LONGITUDINAL CASE STUDIES OVER TEN YEARS

P.G. Coleman

Introduction

In the last few years there has been a very striking growth in awareness among workers with elderly people of the potential importance of reminiscence. The increase in application of what is sometimes called 'reminiscence therapy' in groupwork settings in hospitals, residential homes and day care establishments parallels in some ways the earlier growth of interest in reality orientation. There are also indications that it reflects genuine need. For example in the last number of Ageing Times the author reports that many older people wrote to the Centre for Policy on Ageing after Eric Midwinter's recent TV series: "the interesting feature of many of the correspondents was their obvious need for the chance to recount life histories. Collectively they made a powerful case for more reminiscence groups".

In this context it is therefore all the more important to examine what we know in general about the value of reminiscence in old age, and perhaps to take a more discerning and differentiating view about its nature. There have after all been a number of different theories expressed about the functions of reminiscence. Probably the most influential piece of writing was an article written twenty years ago by the American psychiatrist Robert Butler (Butler, 1963), in which he suggested that the mental process of reviewing one's life was a universal experience in older persons "characterised by the progressive return to consciousness of past experience and, particularly, the resurgence of unresolved conflicts". He coined the term 'life review' and other authors have noted a link with Erik Erikson's description of 'integrity' as the particular task of the last stage of life. Interestingly both Butler and Erikson refer to Ingmar Bergman's film 'Wild Strawberries' in describing their ideas - Erikson (1978). It depicts how a distinguished academic but rather egocentric old man becomes more sensitive to the people around him through a series of dreams and conscious recollections of episodes in his past life. However it needs to be pointed out that there is nothing inevitable about such a positive outcome of the life review. The individual may become obsessed with events and actions he regrets, unable to find any 'solution' to them, and be left with chronic feelings of guilt and depression.

Another train of thought in theorising about the role of reminiscence in the elderly envisages reminiscence as contributing to successful ageing by supporting the self-concept in times of stress. This view has been expressed most strongly by the American psychologist Lewis who investigated this hypothesis in experimental studies - Lewis (1973). The general idea that a greater identification with past life and past achievements might be helpful to elderly people in situations of deprivation and loss seems at least in part to lie behind the present trend to promote reminiscence therapy with groups of elderly people. The past is seen as something positive which an individual possesses, something which can be built upon perhaps in seeking better ways of coping with the present.

Not to be overlooked is the more anthropological notion that reminiscence reflects the traditional role of elderly people as the preserver of memories and thus of traditions in society - McMahon and Rhudick (1967). Even in a fast moving society such as ours with written and other forms of records, it can be claimed that old people should be valued and given a positive role for the live experience of past history they embody. This view is reflected in the fruitful link that has been made between those interested in reminiscence as therapy and as a source of oral history.

A great drawback of much earlier psychodynamic thinking about old age is that it is not based on much in the way of empirical observation. This is something we constantly have to watch for in assessing the relevance of theories of ageing. Both Jung and Erikson, for example, who have written so graphically about the meaning of old age, had their clinical practice with younger groups, Jung with the middle aged, Erikson with adolescents and young adults. Thus, although what they say tells us a lot about the meaning old age could or should have, they do not necessarily tell us much about the usual experience of elderly people. In the same way one must point out that although Butler's notion of the importance of life reviewing was derived from his clinical practice as a psychiatrist with elderly people, it may not indicate the preoccupations and needs of the average elderly person.

A number of general empirical studies were carried out on reminiscence in the late 1960s and early 1970s. These were reviewed recently in two interesting articles, one by Merriam (1980) and one by Kastenbaum (1982). Both contain insightful comments. Merriam's review in particular shows that research on reminiscence has been inconclusive, that the studies considered as a whole have failed to demonstrate that reminiscence promotes adjustment in old age. Quite rightly in my opinion she criticises much of the research for being too simplistic, looking at reminiscence often in a totally undifferentiated way, and posing unsophisticated hypotheses about the value of talking or thinking about the past. She concludes by making a plea for more exploratory and descriptive studies.

My own interest in research on reminiscence is a long-standing one. I was one of the people to carry out a study on reminiscence in the early 1970s - Coleman (1974) - which is included in the recent reviews. I have also had the opportunity recently to reflect more both on the original data and on additional longitudinal data I collected on the same individuals. Over the succeeding ten years I continued to visit them, at first sporadically, but then more systematically - always keeping the same focus on their attitudes to past and present life and the role of reminiscence in their lives. This summer I have had the free time to look at all the material again and to write up a report including detailed case studies of the surviving members of the sample - Coleman (1983). This has led me to formulate certain hypotheses about types of "reminiscers" and "non-reminiscers".

Attitudes to Reminiscence in the Sample

At the time of the original fieldwork in 1970 and 1971 all the people were aged over 65 years and living alone in sheltered housing schemes in five London boroughs. They were of mixed working class and middle class background. I deliberately selected a sample from people living in sixteen housing schemes so as not to interview too many in any one scheme and so as to be able to collect as large a sample of men as women (men being outnumbered usually by three to one in the schemes). In total I approached 68 people and of these I included 51 in the original data analysis - those from whom I had collected a complete set of data. I consciously selected elderly people living alone in sheltered housing because of the ease of interviewing, but also because I judged they would have experienced considerable loss in their lives (e.g. ill health, bereavement, separation from their old environment) such as to provide a good background for discerning any beneficial role reminiscence might play in helping adjustment to loss. Looking back at the data I am particularly surprised by the large number who complained very strongly about life in the sheltered housing scheme and its siting too far from general amenities, and who regretted having made the move. I am surprised that I did not make more comment on it at the time. It also led me to reflect how, only very recently, we have become more prepared to accept a sceptical attitude to the value of sheltered housing - Wheeler (1982).

Over a period of two years I interviewed people on average six times each. I kept a lot of notes on these conversations. One or two hours of conversation with each individual were tape recorded and transcribed. I used a series of standardised questionnaires and interview formats for rating health, change in social roles, morale. I included the life satisfaction index - Neugarten et al (1961) and the depression scale from the MMPI - Dempsey (1964) and general attitudes. I included the attitude to reminiscence questionnaire of Havighurst and Glasser (1972). Over the succeeding years whenever I was in London I continued to visit all these people. In 1980 and 1981, exactly ten years after the original data collection, I deliberately repeated the same interviewing schedules with the eight remaining survivors.

The analysis I originally carried out in the early 1970s was heavily quantitative. The main feature of the analysis was categorising units of conversation in various ways and thus scoring each individual on their conversation characteristics. I could then analyse whether these characteristics could be shown to be intervening variables affecting the very evident association that existed in the sample between degree of loss incurred in recent years and present level of morale. Broadly speaking the tendency to reminisce did not seem to have any particular adaptive value and this finding is consistent with other similar studies. One interesting finding was that for those elderly people who were dissatisfied with their past lives the tendency to analyse past experience did seem to be adaptive, and this could be considered to support the life review notion. But no part of the analysis suggested that reminiscence in general played an important role.

A striking feature of the data was how evenly the group split between "reminiscers" and "non-reminiscers". This was found for objective conversation ratings and observers' ratings, as well as for the individual responses to the attitude questions. A substantial number said they enjoyed thinking about the past and thought it a good and helpful thing to do, whereas an equally substantial number did not enjoy it and thought it a pointless and useless thing to do.

Looking at the data now, however, I realise how inadequate it was just to make a global contrast between "reminiscers" and "non-reminiscers". For statistical purposes I felt I had little choice in a study with such limited numbers but to construct as large groups as possible. As so often occurs in research of this kind, this involved trampling over many important distinctions. First, of course, is the distinction between thinking about the past and talking about the past. They are different phenomena, related but probably fulfilling somewhat different functions. Even more important is the individual's own attitude to reminiscence - whether it has a positive or negative meaning for him or her. Looking carefully at all the data and feeling more confident about using the qualitative evidence available, including most importantly what people actually said about their own reminiscence, I think it is possible to make some interesting distinctions. A crude but indicative typology is show in Table I.

The first group is a large group of individuals who indicated that reminiscence played an important and positive part in their lives. The characteristic the past had for all of them was that of a treasured possession, even with and sometimes because of its difficulties. Significantly a number said to me that they could and would like to write a book! For that reason they were particularly interested in the book they thought I would write about them. It included individuals for whom the past in general was seen as preferable to the present (one said it had "more common humanity") and therefore they were grateful they had lived in an earlier period. But most were not concerned with this comparison but simply gained a great deal psychologically from remembrances of happy times and achievements (concerning for example childhood, family life, collaboration at work and responsibilities fulfilled). All were reasonably well adjusted, but few if any had had easy lives. They referred a lot to coping with,

Table 1 Adjustment and Attitudes to Reminiscence Among Elderly People Living Alone in Sheltered Housing in London 1970-71

GROUP 1: Reminisces and values it	(a) helpful in adjustment	(N = 11)
	(b) insufficient help	(N = 4)
GROUP 2: Reminisces but finds it disturbing		(N = 8)
GROUP 3: Does not reminisce : no point or purpose		(N = 15)
GROUP 4: Does not reminisce because depressing: contrast with present too great		(N = 6)
GROUP 5: Neither clearly a "reminiscer" nor a "non-reminiscer"		(N = 7)

surviving and learning from difficulties. One woman described experiencing her life now as "a pattern, all rolled out behind her". From her own description of changes she had experienced in herself, she appeared to have been through a period of life review, and only comparatively recently to have become "reconciled" to all the difficulties she had encountered in her life: a drunken father who beat her mother, nursing her son, who was born with deformed kidneys, until he died at the age of 15, and caring for her husband too, in his last years, with terminal cancer. Her life, she said, had had much sadness, but what she remembered now was the love. It had become a source of wisdom. She felt she knew now what was important in life. She saw things clearly at last. Old age as a result was a happy time for her. She felt very peaceful. Although one must be careful in interpreting retrospective information about an individual's psychological development, this account is very suggestive of a successful life review process. There was a small subgroup who expressed positive attitudes to reminiscence but indicated that it was insufficient to compensate for present difficulties. Three of the four people in this subgroup had severe problems with their health: one had a lot of pain from a carcinoma of the stomach; one was largely incapacitated by a stroke; one was losing her eyesight rapidly. The fourth member had a history of depressive reactions to loss, had been treated for depression with ECT after losing her husband two years previously, but still felt very depressed.

The second group is particularly interesting because they could be called "compulsive" reminiscers. They reminisced a lot although it made them feel bad about their past lives to a significant extent. They were dissatisfied with their lives as a whole or had significant and troubling areas of regret. They cold not repress their memories.

Interestingly, they were a significantly younger group than the rest of the sample with no one over the age of 78. This group is really suggestive of issues to do with life review. A number had noticeable psychological problems. One man had married late in life, quarrelled with his wife over the upbringing of their children. He had belted a daughter who had been promiscuous and had himself been taken to court as a result. Eventually his wife separated from him on ground of mental cruelty. It drove him mad to think back on it, but he could not help it. Another had served a prison sentence for theft. He said he had to do it to support his wife and family. He still greatly resented that whole episode in his life. His friends had not looked after his wife and family, as they had promised him when in prison, and she had died soon after his release. He was "always thinking about her". He argued with himself over what had happened and what he had done. He just sat and thought and some of his thoughts were "terrible".

Some were troubled memories of wasted chances, failures to marry or to make more of a success of their working lives. Others were troubled by things that had happened to them and permanently affected their lives. One lady born in Belgium, whose father was a well established concert pianist had lost her home in the first world war and fled with her parents to London. Her mother had died soon afterwards. She had never recovered the same standard of life. Her thoughts about the past were full of episodes of "man's cruelty to man". She would rather not have lived. All members of this group were maladjusted to a greater or lesser extent with their lives in old age, and in retrospect may have benefitted from active psychosocial intervention.

The third group is the most heterogeneous. They saw no general value in reminiscence. The majority had found other ways of coping with life. Certainly, and this is important, they seemed no less well adjusted than those in the first group. Some had striking life histories to tell. But they did not feel any need to dwell on them further. This is a noteworthy distinction. A number of writers have referred to the importance of acquaintance with the individual's life history to understanding their needs in their present situation (Johnson, 1978). They have also stress the individual's need to explain himself by describing his past history to an interested hearer. Indeed a number of people in this group spoke a lot about their past lives when I <u>first</u> met them. They seemed to want to tell their life story to indicate how they had become the way they were. One stressed his Quaker upbringing, and the brutalising experiences of the first war. Another analysed carefully the events of his life, and how bad health and accidental events had intervened to prevent his being the success he could have been. But fundamentally their analyses were more dispassionate than those of the previous groups. Life in the present (or future) was important, not the past. There was no point in reminiscence, or as the last man put it "no LSD" (pounds, shillings and pence!).

There was an interesting subgroup of three ladies whose previous lives had been very restricted, being tied down by their husbands and/or work responsibilities. They now very much enjoyed the hobbies and handicraft interests they had developed. They appreciated old age as a time they could at last devote to themselves. They had no need at all for looking back.

The fourth group indicates another important distinction. These were people who, like the previous group, did not reminisce and did not want to reminisce, but, like the second group, their relationship with the past was an uneasy one. They had to avoid reminiscing because it made them feel depressed. This was not because there was anything to regret in the past; on the contrary the past had been fuller and happier, and the contrast with the emptiness of the present made them more sad than they need be. Unlike the third group, they could not find present interests which formed an adequate substitute for their past lives, and the past instead of being a comfort, as with the first group, was a source of depression. Three of the six were men who had recently lost their wives and could not come to terms with living alone.

Longitudinal Data

The people have been followed up over a period of over ten years, so it is possible to analyse what happened to the members of each group. However, this is open to the accusation of being a *post hoc* analysis. I knew, before making the classification already referred to, what did in fact happen to each person in succeeding years. Although I proceeded by first forming this typology from a consideration of data collected between 1969 and 1971 (and only subsequently looked at the later data), the accusation still has weight. The subsequent account, therefore, has more the status of suggestive hypotheses than of established longitudinal findings. Given the scarcity of longitudinal qualitative research on ageing, even data of this kind, biased as they may be, have considerable value - see Table 2.

One general point about the longitudinal data, as other studies have found, is that there is considerable stability in the attitudes expressed over time, both to past and present. Changes are subtle and gradual rather than striking.

Briefly expressed, the large group of those who reminisced, valued their memories highly and found them helpful in coping with life in old age; they appeared without exception to adapt well to the vicissitudes that faced them. None became depressed. They maintained positive attitudes to reminiscence. For one man, his experiences in the first world war had remained in the forefront of his mind. His was a reflective interest which included a striking measure of sympathy for the German soldiers. His continued involvement was such that at the age of 93 he obtained a new book that had come out on the battle of the Somme. The lady mentioned earlier who had had a worrying life continued to draw lessons from it. "Love and friendship were the most important things in life. One should not be too busy". She had been and she had later regretted it. The evidence on this group is so consistent that one can suggest with some confidence that the positive value given to reminiscence seemed to indicate a good prognosis.

Of the small group who valued reminiscence but found it insufficient in coping with personal difficulties, three were in very poor health and all died within a couple of years. One survivor lived long enough to be included in the case studies. By then she had overcome her bereavement and had high morale. The past continued to be very important for her. Thus she had become indistinguishable from the members of the first group. Given her degree of physical frailty and initial level of depression, it seemed in retrospect remarkable that she lived so long. Although one cannot generalise from this example, it suggests that a positive value given to reminiscing can be indicative of survival even when the individual does not have the means to adjust to the immediate losses confronting her.

Table 2 Outcomes for Reminiscence Groups Among Elderly People Living Alone in Sheltered Housing in London Over The Period 1971-1981.

GROUP 1:	(a) Maintained good adjustment (b) Died soon // Recovered good adjustment
GROUP 2:	Deteriorated and/or died soon // Achieved more accepting attitudes to past
GROUP 3:	Mostly maintained good adjustment
GROUP 4:	Deteriorated and/or died soon // Maintained poor adjustment
GROUP 5:	Showed both good and poor adjustment

The second group is particularly interesting since it seems to exemplify the life review process. Five of the eight died within two years. From the evidence I collected it was clear that two at least showed increasing psychological disturbance. According to the reports of wardens and neighbours they had become alcoholics and did not look after themselves. One had become labelled a "nuisance". The other three by contrast survived a long time (two long enough to become case studies in 1981). Two made significant changes in attitude. The Belgian lady who had come to London as a refugee mellowed in her attitudes to life. In particular her attitudes to her past life became more accepting. I recorded how on one occasion she said she was glad she had been a girl and so had been able to look after her father in the disasters that befell him. She took pleasure in showing me photographs from his concert tours in Europe. When I last saw her a few months before she died she spoke very serenely. She could hardly believe her father had been dead so long. He had been a very good companion. Although her outlook on the world was still pessimistic, it was kinder.

Of the two men who survived to be case studies, one was much less critical of himself ten years later. He no longer regretted his lack of a good career or his not getting married. He said that he had not been the type for such a responsibility. He was fortunate in that he maintained good health. The other man by contrast did not resolve regrets of a similar nature. In fact, in 1981 he probably felt them more acutely. Health seemed to be a crucial difference. Ten years later the second man was very disabled by angina and cancer and felt very lonely. He greatly missed not having a family. A comparison of these two cases is instructive and shows the importance of interacting physical, social and psychological factors.

Of the people who discounted the importance of reminiscence, the interesting question is whether they were able to adapt to the vicissitudes of old age as well as the reminiscers. The answer seems to be that they were. One of the fifteen I lost trace of when he moved out of his housing complex, but of the remaining fourteen eleven remained well adjusted until their deaths. Three became depressed and of these two did so in the face of considerable disability. The rest maintained much the same attitudes. They had found successful ways of coping with old age which did not involve reminiscence. Nearly all had plenty of outside interests. They did not feel any need to look back.

From the evidence available, of the six people in the final category who in 1971 did not like to reminisce because of the contrast with their present situation, five were at that time clearly depressed. The sixth was not and is interesting for that reason. She entertained me well and seemed to be content, although I did note down signs of nervous tension. I found out from the warden that she concealed her true feelings about her only daughter who had largely broken off relationships with her for reasons which were unclear. In the circumstances her avoidance of reminiscence seemed to be a significant indicator of maladjustment, of pain on remembering happier times. I did not see her again, but on the warden's account and that of neighbours she became increasingly worried and nervous and had hallucinations. She died one year later in a psychiatric hospital. The other five retained the same negative attitudes to their present life and an avoiding attitude toward reminiscence. Three lived a considerable time and the stability in their attitudes was striking. One man was still making the same incipient but insufficient moves to find a new wife in 1981 as he was in 1971. He and other people might have benefitted a lot from a therapeutic intervention such as could be offered by groupwork.

Conclusions

I hope to have demonstrated that the individual's attitude to reminiscence is an interesting theme in old age. It may be a significant predictor of the ability to cope with difficulties. The data suggest that those who adapt best are either those who indicate that memories of the past offer them significant means of support or those who indicate they have plenty of present interests to take the place of the past. These are probably the kinds of people who can most easily be offered help when they need it: reminiscence groups could satisfy the former, and alternative forms of activity the latter. Problems are much more likely to arise with the other two smaller groups: those who are worried by disturbing thoughts about the past, and those who cannot find means of compensating for the past. We need to be sensitive to such individual differences, and be prepared to provide help on an individual as well as a group basis.

The other point I would like to stress is the great extent of individual variation in orientation to reminiscence. Some people put a very high value of memories as their most treasured possessions - a theme reflected in literature, most especially in Proust. For others the past is gone and unimportant. The development of such a value orientation deserves analysis in its own right. At which point in the life span does it emerge, and how stable is it over time? The way I have presented the subject might suggest that it is an all-or-nothing characteristic. This is not so. Although the vast majority of people do express a clear orientation, seven people in the study have been excluded from the analysis because they seemed neither "reminiscers" nor "non-reminiscers". Their general means of coping with life was based on present activities and interests, but they did not discount altogether the value of the past.

The value an individual places on his past experience is different from being satisfied with one's past life. It is also different from the affective quality of one's memories. It is rather an evaluation of the importance of memories to the individual as a personal possession. Presumably we all value our personal memories to some degree as a bedrock of personal identity, but some put more value on them than others.

Bibliography

Butler, R.N. (1963) 'The Life Review : an Interpretation of Reminiscence in the Aged', Psychiatry, 26, 65-76

Coleman, P.G. (1974) 'Measuring Reminiscence Characteristics from Conversation as Adaptive Features of Old Age', International Journal of Aging and Human Development, 5, 281-294

Coleman, P.G. (1983) 'The Past is the Present. A Longitudinal Study of the Adaptive Value of Reminiscence', Report, University of Southampton

Dempsey, P. (1964) 'A Unidimensional Depression Scale for the MMPI', Journal of Consulting Psychology, 28, 364-370

Erikson, E. (1978) 'Reflections on Dr Borg's Life Cycle', in E. Erikson (ed), Adulthood, W.W. Norton, New York

Havighurst, R.J. and Glasser, R. (1972) 'An Exploratory Study of Reminiscence', Journal of Gerontology, 27, 235-253

Johnson, M. (1978) 'That Was Your Life : a Biographical Approach to Later Life', in V. Carver and P. Liddiard (eds), An Ageing Population, Hodder and Stoughton, Sevenoaks

Kastenbaum, R. (1982) 'Time Course and Time Perspective in Later Life', in C. Eisdorfer (ed), Annual Review of Gerontology and Geriatrics Volume Three, Springer, New York

Lewis, C.N. (1973) 'The Adaptive Value of Reminiscing in Old Age', Journal of Geriatric Psychiatry, 6, 117-121

Merriam, S. (1980) 'The Concept and Function of Reminiscence : a Review of the Research, The Gerontologist, 20, 604-609

McMahon, A.W. and Rhudick, P.J. (1967) 'Reminiscing in the Aged : an Adaptational Response', in S. Levin and R.J. Kahana (eds), Psychodynamic Studies on Aging : Creativity, Reminiscing and Dying, International Universities Press, New York

Neugarten, B.L., Havighurst, R.J. and Tobin, S.S. (1961) 'The Measurement of Life Satisfaction', Journal of Gerontology, 16, 134-143

Wheeler, R. (1982) 'Staying Put : a New Development in Policy?' Ageing and Society, 2, 299-329

Chapter Twenty-one

ASSESSING ATTITUDES TOWARD OLD PEOPLE

J. M. Simpson

Introduction

Early work on attitudes toward old people was characterised by generality. Generalised attitudes were measured towards generalised old people and toward old age in general. Since the mid-seventies researchers have adopted a more analytic approach and the need for a refined conceptual framework has been recognised - Kogan (1979), Lutsky (1980), Bader (1980) and Greene (1981).

Progress is being made in delineating the target areas for attitude studies in this field. Weinberger and Millam (1975) have shown the value of differentiating attitudes toward generalised old people from those toward particular, individual old people. Hickey et al. (1979) contrast attitudes toward OLD AGE with attitudes toward OLD PEOPLE. Bader elaborates this scheme to distinguish three target areas: attitudes toward the PERSON, i.e. old people as people, attitudes toward the PROCESS, i.e. the process of growing old, and attitudes toward the STATE, i.e. the state of old age or of being old. It does not follow that a respondent who holds a low opinion of old age as a state to be experienced will also hold a low opinion of old people themselves. This scheme may be refined to allow for attitudes in each of these target areas to be relevant to either the SELF or to the OTHER. Nardi (1973) proposed a similar refinement but described the subdivisions in terms of "autoperception" and heteroperception". The scheme is detailed in Table 1. Determinants of attitudes toward each of the six groups set out in the table may be investigated in terms of the attributes of the respondents themselves, such as age, sex or personal experience or of the attributes of the target group or process or state.

Table I Categorisation of Areas for Research on Attitudes Toward Old People and Ageing.

PERSON		ABOUT OLD PEOPLE AS PEOPLE.
	SELF	An old person about old people
	OTHER	Younger person about old people
PROCESS		ABOUT THE PROCESS OF GROWING OLD
	SELF	About growing old oneself.
	OTHER	About other people's ageing.
STATE		ABOUT THE STATE OF BEING OLD
	SELF	About the consequences of being old oneself.
	OTHER	About the perceived consequences of being old as it affects old people.

Several reviewers, e.g. Brubaker the Powers (1976), have pointed to the confusion in much of the early work between statements of attitude (which contain an evaluative component) and statements of belief (which are factual). A respondent who agrees that many old people are in residential care does not necessarily dislike old people.

The distinction between attitudes and beliefs is central to an influential paradigm for attitude research familiar to social psychologists - Ajzen and Fishbein (1980). In this model, attitudes themselves are seen as a function of the beliefs a person holds about the target or attitude object. The beliefs are weighted by a measure of their importance to the person himself and it is these weighted beliefs that are seen as predicting the subject's attitude toward the target. Very little work has been done to discover what underlies younger people's attitudes toward old people. By measuring beliefs and respondents' evaluation of these beliefs it may be possible to understand the determinants of their attitudes and thereby reveal ways of changing them.

As part of a larger project, I am measuring medical students' beliefs and feelings about old people as people and investigating change in these attitudes over time as a result of education and maturation. I am using a quasi-experimental design with one set of controls being responses to the same items but referring to people in younger age groups. Most existing methods of examining attitudes toward old people have the disadvantage of not permitting comparisons of this sort as the scale-items are usually specific to the elderly, e.g. Tuckman and Lorge (1953), Kogan (1961), Kafer et al. (1980). An exception is the semantic differential devised by Rosencrantz and McNevin (1969). I focus on beliefs about the consequences for the respondent of "being with old people" as I am assuming that it is something about the way the elderly are perceived to behave that generates positive or negative feelings about them in younger people. This approach therefore differs from others in which attitudinal underpinnings are thought to be stable personality traits that are not easily changed - Bennett and Eckmann (1973).

Construction and Administration of the Scale

Twenty items of behaviour associated primarily with old people were selected from the Tuckman and Lorge scale and from student nurses' and medical students' responses to a set of open-ended questions I have devised. These items are listed in Table 2.

Table 2 Examples of Behaviour to be Rated

1. To be careful about their own personal appearance
2. To have good co-ordination
3. To be selfish
4. To look miserable
5. To have good memories
6. To feel tired
7. To be grateful for what is done for them
8. To be demanding
9. To be absent-minded
10. To worry about unimportant things
11. To be stubborn
12. To have difficulty in seeing
13. To repeat themselves in conversation
14. To be apathetic
15. To like change and new ways of doing things
16. To be withdrawn
17. To be hard of hearing
18. To talk rather than listen
19. To move quickly
20. To grumble

The respondent rates each scale-item twice. The first is a probability rating, he estimates the likelihood of this behaviour being demonstrated by a person in a particular age-group using a seven-point scale from -3 (extremely unlikely) to +3 (extremely likely). Secondly, he or she makes an evaluative judgement of the same behaviour using a similar bipolar scale to rate how pleasant or unpleasant he finds it when a person in a particular age group in whose company he happens to be behaves in this way. These ratings are then multiplied together to yield a weighted score for that particular item. A subject's score on the whole scale is the sum of his weighted belief scores.

Pilot Study

I conducted an exploratory study to examine the usefulness of this method in distinguishing the reactions of different groups of respondents to people in the age groups 20-40, 40-60, 60-80, 80+.

Respondent Groups

The two groups both had experience of working with old people. One group consisted of thirty psychologists, all of whom were working at least part-time with old people and who were interested enough to attend a conference on the care of the elderly. The other was a group of thirty final year medical students, all of whom had scored low on an independent measure of enthusiasm for taking a job in geriatric medicine.

Analysis

Analysis of the results was carried out at three levels : (i) Totals, i.e. the sum of weighted beliefs; (ii) Products, i.e. the weighted belief for an individual item; (iii) Probabilities, i.e. the likelihood rating for an item and Evaluations, i.e. the pleasant/unpleasant rating for an item.

Summary of Results and Discussion

Examination of the totals revealed significant differences between the ratings made by the subject groups and between their assessments of the four age groups. The interaction between subject groups and their ratings of the different age groups was also significant, see Figure 1. The two subject groups differed most in their assessments of the youngest age group not the oldest as had been expected. Overall, the psychologists were less extreme in their views than the medical students. This may be attributable to the wider age range of this group, their greater work experience or to the fact that psychologists are indeed less ageist than the medical students.

Analysis of the individual items showed that among the products only five items - see Table 2 items 2, 5, 6, 16 and 19 - distinguished the respondent groups (all $p<0.009$), whereas all except items 3, 7, 10, 20 distinguished between the age groups at $p<0.05$. For the remainder of this preliminary report I shall focus on the assessments of the different age groups. Of the probability ratings, all but two - items 7 and 18 - did not reveal differences between the age groups rated (otherwise all $p<0.02$), whilst among the evaluations fourteen items showed significant differences at $p<0.01$ (all except items 1,2,7,15,19,20).

Six items on the list are worded in a positive direction, e.g. item 1, "to be careful about their own personal appearance". We may assume that a respondent would welcome such behaviours in another person and rate them as pleasant. The evaluations of only one of these

Figure 1 Mean Total Scores for each Subject Group by Age Group Rated.

Subject group $p < .0058$
Age group rated $p < .0001$
Interaction $p < .0001$

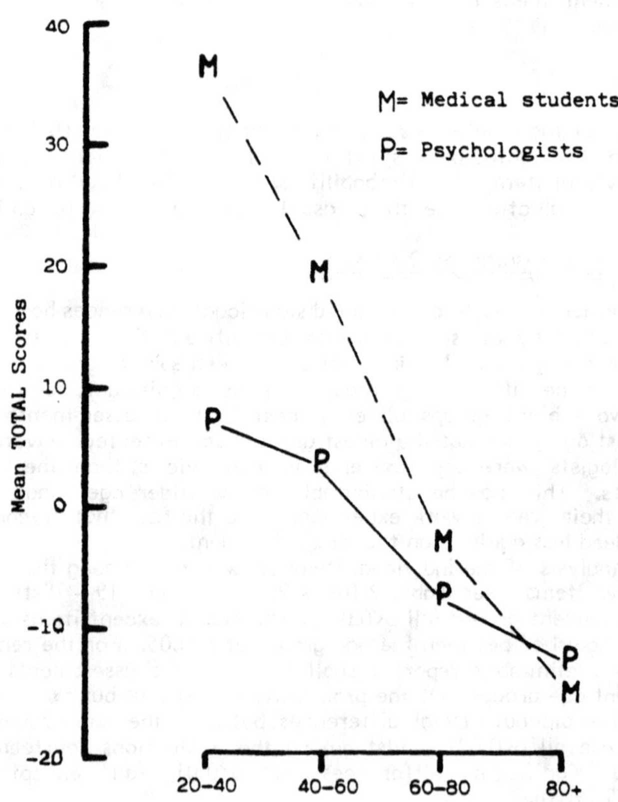

items, number 5, "to have good memories" differentiated significantly between the age groups. Each of those ratings that significantly seperate the four age groups revealed the respondents' greater tolerance of the various behaviours when they occured in old people. The items that differentiated most significantly were those relating to examples of behaviour that might be considered less excusable as they can be seen as a person's own fault: repeating oneself, being apathetic or selfish. But these behaviours were rated as being least acceptable when demonstrated by people in the 20-40 and 40-60 age groups thanin the two oldest groups.

Among the probability ratings, the most significant differences were found amongst items corresponding to behaviour that would seldom be considered a person's own fault: moving quickly, being hard of hearing, having difficulty in seeing and having good co-ordination. In all these cases, as well as in the significantly different ratings of the other, less acceptable behaviours, the elderly were perceived as more likely to behave in ways listed in a positive direction and less likely to exhibit behaviour that was described negatively. For instance the probability that the old would 'repeat themselves in conversation' and not 'like change and new ways of doing things' was rated higher than in the younger groups.

The results of this preliminary analysis suggest that the slightly unfavourable view held of the elderly, especially by some medical students, results from the perceived greater likelihood of old people behaving in ways that are viewed as slightly unpleasant and not because the same behaviour in old people is tolerated less than it is in younger folk. This outcome might be taken to imply that it would be easier to counsel old people on how to modify their ways rather than attempt to alter the values of younger people who work with them. Social skills training for the elderly?

Conclusion

Studies of attitudes toward the elderly have failed to exploit the progress in attitude research in social psychology. Greater precision in defining target areas is advocated with the aim of identifying underlying mechanisms thereby aiding the development of successful programmes of change. The work reported here reflects one possible approach. It remains to be seen just how fruitful it will be.

Acknowledgement

I wish to thank Dr. Sheila Chown for all her help and guidance.

Bibliography

Azjen, I. and Fishbein, M. (1980) Understanding Attitudes and Predicting Social Behaviour, Prentice Hall, Englewood Cliffs, New Jersey

Bader, J. (1980) 'Attitudes Towards Aging, Old Age and Old People', Aged Care and Services Review, 2, 1-14

Bennett, R. and Eckman, J. (1973) 'Attitudes Towards Aging: a Critical Examination of Recent Literature and Implications for Future Research', in C. Eisdorfer and M. Lawton (eds), Psychology of Adult Aging and Development, American Psychological Association, Washington, D.C.

Brubaker, T. and Powers, E. (1976) 'The Stereotype of "Old". A Review and Alternative Approach', Journal of Gerontology, 31, 441-447

Greene, S. (1981) 'Attitudes and Perceptions About the Elderly: Current and Future Perspectives', International Journal of Aging and Human Development, 13, 99-115

Hickey, T., Bragg S., Rakowski, W. and Hultsch, D. (1979) 'Attitude Instrument Analysis: an Examination of Factor Consistency Across Two Samples'. International Journal of Aging and Human Development, 10, 359-375

Kafer, R., Rakowski, W., Lachman, M. and Hickey, T. (1980) 'Aging Opinion Survey: a Report on Instrument Development', International Journal of Aging and Human Development, 11, 319-333

Kogan, N. (1961) 'Attitudes Toward Old People: The Development of a Scale and Examination of Correlates', Journal of Abnormal and Social Psychology, 62, 44-54

Kogan, N. (1979) 'Beliefs, Attitudes and Stereotypes about Old People: a New Look at Some Old Issues', Research on Aging, 1, 12-36

Lutsky, N. (1980) 'Attitudes Towards Old Age and Elderly Persons', in C. Eisdorfer (ed), Annual Review of Gerontology and Geriatrics, Vol 1. Springer Publishing Co., New York

Nardi, A. (1973) 'Person-perception Research and the Perception of Life-span Development', in P. B. Baltes and K. W. Schaie (eds), Life Span Developmental Psychology, Academic Press, New York

Rosencranz, H. and McNevin, T. (1969) 'A Factor Analysis of Attitudes Towards the Aged', Gerontologist, 9, 55-59

Tuckman, J. and Lorge, I. (1953) 'Attitudes Towards Old People', Journal of Social Psychology, 37, 249-260

Weinberger, L. and Millham, J. (1975) 'A Multidimensional, Multimethod Analysis of Attitudes Toward the Elderly', Journal of Gerontology, 30, 343-348

Chapter Twenty-two

RESIDENTIAL SEPARATION AND VISITING BETWEEN RETIRED PARENTS AND THEIR SONS AND DAUGHTERS

A. M. Warnes

Introduction

During the summer of 1983 a social survey of the visiting patterns of retired married couples living without others was carried out in four districts of England: Maidstone, Kent, Melton Mowbray, Oakham and two villages in Leicestershire; the Metropolitan District of Stockport; the London Borough of Merton. This paper presents a small selection of the preliminary descriptive results from the 432 completed questionnaires. As a first report at an early stage of the analysis and in the limited space available, the opportunity will be taken to explain some of the empirical questions that the survey has addressed and to identify early lines of investigation that are being pursued.

The background to the research had been an interest in the environmental or, more specifically, geographical influences upon the lives of retired people - Warnes (1982). Studies of the implications of retirement migration upon contact with relatives had raised questions about the impact of increased residential mobility and geographical separation of relatives and friends on their social interaction. Do either improved personal mobility through wider car ownership and faster roads or more accessible telcommunications compensate for physical separation? To what extent can social mobility or social class be related to residential separation or, from a contrasting perspective, to what extent can geographical distance be identified as an independent influence upon social interaction? As well as of intrinsic geographical concern, these questions can be related to several normative and policy issues.

Despite the many merits and accomplishments of the literature on social interaction, some dissatisfaction was felt at its treatment of spatial influence. Frequently a relationship between the distance separating individuals and the temporal structure and the content of their contacts had been recognised but understandably investigators from academic, sociological or psychological backgrounds were rarely prompted to tenaciously analyse this factor - Took (1984).

Accordingly, the present survey was designed to collect detailed information on retired couples' residential histories and on their present social contacts. - Warnes (1984). A focus on intergenerational consanguineal relations was adopted. It is recognised that we are taking on an inherently complex problem for which multivariate analytical and conceptual methods will be necessary - Howes (1984). The influences of socio-economic status, marital status, competing social opportunities or social network topology and other factors will have to be taken into account.

Frequency of Visiting

Approximately four in ten of the retired couples' children were reported as making visits to their parents at least once a week and only two in ten visit less than four times a year (Table I). Hardly any difference exists between the first and second children. Parents, however, visit their children's homes much less frequently, with one third making less than four visits a year. Their frequency of weekly visits is approximately one half of that from children to parents. Eight per cent of the children never receive visits from their parents and there was insignificant differentiation between first and second children.

Table I Frequency of Visiting Between Retired Parents and Their Children

Visitor and visited	Sample size	Once + a week	Once + a month	4+ times a year	Less often	Never
		Cumulative freqeuncy (%)			%	%
CI to RC	432	38.2	62.0	79.6	18.2	2.1
C2 to RC	432	40.0	65.2	77.9	19.4	2.5
RC to CI	432	22.9	45.6	64.6	26.9	8.6
RC to C2	432	22.4	48.6	66.0	26.2	7.9
MC to RC	419	37.8	61.0	78.7	19.3	2.1
FM to RC	445	40.0	66.2	79.0	18.4	2.5
RC to M	419	17.9	38.4	59.2	30.8	10.0
RC to FM	445	27.2	55.3	71.0	22.5	6.5

Notes: CI first children; C2 second child; RC retired couple together or husband alone or wife alone; M sons; FM daughters.

Although it is clear that the birth order of a child has little relationship with the frequency of their visits to and from their parents, some differentiation between sons and daughters was revealed. Somewhat surprisingly there is no evidence from the survey that daughters visit their parents more frequently than sons: the differentiation occurs rather among the retired parents in respect of visits to their children's homes. As many as one in ten of the sons are not visited and only 38 per cent receive visits from their parents at least monthly in comparison to 55 per cent of the daughters (Table 1). The frequencies of parental visits to sons and daughters were significantly different according to a chi-quare test (dichotomised frequencies at least or less than once a month; (calculated $X^2 = 24.60$; critical value $X^2 = 6.64$, df=1, $p<0.01$).

It will be possible to disaggregate further the information on visiting by the marital status of children, the number and ages of grandchildren, the separate frequencies of visits by husbands, wives and married couple and other variables. Some may be found to be of little significance, as appears to be the case with birth order, and gradually our attention will be directed towards the most influential or particularly interesting effects. Special interest attaches to the distance between the homes of retired couples and their children.

Age and Distance of Children's Separation

Individual sons and daughters left home as early as nine years of age and as late as 51 years but at an average age of 23.0 years. No differences between first and second children emerged without taking into account their sex; sons left their parents' homes at 23.7 years, approximately 17 months later than daughters. In this case the combination of birth order and the sex of a child produces statistically significant differences in behaviour. On average male first children were most reluctant to leave home, at an average age of 24.1 years, but female first children left soonest at 22.0 years, the discrepancy is highly significant in a difference of means test (calculated $t = 4.61$; critical value $t = 3.33$ df = 419, $p < 0.001$). Second children showed an intermediate position, although sons similarly left home at a later age (23.4 years) than daughters (22.6 years), a small difference but one which remained statistically significant (calcualted $t = 2.08$; critical value $t = 1.97$, df 437, $p < 0.05$).

The distance presently separating children from their parents again has considerable variation, from a few cases of living next door to a scatter throughout Great Britain. Some children living in North-West Europe were also included in the eligible sample - it is as easy to travel between Maidstone and, say, Cologne as between Maidstone and Cornwall. On average first children are significantly closer (54.2 km) than second children (60.5 km) but a greater contrast exists between daughters (51.3 km) and sons (63.8 km). Put in very general terms, the younger the age at which a child leaves home, the more proximate they are likely to be during their parents' retirement. Clear differences between the survey districts are apparent, ranging from a separation of over 80 km in Maidstone to under 55 km in Stockport and approximately 45 km in Merton.

A preliminary inspection of the relationship between proximity and the frequency of visiting concludes this short report. It is of course not at all surprising to find that adjacent relatives visit each other more frequently than widely separated kin but it is commonly not realised how sharp the changes in frequency are with small increments of distance. Whereas 72 per cent of the first children living within 5 km of their parents visit their parents at least weekly, only 42 per cent of those living between 5 and 25 km match this frequency of contact. Among those living beyond 25 km, 62 per cent visit less than four times a year (Table 2).

Table 2 Frequency of visits by Distance of Separation

Frequency of Visits	Distance of separation (km)			
	0-4.9	5-24.9	25-99.9	100+
First children to retired parents	%	%	%	%
At least once a week	72	42	10	3
At least once a month	17	41	34	8
At least once in 3 months	6	12	36	26
Less often	5	5	20	63
Retired parents to first children	%	%	%	%
At least once a week	45	22	4	3
At least once a month	24	41	18	6
At least once in 3 months	16	17	28	18
Less often	15	20	50	73
Sample size	157	95	90	90

These are not long distances, 25 kilometres is $15^{1/2}$ miles, but for visits both by and to retired parents a few kilometres exerts a strong relationship with existing frequency. In comparison to the measures of association with other variables such as sex, marital status and the retired husband's social group, relatively high values are generated by the distance variable (Table 3).

Table 3 Associations With the Frequency of Visiting

		Description of visits			
		RC to C1	RC to C2	C1 to RC	C2 to RC
Variable	k	Cramer's V measure of association			
Sex of child	2	0.24	0.16	0.13	0.10
Marital status of child	4			0.20	0.20
Social group of RC	5	0.13	0.14	0.13	0.14
Distance of separation	5	0.36	0.37	0.43	0.46

Notes: RC retired couple, C1 first child, C2 second child, k number of categories. Frequency of visiting has nine categories

Conclusions

Of the small selection of aggregate influences upon the frequency of visits between retired parents and their children that have so far been examined, the distance of separation has emerged as relatively important. The challenging questions that we face include: To what extent is frequency a control upon the value and the satisfaction produced by visits for their participants? To what extent is physical separation a causal factor, as opposed to an expression of either the closeness of interpersonal relations or exogenous factors (such as the location of employment and housing opportunities)? It may be that the duration of visits varies in a complementary way to their frequency or that the satisfactions which attach to an individual visit are an inverse function of their frequency. These topics will be investigated thoroughly along with attention to the content of visits and their evaluation by retired people.

Acknowledgements

This project has been funded by the Economic and Social Research Council and carried out in the Department of Geography at King's College London. Many individuals and organisations have assisted during the course of the project. Particular thanks are due to all our respondents in Maidstone, Melton Mowbray, Oakham, Stockport and Merton. The following acted as interviewers on the project and we are grateful for their enthusiastic help: Rodney Bungey, Simon Corley, Geoffrey Crothall, Vivien Crump, Janet Kerber, Christine Ogden,

Susan Sayer, Garry Tobiss, Elizabeth Took, Peter Wade (assistant) and Else Zapletal. The full time staff of the project are David Howes and Laurance Took.

Bibliography

Howes, D. (1984) 'Analysis of Categorical Data: Discussion and Examples', Department of Geography, King's College, London

Took, L. (1984) 'Social Interaction and the Study of the Elderly', Department of Geography, Occasional Paper, 19, King's College, London

Warnes, A. M. (ed) (1982) Geographical Perspectives on the Elderly, Wiley, Chichester

Warnes, A. M. (1984) 'Residential Proximity, Intergenerational Relations and the Support of the Elderly: a Research Proposal', Department of Geography, Occasional Paper 18, King's College, London

Chapter Twenty-three

CHANGING IMAGES OF RETIREMENT. AN ANALYSIS OF REPRESENTATIONS OF AGEING IN THE POPULAR MAGAZINE RETIREMENT CHOICE

M. Featherstone and M. Hepworth

Introduction

Recent sociological studies of the history of ageing and retirement in Britain and the United States have argued that retirement is essentially the product of economic and political decisions to which individuals are required to adjust as they grow older - Graebner (1980), Phillipson (1977, 1982). The more societies find it necessary to restrict the employment of older workers the more they find it expedient to make retirement a palatable and attractive experience. By the closing years of the nineteenth century it was recognised that a basic requirement for satisfactory retirement was a minimal degree of financial security and from this basis the idea of providing various positive inducements to retirement was slowly elaborated into the conept of retirement as an active lifestyle: a concept which has been more speedily developed during the last two decadès under the influence of an expanding consumer culture.

Analysis of Trends in a Retirement Magazine

Whilst there have been several analyses of the politico-economic origins of retirement policy in advanced capitalist societies, there have been relatively few attempts to document constituent elements of the contemporary retirement lifestyle. In this paper we report on a study of the lifestyle imagery in the British retirement magazine Choice which first appeared in October 1972 under the title Retirement Choice and is the only monthly commercial magazine devoted to preparation for retirement on sale on newstands throughout the United Kingdom. Linked with the Pre-Retirement Association of Great Britain and Northern Ireland, Choice is currently distributed to an ever increasing audience of readers. The magazine now describes itself as, 'The magazine for leisure and retirement planning' and suggests that some companies find that 'Choice is a complete preparation for retirement itself.' (Nov., 1980 p. 3) For a number of reasons, therefore, Choice can be seen as a key source of information for students of representations of retirement in contemporary Britain and in this paper we present the result of an exploratory study of the major changes in the imagery of retirement which have occured in this magazine since its first appearance in October, 1972.

From its inception in 1972, Retirement Choice mounted an attack on the traditional image of retirement in Britain. In the second issue (November) Lord Raglan, the then president of the Pre-Retirement Association, emphasised that Society, 'arbitrarily imposes the rules of retirement, and, therefore, society should play its full part in providing pre-retirement education to help people adjust to a new way of life, at what after all is a time in life when change is proverbially difficult.' In addition readers were sternly advised that 'in the interests of the community there must be a quite dramatic change in attitudes to the whole question of retirement.' (Nov., 1972, p. 2) The problem was that for too long retirement had been associated with useless and passive old age and it was now the responsibility of society to transform retirement into a positive stage of life. The section on women's fashion was particularly interesting since it adopted an especially militant stand towards the image of retirement. In a piece entitled 'Strictly Between Women - Yes, You can Wear These Clothes', women readers were told that they need no longer dress themselves in the 'dull uniform' of the retirement, 'Time was when, once you were forty or so, you could climb into a "uniform" of long black skirt, severe blouse and sensible shoes, sit back and officially enter old age for ever.' By contrast, the grandmothers of 1972 were praised for their modern outlook. The days were gone when they could skimp on make-up and wear something old and comfortable around the house. 'Now, when your husband is going to be home most of the time, is the moment to make him sit up and take notice of your elegant new image.' Perhaps as an added inducement the photographic models demonstrating fashionable aids to his new image were much younger women than the presumed readership (Nov., 1972, pp 18-19).

Promotion of this new image of retirement continued to appear throughout the lifetime of Retirement Choice. In December, 1972, readers were invited to contribute to a new series called 'Then and Now' which, as a photographic celebration of the passage of time, also doubled as a convenient medium for the new message. A set of photographs showed how the pressure on men and women to dress in an elderly fashion in the 1880's had been reduced in the 1960's when liberation seemed for the first time to be at hand. The brief text accompanying the photographs is a plea to free men and women 'from their chronological bonds'. To remove those external pressures which make people feel old, 'whereas past generations of older people were expected to conform to a rigid age pattern, today we are trying to let in a healthy gust of air to blow these wretched cobwebs away.' (Dec., 1972, p.8)

In February, 1973, the editorial expressed a continuing sense of grievance over the association of 'old age' with retirement, 'We no longer wear the kind of clothes which earlier generations of elderly folk donned simply to denote that they were 'elderly'. Yet at the same time older people in spite of their maturity and experience, 'still remain trapped within a fence of outworn stereos'. 'Isn't it about time the news got around that nowadays people stay younger and are not old in the same way that people were old in times of yore?'... 'The ageing processes were', the editor concluded, 'inevitable enough without officialdom giving them a shove along with an outdated vocabulary.' (Feb. 1973, p.3) On the inside pages of this issue was a reference to Newport and Monmouthshire Retirement Council which had issued a brochure including a lively sketch of an old man with a red nose and fringe of white hair leapfrogging a GPO pillarbox, 'Don't be a Mouldy Ouldy. Be a Lively Sixty Five!' (Feb., 1973, p.5).

At a press conference organised to mark the first birthday of Retirement Choice, Dr Wright, Chairman of the Pre-Retirement Association, told reporters and journalists there was still widespread ignorance of the financial and philosophical problems of retirement. To reinforce his message an enormous gold pocket watch made from plastic, plaster and wire was ceremonially destroyed with a hammer. On the cover of this issue was a photograph of this ceremony described as 'breaking a golden spell'. (Oct., 1973, p.11) It was announced that for the first time the magazine, previously available to members of the Pre-Retirement Association, was now available at newsagents and bookstalls throughout the country.

Between October and November 1974, the format of the magazine changed dramatically. The title was changed from Retirement Choice (with the cover design highlighting the word Retirement) to Pre-Retirement Choice (with the emphasis on the word Choice) and it was published in glossy covers which for the first time featured close-ups of faces of celebrities from politics, show business and the media - all of whom were in their late 40's, 50's and 60's. The publication of the journal was now in the hands of a commercial organisation which further concentrated the focus of the magazine on preparation for retirement and on leisure and the exercise of choice, all of which were juxtaposed alongside a more youthful, dynamic image. Examples included politician Margaret Thatcher (Dec., 1974), singer Vera Lynn ('How Vera Lynn defeats middle-age') (Jan., 1975), popular comedian Eric Morecombe ('Laughing off a heart attack') (Feb., 1975) and trade unionist Tom Jackson (May, 1975).

The rationale for this transformation was to create 'a magazine which will become essential for all caught up in preparing for retirement' (emphasis ours) (Oct., 1974). The intention was to expand the concept of pre-retirement to include a younger audience, i.e. the middle aged. For 'people looking ahead to retirement', the publishers announced, 'We shall be covering a wide range of topics of special interest to men and women who know that sooner or later they have to fashion their lives afresh' (Oct., 1974).

In the first issue the editorial pointed out that the Pre-Retirement Association had endured a 'long hard struggle for survival and solvency'. A government grant in 1973 and help from the Parkhill Trust had provided some relief and some of that money had gone into this 'brave and exciting attempt to produce and run an entirely new magazine.' Although the previous magazine had 'done reasonable well', it had, nevertheless, lost money and did require the strength of 'an overt publishing organisation' behind it. It was still, however, in its expanded format linked with the Pre-Retirement Association and its philosophy would be much the same as before (Nov., 1974, p.5). To reinforce the new image an item on the back page announced that forthcoming attractions would further the cause of 'Putting real CHOICE into Pre-Retirement' and December's new improved issue was, for example, to contain more 'informative and entertaining features' including 'down to earth advice on keeping your body in trim in middle age' (Nov., 1974).

Between May and June 1975 'choice' was further highlighted when the word 'Pre-Retirement' was finally dropped from the front cover and the magazine renamed simply Choice and subtitled, 'The only magazine for retirement planning' (June, 1975). The most recent change took place in 1978 involving a merger with the Over 50's Club which had been formed in 1977 (Oct., 1978) and Choice continues to present retirement as an extended lifestyle with little or no mention of geriatric old age and death.

One important consequence of the developments outlined above is the increasing definition of retirement as a consumer lifestyle. The earlier attempts of Retirement Choice to create an active and more positive image for those entering retirement found its expression through modest hobbies such as gardening, painting, photography, watching sport, keeping pets, model soldiers, where the stylisation of the body, presentation of a youthful appearance and the cultivation of an expressive lifestyle were given relatively low priority. Despite the avowed intention of refurbishing and updating the image of retirement the illustrations in Retirement choice from time to time lapsed into the more traditional portrayal of retirement as a time of tranquil inactivity and disengagement from active life, e.g. Retirement Choice (May, 1973; Aug., 1973; Nov., 1973)

From November 1974, however, the magazine has become unashamedly concerned with images of an active consumer lifestyle as a means of separating retirement from any of its previous associations with a decline into traditional old age and social disengagement. None of the celebrities whose photographs now appear on the cover of the magazines have any intention of lapsing into passive retirement; indeed, several of the men and women interviewed have no intention of retiring at all. In July 1975, for example, Lord George Brown, former Deputy Leader of the Labour Party, proudly stated that he had no outside interests 'apart from work, politics, and watching West Ham win the Cup occasionally.' He stressed the importance of continuing in employment to make sufficient money to live comfortably and expressed no intention of retiring from active involvement in his various business interests - Choice (July, 1975, p.25). In cases where celebrities have featured in Choice and retired from one occupation they have usually lost no opportunity to take up alternative employment and such involvement had the effect of reinforcing the new image of ageing as a vigorous, lively and above all enjoyable avenue of self-realisation.

In the context of an overall transformation of a particular medium the question inevitably arises of the relevance of this particular image to the majority of the population in a society characterised by great inequalities in income and opportunity. In a society which still has to make revolutionary changes in pre-retirement and continuing education - retirement means enforced idleness for many and in particular the absence of an adequate income to pursue many of the consumer values central to our society. In January 1974 Retirement Choice was prompted by two published letters from readers to include an article asking 'Are We "Middle Class"?'. One correspondent wrote that he had 'yet to read a letter or an article describing his plans for retirement and life after retirement from, say, an agricultural labourer, a builder's labourer, factory hand or one of the very large class who on retirement have for income the state pension' The correspondent added, 'My finance will not permit me to indulge in some of the hobbies enjoyed by some of your correspondents.' The second correspondent indicated a confusion about the aims of the magazine. He felt that people whose only source of income was the old age pension could not afford to buy the journal and added, 'My guess is that your readers are chiefly those who are getting or will get two pensions. I suggest that, therefore, your appeal should be to the middle class and less often to the old age pensioners who may be are eligible for supplementary benefit.' The editor replied that his task was to provide a service of information for readers before and after retirement who were living in all kinds of social circumstance. He was, he implied, attempting to steer a course between 'a genteel, mild glossy publication slanted at the well-heeled' and 'a kind of old folks comic cuts, full of bingo and telly, deliberately keyed to the mass market.' (Jan., 1974, pp. 14-15).

Conclusions

In spite of these laudable intentions, the magazine has depended for its survival on fostering specific elements of consumer culture: the cultivation of youthfulness and an energetic outlook, fitness, beauty, self-expression, hedonism, fashion and style - Hepworth and Featherstone (1982) - all of which are closely connected with a disposable income; in other words an active role in a market economy. In working towards the dissociation of retirement from late ageing and in effect extending the plateau of an active middle age -Featherstone and Hepworth (1982) - the magazine has had no choice but to ally itself with consumer industries. In a society characterised by socio-economic changes which do not reward the inactive and the obsolete, one unintended consequence has been the creation of two nations in middle and old age: those with the resources to prepare and retire with dignity and style (some of whom feature prominently in the pages of a magazine like Choice) and the large number of men and women who do not have the resources and whose lives consequently do not feature in the magazine.

Acknowledgements

An earlier version of this paper was presented to the Systed '83 Conference, Montreal.

Bibliography

Featherstone, M. and Hepworth, M. (1982) 'Ageing and Inequality: Consumer Culture and the New Middle Age' in D. Robbins et al. (eds), Rethinking Social Inequality, Aldershot, Gower (See also the special Issue of Theory, Culture and Society, 1, 3, 1983, on 'Consumer Culture')

Graebner, W. (1980) A History of Retirement: The Meaning and Function of an American Institution, 1885-1978, Yale University Press, New Haven and London

Hepworth M. and Featherstone, M. (1982) Surviving Middle Age, Basil Blackwell, Oxford

Phillipson, C. (1977) 'The Emergence of Retirement', Working Papers in Sociology, No. 14, University of Durham

Phillipson, C. (1982) Capitalism and the Construction of Old Age, Macmillan, London

Chapter Twenty-four

EDUCATIONAL GERONTOLOGY. TOWARDS A NECESSARY DISCIPLINE?

F. Glendenning

Introduction

Educational gerontology has found little favour in Britain although it has been in use in the United States since 1970. Glendenning (1983) traced the development of the concept in the United States, and the development of practice in the UK. Attention was drawn to the absence of a coherent academic discipline researching the teaching-learning process in relation to older people in this country. Descriptions of experiments and anecdotal material find their way into bulletins, information sheets and into books, such as Glendenning (1980), Midwinter (1982) and Johnston and Phillipson (1983). The useful bulletin provided by the Forum on the Rights of Elderly People to Education also acts as a sounding board for practical developments in this field. This is all very well, but we will make little progress in social policy terms as long as we lack evaluative research; without such evidence it is difficult to make a case for extension in educational programmes. It is not sufficient to assume that because an enterprise is 'educational' it must therefore be worthy of financial and policy support.

Review of Literature

Jones (1975) identified three categories of educational experience to be found within the elderly population which have often been quoted since: (1) those who had received substantial education after 18, (2) a fairly large proportion who left school at 16 and would nowadays go on to college or university, and (3) a much larger group who left school between 12 and 14 years of age and spent most of their working life in manual occupations. Bromley (1970) said that: 'Adult Education as a sub-discipline within gerontology could become an important influence contributing to the content and significance of human activities in late life'. He accepted the view that 'persons with higher intelligence are more likely to have better formal education and appear to deteriorate at a slower rate and to live longer than persons of lower intelligence'. This agrees with the findings of Kahn et al. (1961) that 'mental functioning is only minimally related to age, but is more highly related to psychiatric status, physical condition and educational level'. Agruso (1978) agrees as do Jones (1982) and Tyler (1978). Older people can and do exercise cognitive skills throughout their lives - see Allman (1981, 1982, 1983). The task of the educator is to create opportunities especially where the gaps in knowledge created by the technological revolution can be closed. Havighurst (1972) has defined "the developmental tasks of life' as those things that a person must learn in order to adapt to situations and realise a measure of happiness. The tasks of early adulthood are different from those of middle life, which in turn are different from late adulthood when one is adapting to so-called 'retirement' and possibly to an increase in health problems and a decrease in economic security. Houle (1974) believes that viable education programmes are required at different periods of life and he cites, as his age periods, 20-35, 35-55, 55-75 and over 75. He sees the need for assisting people in the 55+ group to learn how to disengage from former life patterns, and re-engage in new interests, having learnt new strategies for living. For the over-75s, he sees the statistical possibility of physical illness or decline, i.e. the erosion of physical autonomy, but even this may release a new personal autonomy through intellectual stimulation and educational involvement.

In this country, Jones (1983) and Walker (1976, 1983) have demonstrated the power of intellectual stimulus in long-stay institutional situations. (Jones (1982) must be the only educational treatise in history which carries a complete chapter on incontinence!) Jones and Walker have demonstrated the significance of educational input both for physical and mental improvement as well as for increased social interaction in the hospital ward or residential home. Jones has produced evidence to show the effect of educational stimulation on incontinence. Mulford, a practising adult educator in Lancashire, has demonstrated the helpfulness of stimulation in overcoming types of behaviour and physical difficulties; Mulford witnessed very positive results in a psycho-geriatric unit - see Jones (1983).

Poulden (1980, 1983) has done remarkable work with painting and sculpture in London geriatric units. Others, working quietly away in different parts of the country, have reported similar confirmation of improved quality of life. Walker (1976) reviewed residential homes for old people in Leicestershire. His argument was based on what he called the 'philosophy of care' in residential homes, on existing social policy statements from governments in Britain and on the work of researchers who have committed themselves in this area of interest. He saw the establishment of learning networks as fundamental to the philosophy of care which encourages the maintenance of personal dignity and independent life-styles. This means forging links between residential homes and the local community, participation and involvement in the institution and a degree of mutal self-help. He has since amply demonstrated that the establishment of learning networks for older people in residential setttings is feasible given a cooperative infra-structure, and greatly appreciated by the residents who take part, as well as by their relations and carers.

Jones has gone a good deal further. He has mounted tests and experiments in geriatric units with the cooperation of consultant geriatricians. They tested the effects of an educational programme over a four-year period. Jones (1983) says, 'Testing showed that half of them retained their intellectual abilities as tested at the beginning of the programme, deterioration of a physical nature was held at bay and one patient actually improved in health over the period. Mood state and social interaction improved. Incontinence showed little or no deterioration.' What he is suggesting is that it is not the education programme alone which brings benefit to the patients, but the actual participation itself that affects the total personal situation of patients. Jones (1982) has described the remarkable response and support he received from the staff of the hospital who were unexpectedly seeing their patients as students as well.

Much of the interactive success of this programme would be parallelled by others. Cooper (1980) is a prime contribution to this particular area of interest. Jones has been able to carry out at least three research programmes in geriatric hospitals - one in poetry, one in art and one in French conversation. He has also studied older learners in two other hospitals and a day centre and those who came to his courses at the Polytechnic of North London in 1981-82. What emerges from his work is that, whether education takes place within the sphere of higher education or in geriatric institutions, education for older people does more than teach history or music and movement. It achieves more than gaining knowledge or acquiring skills. There is personal change, when the learning is successful, change often of a physical, social and psychological character. Jones (1982) has invented the term 'meta-learning' to describe this process. He does not discuss education for the housebound and the possibility of experiments in distance learning in such situations or the adult centres and colleges of Further Education which are creating education possibilities for housebound people.

Throughout his work, he has placed great stress on a thorough understanding of the psychology and physiology of ageing. The core of his findings may be summed up by these words of Exton-Smith (1978), 'Whatever be the relative importance of vitality in each bodily system, the continued integrity of functions in the nervous system must be of over-riding significance. Not only does it influence function in other systems but the maintenance of acquired skills and the retention of intellectual powers enable the individual to make satisfactory adjustments to environmental hazards.' Jones concluded that central to the whole educational experience of older adults is what he calls the 'self-concept'. The integrating factor in the physical, social and psychological outcomes of the educational experiences which he describes <u>is</u> the self-concept: 'The conquest of helplessness, through acquiring competence and a sense of achievement', 'Feeling a sense of power'. A person's self-concept is affected in two ways according to Jones. One knows that one has learned and others know that one has learned. There are positive developments: the learner feels more capable, discovers goals and purposes, finds a role where there had been none, is regarded more positively, reacts to others more positively. All this affects the social life of the person concerned. There is more interaction. A more positive self-concept is reflected by more positive attitudes and behaviour generally. The self-concept is at the centre of motivation.

Jones believes that exercise is of immense importance to the brain and this underlines the importance of regular controlled exercise throughout life so that when mind and body can continue to be exercised, the nervous system benefits, becomes more efficient and the proportion of people who need institutional care is reduced. The importance of Jones's work lies in the fact that he is one of the few of people in the UK who have begun to contribute to the literature on educational gerontology. Allman has warned against the tendency in America to argue from results derived from studies of institutionalised old people. Although old people in institutions do loom large in Jones's research results, he is working with fit and able-bodied older people as well, as his recent reports indicate. Tyler (1978) bases his work substantially on secondary sources, bringing together the broad sweep of the issue. He places the ageing process, the sociology of ageing and the intellectual aptitude of older people alongside a thorough discussion of physical resources and needs, i.e. locations, premises, heating, furniture, aids, accoustics, times of meeting, curriculum development and teaching strategies. He provides a detailed discussion of the segregation/integration issue and concludes that both types of provision can profitably co-exist. What he does omit, however, is the problem of transport.

I shall not deal with pre-retirement education in detail. The most effective evaluation research in this field has been done by Phillipson and Strang (1983) and to a lesser extent by Coleman (1982). The results of both research projects point towards necessary and inevitable changes in teaching method and curriculum development or else to a total irrelevance of the genre. This is because a substantial amount of pre-retirement education has been in the hands of non-educators for twenty years.

The situation in relation to adult education and older adults in general is somewhat different. Traditionally, 18-20 percent of students in adult and continuing education classes have come from the over-60s. They have been professionally taught in part-time and full-time courses and have, on the whole, reponded well. No one has stopped to ask how or why. Only in the last seven or eight years has attention been focussed on the <u>special</u> educational needs of older people. The work of Arenberg and Robertson-Tchabo (1974) in America and Harwood and Naylor (1972) in Australia suggests that there has to be some modification of learning styles. More time is required to take in new information, with smaller amounts of information at a time, more frequent repetition and feedback of progress. I am unaware of any work of this character having been carried out in depth in this country apart from that of Cohen quoted in Abrams (1980). Allman is virtually alone in writing of the older learner within the context of lifespan developmental psychology.

The issue of the older adult has come to the fore because of the increasing awareness that we belong to a society with a rapid growth in numbers of people who are over 65. Older people nowadays are breaking the stereotype of 'old age', i.e. over 60 or 65, as a period of inevitable and irretrievable decline. The absence of government resources to expand an educational programme for older adults was made clear by a Labour Government spokesman as long ago as the first Keele seminar, in 1975. The self-help education movement has begun to establish itself. If it is to prosper and if further and higher education are to make professional contributions, also, it is necessary to underpin these developments with secure academic foundations. Self-help education should be no less rigorous than ordinary, professionally tutored adult education courses. While it is true that a large number of the older population reject the possibility of joining education courses, a number might welcome the possibility. We have moved rapidly in the last few years into a society where redundancy and early retirement are commonplace, leaving many with nearly one third of their life to live. Abrams (1980) reminds us that for those aged between 50 and 59, two-thirds completed their schooling at 14 or less, and only 17 percent have a terminal education of 17 or more. It is no wonder that Laslett has called us the worst educated country in Western Europe.

In 1982, the Centre for Policy on Ageing inserted a question in the Quota Omnibus Survey of the National Opinion Polls Market Research Ltd. The question was: 'Are you at present undertaking a part-time educational course, for example, by attending an evening class, doing a correspondence course or an Open University course?'. Of those who were over 60, 2 percent claimed to take part in a course. Previous educational and current professional status proved to be critical. In the 15-71+ age groups, there was a drop from 9 percent in class A to 2 percent in Class E. These findings are similar to those of Abrams (1980) when he reviewed the General Household Survey of 1976/77. Todd in Midwinter (1982) has reminded us that educators need to study more closely the social and cultural factors which make up distinctions in test findings. What is the relation between intelligence and class? Townsend and Davidson (1982) have made some gestures in this direction in relation to class and mortality. If it can be proved beyond all reasonable doubt that the abilities of older people have been held in check by limited opportunities when they were young, then we have some support for the argument that older people have had the worst possible deal in educational terms.

Commentary

The development of educational gerontology as a discipline in Britain has not been raised as an issue for debate before. Now, however, we have the beginnings of a literature. The contributors I have referred to - Walker, Jones, Tyler, Phillipson and Strang, Coleman and Midwinter -have presented us with the beginnings of a framework within which to develop educational gerontology as a necessary discipline.

The term 'educational gerontology' (first used in Michigan in 1970) was defined by Peterson (1976), as follows:

> 'a field of study and practice that has recently developed at the interface of adult education and social gerontology. The parameters of the field are defined as including three major components; (1) educational endeavours for middle-aged and older people; (2) public education about ageing which will improve general attitudes toward older people; and (3) pre-service and in-service education of professionals and practitioners for work in the field.'

Some of us have tried systematically for several years to keep all three parts of the whole in lively relationship within our programmes, but what we need are evaluation studies, especially in the area of curriculum development, memory and intelligence.

Just before he died a year ago McLusky (1982) wrote:

> 'Older people have a vital need for that kind of education that will enable them to exert influence in protecting and improving their own situation and also in contributing to the well-being of a larger society.'

In Britain, practically all the evidence to support such an assertion is descriptive or anecdotal. There is a dearth of research on education and older people. There is, however, growing support for the rights of elderly people to education. Evaluation studies are required to enable us either to give up the idea, or to ensure that it is permanently on the social policy agenda.

We need to improve society's perception and understanding of ageing. There is a great deal in media presentation that leaves much to be desired. Content analyses are required of TV programmes and of newspaper journalism. Children's books and adolescent books need to be studied for ageism as vigorously as we have tried to examine them for racism and sexism. We need to raise the community's awareness, so that there can be a visible and continuing improvement in the quality of life of older people. We need to disseminate knowledge about the processes of ageing and to develop a deeper understanding of, and realistic image of, later life. Programmes for professionals and practitioners and para-professionals are urgently required. The considerable growth in academically based gerontology programmes in America has not been paralleled here. We need detailed, systematic, regular courses for all the different sorts of people engaged in work all with the elderly. Further and higher education and the agency training departments need to work out plans locally and regionally. This raises numerous issues: the model of teaching, the purpose of the courses, the intended benefit in terms of qualifications and educational experience, the actual structural strategies applied to enable such courses to take place. Programmes should include the process of ageing, the stereotypes and myths of old age, the dignity of ageing, the dissemination of knowledge and skills, legislation and existing service programmes, welfare rights, strategies for service delivery, how to solve the problems of older people, training in recording, research and teaching skills, sensitising professionals and para-professionals to the needs of older people.

A Model for Educational Gerontology

Peterson's (1976) definition of educational gerontology strikes definite chords for those of us involved in this necessary discipline. Peterson (1980) refined his model. A year ago, I believed that it pressed us in Britain too far and that the academic infrastructure was not available. Affairs have moved so fast that I now feel we could apply ourselves to the revised model. This includes two sections to each of his three categories:

1. Educational for older people: (a) instructional gerontology, i.e. research into how we teach older people; (b) senior adult education (education for older people).
2. Education about ageing: (a) social gerontology (research-based understanding of the condition of older people); (b) advocacy gerontology (informing the public about older people).
3. Education of professionals and para-professionals: (a) gerontology education (instruction of professionals and para-professionals); (b) professional gerontology (post-experience training of gerontologists).

We could expand the model a little, as follows, with clear acknowledgements to Peterson:

1. Instruction of older people:

(a) Instructional gerontology. This is research into the ènvironmental context in which older people function and the circumstances in which they can learn most effectively and efficiently. It includes the following: the educational needs of older people; the motivation of older people to take part in education; the ways in which those who have had no contact or interest in formal education for the last 40 or 50 years can be brought into a learning situation; changes in intelligence during the life span; the effectiveness of instructional methods; programme models and what Peterson calls 'delivery system characteristics' in the education of older people.
(b) Senior adult education. This is the practice of instruction of older people to increase their knowledge and skills, so that they may enjoy life more and increase their competence to cope with contemporary life. This is what most people who use the term would mean by 'educational gerontology'. Senior adult education involves an assessment of the needs of potential participants, recruitment and training of tutors, developing the curriculum, assessing the level of instruction required, designing effective delivery systems and methods for evaluating the programme.

2. Instruction about older people:

(a) Social gerontology. This is using research and theory to describe the condition of older people and the methods required to communicate this knowledge to families, policy makers, agency workers, volunteer carers. It is an attempt to enable the community to understand the experience of elderly people through the exploration of methods and approaches; a study of roles, stereotypes, myths and attitudes associated with ageing; the development of teaching models which are relevant to the attitudes and perceptions of people in general. Peterson sees this as a necessary component, but it has to be recognised that social gerontology has established itself as a discipline in its own right over the last 20 years.
(b) Advocacy gerontology. This means informing the general public about older people and the conditions under which they live: designing programmes to increase public awareness; using the mass media to change attitudes and stereotypes; providing information and skills for families; sensitising those who work with older people as well as young people at school.

3. Instruction of professionals and para-professionals:

(a) Gerontology education. This refers to the instruction of those who are preparing for employment in the field of ageing, meaning social workers, doctors, nurses, officers-in-charge, care assistants, managers of day centres, wardens of sheltered housing schemes, and their supervisors. Even in America, little research work has been done in this field.
(b) Professional gerontology. This covers the development of groups of practitioners who can design, implement and carry out the services required in educating older people. These services include meeting their social welfare and health needs, changing society's attitudes and helping individuals and their families to maintain their viability. This is a neglected aspect of higher and further education. Other potentials in this category include in-service education in planning and service delivery agencies.

These six components of educational gerontology describe what we have begun to evolve in our pragmatic programme at Kele and in North Staffordshire. In adition, there is the whole complex of self-help. We can call it self-help gerontology: peer group counselling, legal advocacy, i.e. para-legal counselling by elders themselves, self-help health care, as well as a reassessment of values to provide more coherence during the later years of life. All this is open to much more encouragement and development and requires of necessity an educational programme.

What I would like to see emerge is a group of researchers and practitioners committed to dialogue and committed to developing this discipline. Social gerontology has been slow to develop in Britain and it is not surprising that educational gerontology has barely spoken its own name. At the moment, it is a lonely responsibility to describe its potentiality.

The term 'educational gerontology' may not attract some of our pragmatically orientated colleagues. But academically, it is nonetheless a concept which is going to be accepted increasingly in the international educational philosophy of the Western world and it is a necessary discipline needing urgent attention in Britain.

Bibliography

Abrams, M. (1980) Education and Elderly People, Age Concern Research Unit, London

Agruso, V.M. (1978) Learning in the Later Years, Academic Press, London

Allman, P. (1981) Adult Development: An Overview of Recent Research, Department of Adult Education, University of Nottingham

Allman, P. (1982) 'New Perspectives on the Adult: An Argument for Lifelong Education', International Journal of Lifelong Education, 1, 1, Falmer Press, Lewes

Allman, P. (1983) 'The Potential for Learning in Later Life' in D. Jerrome (ed.), Ageing in Modern Society, Croom Helm, London

Arenberg, D.L. and Robertson-Tchabo, E. A. (1974) 'The Older Individual as Learner' in S. M. Grabowski and W. D. Mason (eds.), Learning for Ageing, Adult Education Association of the USA, Washington, D.C.

Bromley, D.B. (1970) 'Age and Adult Education', Studies in Adult Education, 2, 124-138

Coleman, A. (1982) Preparation for Retirement in England and Wales, National Institute of Adult Education, Leicester

Cooper, J.D. (1980) Social Groupwork and Elderly People in Hospital, Beth Johnson Foundation, Stoke-on-Trent

Exton-Smith, A.N. (1978) Opening address, Symposium on 'Mental and Neurological Disturbance in the Elderly', Age and Ageing, 7, Supplement

Glendenning, F. (ed.) (1980) Outreach Education and the Elders: Theory and Practice, Beth Johnson Foundation in association with Department of Adult Education, University of Keele

Glendenning, F. (1983) 'Educational Gerontology: A Review of British and American Developments', International Journal of Lifelong

Education, 2, 1

Harwood, E. and Naylor, G.F.K. (1972) Derivation and Inference of Need From a Longitudinal Study of Psychological and Educational Factors in theNormal Ageing Population, (mimeo) BSSBG, 25 March, London

Havighurst, R. (1972) Developmental Tasks and Education, David McKay, New York

Houle, C.O. (1974) 'Changing Goals of Education', International Review of Education, XX, 4, Hamburg

Johnston, S. and Phillipson, C. (eds.) (1983) Older Learners: the Challenge to Adult Education, Bedford Square Press, London

Jones, S. (1975) 'Education and the Elderly' in F. Glendenning and S. Jones (eds.) Education and the Over-60s (2nd edition, 1980), Beth Johnson Foundation in association with Department of Adult Education, University of Keele.

Jones, S. (1982) Learning and Meta-learning with Special Reference to Education for the Elders, unpublished Ph.D. thesis, University of London

Jones, S. (1983) 'Education and Life in the Continuing Care Ward' in M.J. Denham, Care of the Long-stay Elderly Patient, Croom Helm, London

Kahn, R.L., Pollack, M., Goldfarb, A. (1961) 'Factors Related to Individual Differences in Mental States of Individual Aged' in P.H. Hoch and J. Zubin, (eds.) Psychopathology in Ageing, Grune and Stratton, New York

McLusky, H. (1982) Education of Older Adults, (unpublished paper), University of Michigan

Midwinter, E. (1982) Age is Opportunity: Education and Older People, Centre for Policy on Ageing, London

Peterson, D.A. (1976) 'Educational Gerontology; the State of the Art', Educational Gerontology, 1, 61-73

Peterson, D.A. (1980) 'Who are the Educational Gerontologists?', Educational Gerontology, 5, 65-77

Phillipson, C. and Strang, P. (1983) The Impact of Pre-retirement Education: a Longitudinal Evaluation, Department of Adult Education, University of Keele

Poulden, S. (1980) 'Art for the Elderly in Hospitals and Residential

Homes: Some Proposals' in F. Glendenning (1980), op.cit.

Poulden, S. (1983) 'Art Education' in M.J. Denham Care of the Long-Stay Elderly Patient, Croom-Helm, London

Townsend, P. and Davidson, N. (1982) Inequalities in Health, Pelican, Harmondsworth

Tyler, W. (1978) The Educational Needs of the Elderly, unpublished M.Phil. thesis, University of Nottingham

Walker, I. (1976) Old People in Homes and the Education and Caring Services in Leicestershire, Beth Johnson Foundation (mimeo and out of print), Stoke-on-Trent

Walker, I. (1983) 'Institutional Care: the Creation of a Learning Environment', in S. Johnston and C. Phillipson (eds.) (1983) op.cit.

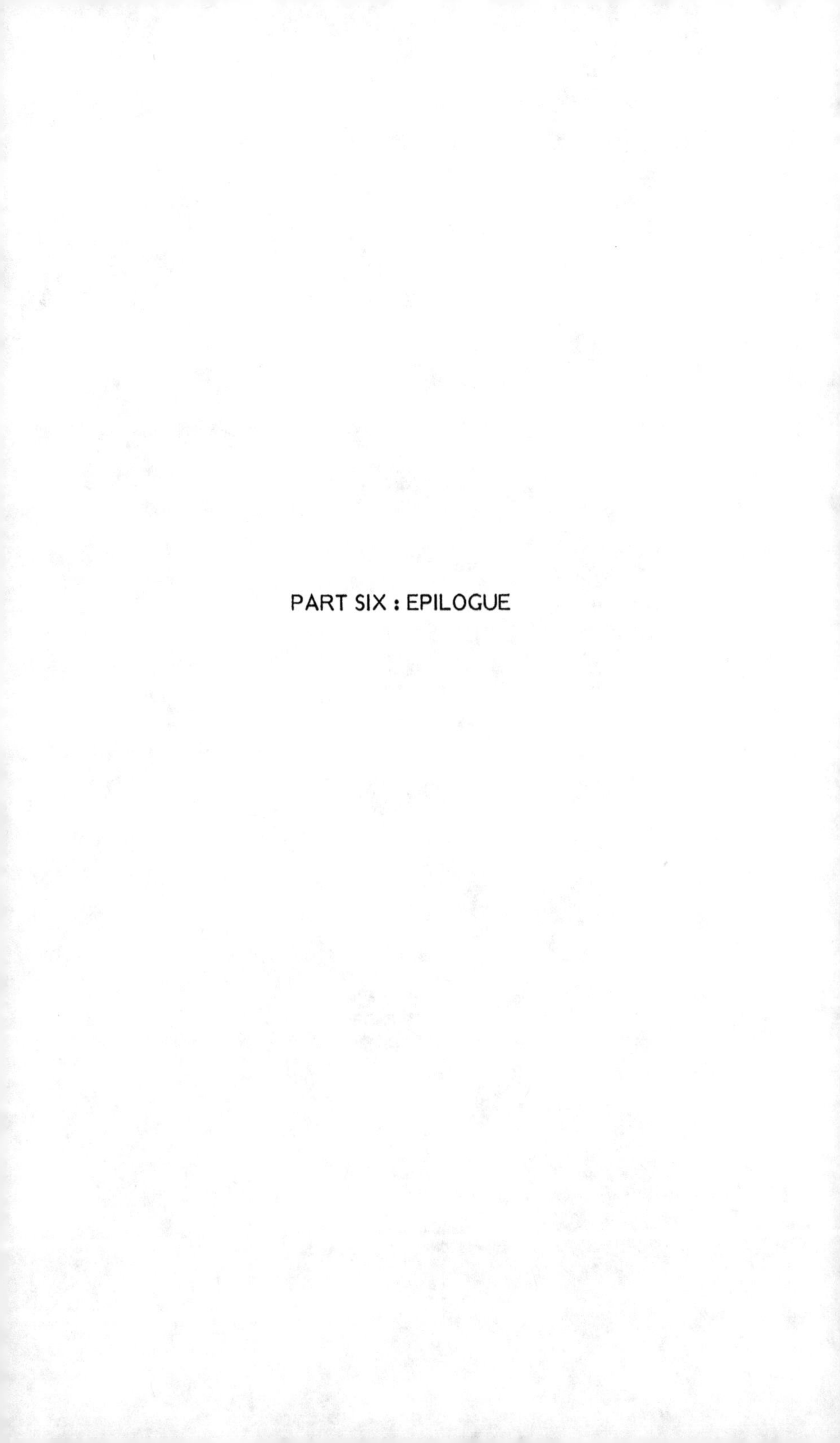

PART SIX : EPILOGUE

Chapter Twenty-five

RESEARCH UTILISATION. ANOTHER CINDERELLA?

A. Osborn

Introduction

This paper takes as its starting point the position that policy, management and practice in the health and social services will benefit by the application of relevant research. Why, then, does the utilisation of research attract so little attention and have relatively low status within the social research community and why do potential users under-exploit research? This article presents some observations about researchers and users. These are based on experience of local utilisation gained whilst working in research and development within the health service, local authority social service and social work departments and, latterly, as an intermediary research user with a national charity. Not everyone will agree with the values and assumptions implied in this paper, but I hope it will stimulate further discussion. The paper is not about the more global issue of the researcher's contribution to national policy debates, so ably addressed by Taylor elsewhere in this volume.

What is Research Utilisation?

Research utilisation is the appliction of research to promote change in policy practice and attitudes. The modification of attitudes and outlook, the assimilation of research into the body of informed debate are as important as the dramatic and immediate implementation of 'major findings'. The slow cumulative impact of research creates climate for change, and needs both research-minded users and user-minded researchers. Some of the factors inhibiting both will be illustrated in later sections.

Research use is not confined to the use of the results. The research process itself can be an extremely powerful development tool. Research can influence thinking about policy and practice from the stage of early identification and negotiation of the research problem. Some research has achieved its desired impact even before the research has been fully documented. This is why some 'internal' research is inadequately written up, which is a matter of much regret.

Research Utilisation. Another Cinderella?

Research utilisation also means researcher utilisation. It is difficult to separate the skills, style, influence and insights of the researcher from the impact of the research itself. Furthermore, the researcher's knowledge of the topic can be considerable and go beyond that directly presented within the specific research study. There will be literature searches, contact with others researching in similar fields, knowledge of service and policy developments, problems and trends elsewhere.

Research use does not always resolve uncertainties or provide unequivocal answers. Users may well feel cheated when faced with uncertainties that have been sharpened and clarified rather than obliterated. Researchers themselves may find it difficult to work with uncertainty or to present conditional results confidently and constructively. One barrier to continued research use may be the unrealistic expectations of research held by potential users combined with, at times, over-optimistic or unduly obscure research presentations.

Where is the Research?

A user organisation may have its own research capability in-house, may be playing host to researchers from elsewhere or it may need to look at research that is quite independent of the organisation. In-house research should be the most accessible. On the other hand, the opportunity will need to be taken to ensure that the research of others occuring on site is, in the nicest sense, fully exploited. Service-giving agencies are heavily used as field sites by academics who can usually be persuaded to give something back to the agency. In-house research and development staff can increase the mutual relevance of this to the agency and the outside researcher. Finally, a wealth of existing research conducted elsewhere can be hooked in, sometimes along with the researcher. The excellent research register produced by the Centre for Policy on Ageing (1955 et seq.), research reviews such as Goldberg and Connelly (1982), the Research Highlights series, e.g. Reinach (1982), which was originally proposed by the Social Services Research Group to meet such needs; other published sources and use of networks such as the British Society of Gerontology are all means of tracking down useful work - see BSG (1979 et seq.), CPA and BSG (1981 et seq.) and Jerrome (1983 et seq.).

Those designing research to address a particular issue, or looking for existing work to inform a problem, can draw on whatever method or discipline is best suited to the task. The help, good will and in-depth expertise of many different specialists in their fields can be called upon. Cross-fertilisation between disciplines can be an outcome, although it is sadly under-developed. There are great benefits in being a Jack-of-all-trades; mastery of the eclectic method is perhaps underrated.

The Varying Roles of Researchers

The research world that impinges upon policy and service development is not one of homogeneity and consensus. The inclination and freedom of researchers themselves to undertake utilisation work is not uniform. It depends upon the definition and limits put upon research activity by the researcher and the research funder, the employing organisation (if different) and the user groups and organisations targetted by the research. There will be major differences between researchers employed by service-giving organisations and researchers based in other settings as well as considerable variation within these two groups.

Researchers employed in service-giving agencies are expected to consider possible application of the research from the time at which the work is originally negotiated. These researchers generally contribute to the devising of the research programmes and the selection of the research priorities. These programmes are justified in terms of their utility to the organisation. Action research and research and development are available options. In-house researchers (employed within the user organisation), in theory at least, will have fewer problems of continuity and more scope for seizing the right time and opportunity to use research knowledge than will external researchers. However, a potential charge against in-house research is that of reduced methodological rigour. There is little to suggest that in-house work is generally unsound. Some may be cheap and cheerful but it tends to be used within its limits. In-house researchers are sometimes accused of 'going native' but research is greatly eased by good contact with users and some degree of shared commitment. More research-minded 'natives' are needed rather than fewer user-minded researchers.

The availability and willingness of researchers to involve themselves in direct utilisation is affected by many factors. Not all researchers see policy makers and practitioners as their primary audience. Some address their academic colleagues; others report to their funders, who may not be in a position to apply the resarch they are supporting. Some primarily address potential future funders. Not all assess their own success in terms of the the use made of their work in the field. For some the contribution may be to methodological advance rather than to an issue of policy or practice. Those on short-term contracts may have other preoccupations and may not have time or funding to devote to utilisation. In the academic world plagiarism can be a dirty word and may inhibit an open flow of material or ideas, particularly in advance of publication. The service-based research community enjoys a generally free and willing exchange but, conversely, its work is less widely available in published form. It would be easy to speculate further, but the main point is that not all researchers are in a position to take part in research utilisation directly and not all would see this as a major or legitimate role.

Inappropriate Application of Research Findings

Researchers may fear that the integrity of their work or their own reputations could be compromised by the use to which their work might be put particularly if this lies outside their control. There are risks involved in the application of research findings. A positive impact on development and change is not easily achieved. The attempt may fail and perhaps the research may be blamed. A major barrier to the appropriate use of research is the failure to appreciate the context and limitations of a piece of research. Both researchers and users can misapply the results of research work. Some examples of research abuse are given below.

The Square Peg in the Round Hole

This is research used out of context. One bizarre example of misapplication was the plan of a social services manager to respond to a careful random sample household survey of chronic sick and disabled persons by mounting a full enumeration. This was not, as one might assume, a planned response to the amount of need now expected, but merely a check on the survey estimates. The second example relates to the inappropriate use of indicators. Need indicators are useful for strategic planning but are prone to misuse as definitive measures of individual needs. One Scottish Region assesses the geographical distribution and extensiveness of 'vulnerability' within its elderly population by looking at the proportions who are aged 75 years and more, live alone, social class IV or V. These are valuable as planning and management data. It would be unhelpful to allocate or refuse service to an individual older person solely on the basis of these factors, but some users, convinced of the planning arguments, are tempted to adopt this as a simple rule of thumb.

The Rack

It is not original to say that any research results will eventually submit under torture. Stretching results to fit inappropriate situations does occur and can appear plausible to those who did not witness the application of undue force. The results of a population survey conducted in town A will not necessarily apply to town B in another part of the country merely because a scientific random sample was drawn in town A, and yet attempts to do this are seen. To take another example, work on criteria setting often becomes more rigidly applied in practice than was the intention. Research suggests that a useful guideline in the allocation of home-help service can be the need for assistance with shopping. When this results in denial of service to someone with arthritic hands who can shop but do little else, or when it results in an old man who is unable to bend to do housework being told that he will only get help if he agrees to stop doing his own shopping, then something is amiss.

Tablets of Stone

It is as alarming for research findings to be given an authority they do not justify as it is depressing to have them totally ignored. Sometimes this occurs when a blunt instrument is needed with which to subdue an opponent, as when the popularity of sheltered housing is used as the argument to silence its critics. At other times it shows a touching faith in anything 'scientific'. Sometimes findings are made immutable by incorporation into legislation, as for example occurred with research on the length of time children spend in care.

The Selection Box

This means taking the appealing items whilst ignoring the rest. The approach is well illustrated by the use of meals-on-wheels research to finely-tune what is possibly the wrong engine, or by work on community alarms which may be examined to pull out information that helps in choosing between competing technologies whilst leaving untouched the aspects that raise more fundamental questions.

The Ostrich

This is active non-utilisation. The research is definitely not to the user's taste and is ignored. This may be combined with the selection box approach but suggests greater antipathy to the unpopular bits. Consider again community alarms. Questions about the objectives, relative priority and actual effectivness of these systems makes such research prone to gather dust.

The Sceptical User

The factors suggested above might make some researchers a little twitchy about their work and possibly their name being used 'in anger', although researchers themselves are not immune to these pitfalls. A certain wariness may also exist on the side of potential users. Here are some reservations which will be familiar to anyone who has worked with policy makers, managers or practitioners to utilise research, either by conducting in-house work or seeking to apply work done elsewhere:

(a) "We tried it before and it didn't work." One example is the seemingly chronic negative attitudes to the use of volunteers held by many social workers.

(b) "But we are doing it already." For example, bodies involved in pre-retirement education may believe that they reach a wider sector of the population than is the case and make greater use of informal group learning methods than is found in practice.

(c) "Very interesting, but it is nothing to do with us." Staff in old people's homes can have some effect on patterns of drug prescribing, although only the medical practitioner can actually prescribe. They may be reluctant to recognise their own influence.

(d) "We'd love to act upon it but 'they' won't let us." For example, if managers do not consider older people to have drink problems, then their staff will not be trained to recognise and cope with these problems even though they feel they need training.

(e) "It's not our priority or most pressing problem." Despite the likely benefits of a mangement for continence programme, care-staff may feel that pressure of work will not allow them to vary their routines, many of which are dominated by the changing and cleaning of incontinent residents.

(f) "We're different and the research does not apply to us." There are many variations such as, "We're unique, so research done elsewhere cannot be relevant"; "The research location was unique and so says nothing about us". A voluntary group running a day centre initially showed no interest in a piece of day centre research. The group was then intrigued to see that the other day centres also experienced problems of overloading and conflicting expectations. Although not all the findings accorded with their experience they found the insights useful.

(g) "But it doesn't allow for .... the extreme or rare case." For example, any form designed to monitor anything at all can meet with this objection.

(h) "It can't be trusted because you're not one of us." The thoroughly researched assessment schedule known as CAPE asssists in clarifying mental and physical status. Although it has been tried and tested by many groups of staff, social workers were initially very wary of something produced by a clinical psychologist.

(i) "We can't understand the jargon." Dare it be suggested that there may be examples in this present volume?

(j) "The last researchers gave us nothing back." Shame on them.

(k) "People are unique individuals and we cannot allow them to be codified." This can inhibit use of case-finding and 'at-risk' research designed to benefit individuals.

(l) "My colours are already nailed to the mast." Research evidence can be too late and elected members may take up their position very early on.

(m) "We'll change it a bit and then use it." Staff interested in using CAPE went through a phase of trying to rewrite the questions or even trying to introduce the questions into a 'normal' conversation, being on the receiving end of which would certainly have induced confusion. After passing through this phase the assessment was in fact applied correctly.

(n) "We would rather not know; our jobs are too stressful anyway." Research highlighting poverty in old age or the situation of many with senile dementia can paralyse rather than motivate some staff who feel overwhelmed and powerless to influence the situation.

(o) "But what we need is more research." This may sound like music to many ears, perhaps, but researched action may be needed to move the issue forward, for example, on the non-use of aids supplied by occupational therapists.

Concluding Comments

Anecdotal evidence has been used above to refer to some of the factors which can inhibit the utilisation of research. Anyone who has worked to put research to use will recognise the kinds of situation which can arise. Those without such experience might be tempted to dismiss these problems as trivial or easily overcome, yet they account for much under-use of research.

Fairly simple and basic improvements in utilisation skills could greatly enhance the interplay between research and service provision, even though the policy and practice situations that researchers hope to influence are themselves complex and multi-faceted. Some suggestions are implied above. Here, in conclusion, are some general observations:

(a) Research tailored to use will be easier to apply than that designed for other purposes. (b) Research that has involved users from the start is likely to generate commitment to its use. (c) Replicated work is rare, yet permits an accumulation and sharing of experience. (d) Practitioner research in many disciplines is in its infancy, yet has clear benefits to users. (e) Research use requires people available and able to link the research to it application. These could be the original researchers, development staff, research brokers, research-minded policy or practice staff. (f) It takes time and resources to use research and continuity of follow-through is important. (g) Dissemination of research via registers, reports prepared for users, meetings and so on are necessary, but on their own are unlikely to be sufficient to stimulate a continuing process of utilisation. (h) Policy makers, managers and practitioners need better training to enable them to evaluate and use research or to conduct their own. Trainers of the service providers also need these skills and some incorporate too little research into their own teaching material. (i) More demystification of research is needed. (j) Research, both as a method of enquiry and as a producer of results, offers a vehicle for review and reflection. (k) Research can do more to demystify policymaking and service provision issues. (l) Serendipity and opportunism may be very beneficial and some flair is needed to seize the benefits. (m) The 'water on the stone', i.e. the slow steady impact on assumptions and attitudes, is probably the major contribution of research. The 'apocalypse', i.e. the major burst of findings which revolutionises the situation in an instant, is rare.

Bibliography

British Society of Gerontology (1979 et seq.) Ageing Times (BSG members' house journal)

Centre for Policy on Ageing (1955 et seq.) Old Age. A Register of Social Research, Centre for Policy on Ageing, London

Centre for Policy on Ageing and British Society of Gerontology (1981 et seq.) Ageing and Society, Cambridge University Press, Cambridge

Goldberg, E.M. and Connelly, N. (1982) The Effectiveness of Social Care for the Elderly: An Overview of Recent and Current Evaluative Research, Heinemann Educational Books, London

Jerrome, D. (ed.) (1983) Ageing in Modern Society: Contemporary Approaches, Croom Helm, London

Reinach, E. (1982) 'Developing Services for the Elderly', Research Highlights, no 3, Department of Social Work, University of Aberdeen

DETAILS OF CONTRIBUTORS

R. Abed, Department of Psychiatry, University of Liverpool.

M. G. Binks, Department of Psychology, University of Liverpool.

J. Bond, Health Care Research Unit, University of Newcastle upon Tyne.

D. B. Bromley, Department of Psychology, University of Liverpool.

C. Cantley, Unit for the Study of the Elderly, Department of Community Medicine, University of Aberdeen.

S. Clayton, Department of Social Administration, University of Lancaster.

P. G. Coleman, Department of Geriatric Medicine and Social Work Studies, University of Southampton.

J. R. M. Copeland, Department of Psychiatry, University of Liverpool.

C. Crosby, Department of Psychiatry, University of Liverpool.

A. D. M. Davies, Department of Psychology, University of Liverpool.

M. E. Dewey, Department of Psychiatry, University of Liverpool.

D. R. Fabian, P.O. Box 455, Augusta, Maine 04330, U.S.A.

M. Featherstone, Department of Administrative and Social Studies, Teeside Polytechnic.

D. M. Forshaw, Department of Psychiatry, University of Liverpool.

F. Glendenning, Department of Adult Education, Keele University.

E. M. Goldberg, 27 Ringshall, Berkhamsted.

M. Hepworth, Department of Administrative and Social Studies, Teeside Polytechnic, Cleveland.

D. J. Hunter, Unit for the Study of the Elderly, Department of Community Medicine, University of Aberdeen.

C. Itzin, 19 Knatchbull Road, London.

M. L. Johnson, formerly at the Policy Studies Institute, London, now at the Open University, Milton Keynes.

P. McCoy, Social Services Department, Suffolk County Council, Ipswich.

P. P. Mayer, West Midlands Institute of Geriatric Medicine and Gerontology, Birmingham.

A. Merriman, Department of Social Medicine and Public Health, University of Singapore.

M. S. Muthu, Department of Psychiatry, University of Liverpool.

A. Osborn, Age Concern Scotland, Edinburgh.

L. Sawyer, 5 Cottenham Park Road, London.

R. T. Searle, Department of Psychiatry, University of Liverpool.

V. K. Sharma, Department of Psychiatry, University of Liverpool.

J. M. Simpson, Geriatric Research Unit, University College Hospital, London.

R. C. Stevenson, Department of Economic and Business Studies, University of Liverpool.

H. Taylor, Centre for Policy on Ageing, London.

C. R. Victor, Research Team for the Care of the Elderly, Welsh National School of Medicine, Cardiff.

A. M. Warnes, Department of Geography, King's College, University of London.

N. Wood, Department of Psychiatry, University of Liverpool.

SUBJECT INDEX

For Product Safety Concerns and Information please contact our EU
representative GPSR@taylorandfrancis.com
Taylor & Francis Verlag GmbH, Kaufingerstraße 24, 80331 München, Germany

www.ingramcontent.com/pod-product-compliance
Lightning Source LLC
Chambersburg PA
CBHW050414280326
41932CB00013BA/1860

* 9 7 8 1 0 3 2 7 0 9 9 6 3 *